Rangerchick
At Work in the Woods

Frances Reneau

ISBN: **1502511665**
ISBN 13: **9781502511669**

Acknowledgments

I am greatly indebted to Becky Bach and to Carol Pechler for long hours of reading and editing. Also thank you to Michael Newburn, Annette Coleman, Garth Harwood, Christine Witzel, Cindy Roessler, and my husband, David Reneau.

Dedicated to my mother and father,
Calvin and Louise French

Contents

Forward

Unlike many writers of the ranger genre, I do not work for the National Park Service, but rather am very proud to serve the Midpeninsula Regional Open Space District, a unique, local, public agency on California's San Francisco peninsula. Midpenn, as it is affectionately known, is supported by local property taxes, and governed by an elected Board of Directors. We just celebrated our fortieth anniversary. We have about 120 permanent employees—planners, analysts, administrative assistants, lawyers, IT people, docent and volunteer coordinators, and exactly 20 rangers. Our place of work, the beautiful Santa Cruz Mountains, is threatened by development on all sides, primarily by Silicone Valley burgeoning on our eastern flank, but also from the west where development eats away at the pastoral ranchlands south of Half Moon Bay. The District now encompasses some 62,000 acres of undeveloped land and works with other local agencies, public and private, to preserve and restore these last remnants our bygone wilderness, and to manage them for public access.

Although I never set out to be a park ranger, or a writer for that matter, I did start keeping a work journal sometime during my first year on the job, partly as self-expression, partly a place to record not just the facts of an incident and what I did, but of how I felt about them. The two other forms of written record--

deadly dull daily patrol logs stating where I was and what I was doing, and stilted and stylised incident reports detailing medicals and law enforcement contacts--just didn't satisfy my need for narrative storytelling. After a decade on the job, I had a stack of 8.5X11 notepads ten inches tall, which I knew I would either need to compile into a book, or throw into the recycling. Who was going to read them otherwise? So now my old journal entries form the foundation of this book, along with some amended incident reports, all of which appear in italics. I have given all my co-workers, and, of course, suspects, neighbors and accident victims, fictitious names.

Looking back over some old entries now, I wish I had written more, and more often than once or twice a week. Times change and this job has changed subtly even in the ten short years that I have been here. Certainly many of the stories that follow I would have forgotten had I not written them down. Other rangers, some of whom have been with the District nearly from its inception, tell me they wish they too had kept journals all those years ago. I wish they had too.

1. Rangerchick

One day some years ago I was on patrol headed into El Sereno Open Space Preserve crawling along in my patrol truck with no real agenda when movement caught my eye on the left. I hit the brakes, heard the screeching of bike brakes, and saw this older man with puffy, Einstein-like white hair, still aboard his bike about five feet away from my left front bumper. He was still flying along, now turning toward Montevina Road. He had no helmet, but was an old guy, probably not a regular rider and probably clueless about the helmet regulation. I supposed he just needed a verbal warning, a little talking to. I hopped out of my truck, imagining that I'd be assisting a scared and shaken grandfatherly sort of man. I didn't even put myself 10-95 (pedestrian stop) with dispatch before calling out, "Are you okay?"

To my surprise, I was greeted with a barrage of criticism and abuse. "You idiot! You weren't paying any attention! You almost hit me!" What? He was the one who almost ran into me, having obviously come speeding down the little hill from the Bohlman Road entrance. I saw no point in getting into that now. Despite the obviously confrontational nature of the contact so far, I somehow still hadn't mentally clicked over from verbal warning mode to citation mode, or tone of voice. I was still recovering from the near collision of a few seconds before. "Park Ranger.

Peace Officer. Stop your bike. I need to talk to you. You have to wear a helmet in the preserve," I called. I was still fumbling and confused. "Oh, I know all about that," he yelled, riding away out of earshot. I was finally catching on. "Stop your bike now or I will call the čops." (Supervisor Tony pointed out later that this was a rather stupid thing to say since, technically, I am the cops. I suppose I meant Los Gatos Police, but that's not what came out.) "You do that." And he was gone. The whole contact had lasted maybe 15 seconds.

Damn! I sure messed that one up. What was I thinking? How could I be such a dimwit? I fumed for 30 seconds or so before turning Dumbo, my patrol truck, down the hill after him. At least I had managed to get the words "peace officer" (that is to say law enforcement in legal parlance) out of my mouth, and what with my standing there in full uniform beside my Code 3 truck, he couldn't very well claim that he didn't realize he was being legally detained. A bike can way outpace a truck going downhill on a steep, windy mountain road; still, he was worth pursuing. Maybe he would crash, or get a flat or something. I called in my attempted stop and fleeing suspect (Penal Code 148: Delay or Obstruct a Peace Officer, a misdmeanor) information to dispatch and asked them to alert Santa Clara County Sheriff as well as Los Gatos Police. Be on the lookout (B.O.L.) for an old guy on a bike headed down Montevina Road. Probably pretty hopeless, except for the very distinctive puffy white hair.

Then Ranger Terry came up on the radio offering to fill (assist), and asking where he should go, but he was at least half an hour away, coming all the way from Rancho San Antonio Open Space Preserve outside of Cupertino. Suddenly I had a brilliant realization: as my suspect was now headed down Montevina Road, the only place old Einstein Hair could really be going was downtown Los Gatos, and, from the bottom of Montevina

Road, there were only two possible routes to get there. Either he had to take the high road on the Jones Trail through St. Joseph's Hill Open Space Preserve, or the low road, on the Los Gatos Creek Trail through Lexington Reservoir County Park. I saw a glimmer of hope. Terry could station himself on the Los Gatos Creek Trail just north of the Main Street entrance in Los Gatos, while I drove through St. Joseph's Hill on the Jones Trail.

Twenty minutes later, as I was doggedly making my way along the Jones Trail crowded with dogs, strollers, and oblivious ear-bud wearing athletes, I saw him! I couldn't believe it, but there was no mistaking that hairdo. From a couple spots on the Jones Trail there is a bird's eye view down to the Los Gatos Creek Trail and that's how I saw him, and how he got caught. Terry arrived in the nick of time and was just pulling off of Main Street when I radioed that our suspect was coming south, headed directly for him.

From Terry's Supplemental Incident Report: I observed the suspect riding towards me who matched the description that I had received from Ranger Reneau. I put on my Code Three lights, positioned my truck so as to block most of the trail, stepped out of the truck and stopped the suspect at approximately 1330 hours. I identified myself as a Ranger Peace Officer and told him to get off his bike, which he did. I told the suspect that I was looking for someone who matched his description who had fled from another ranger and that he needed to wait with me until the ranger arrived and that if he was not the one they were looking for, he would be free to go.

The suspect stated (statements are not exactly verbatim) that he had been "putting up with this kind of crap from us rangers for years," that he knows about the helmet rule and had been cited "three or four times" for not wearing one. He said that he had just been riding in the El Sereno Preserve and that there had been a woman ranger there and that she had told him that she was going to call the police on him. The suspect then tried to go around my truck, but I was blocking his path and I told him to stop and again that I was a Peace Officer. He said," If you are a cop, where is your gun?" Then he said that he had just been trying to get out of the sun into the shade. He then tried to go around the other side of the truck with his bike, but I told him there was no shade on the trail, blocked his path and told him to stay in front of the truck. He said he wasn't going to wait much longer.

Ranger Reneau arrived and said he was the suspect who fled from her, and she asked for and received identification.

The suspect, who had now been identified as Mr. Ho, then started to leave again and came at me as I was standing by the truck. I told him to stop, put one hand on suspect Ho's bike handle bars to stop them from hitting me and suspect Ho then put one of his hands on my chest to push me and said," Get the fuck out of my way!" I told him not to touch me and he backed off and said," Get your hands the fuck off my bike." At no time did I put my hand on suspect Ho. He then told me that if he had really wanted to get by me that there was no way that I could have stopped him since he had been a boxer and was a black belt.

When Ho tried to push past Terry, I requested Los Gatos Police respond to our stop, and two officers on motorcycles finally arrived, just as I finished filling out the citation, which he then signed without further ado. All this fuss was for an infraction helmet citation, which now had morphed into a misdemeanor PC 148 violation. We later also made a request to the District Attorney to add an "assault and battery" charge for his putting his hand on Terry's chest to push past him. Who would have thought that a 72-year old wouldn't have acquired more sense? Such headstrong, impulsive, aggressive behavior is more to be expected when stopping a 22-year old!

Back at the office doing the paperwork, I got motivated to find the incident reports from our suspect's previous cites, especially since Supervisor Tony thought he remembered this guy. Finding old records from the pre-computerized reports era is not easy. I scanned (using my God-given anatomical scanners) years of old incident reports and finally found Ranger Sandy's 1996 Ho helmet citation, and another one by Tony in 2006. Sandy's report noted that Ho was "uncooperative and never came to a complete stop." Both noted a generous use of expletives: "Fuck you," "You are a fucking punk," and "I'll kick your ass if I ever see you on the street." Some people never learn.

Several weeks later I got an email from one of the Skyline rangers, Lane, containing a link to the archives of a lawyer call-in show on a local radio station, KGO. I opened the link and was soon laughing out loud. I later replayed it for Terry and some of the other rangers. Our suspect, Ho, as irascible and outrageous as ever, but not so profane, was on the air bragging about his prowess as an athlete, complaining about the District's helmet regulation, and telling the story of our recent encounter. I loved it, particularly the part where he described being pulled over by "this rangerchick!" Wow, I sounded rough and tough, and youthful. He probably meant it as a sexist slur, but I didn't hear it that way. I guess the KGO lawyer did, because he immediately pegged Ho as a firebrand. He told Ho that if he went into court talking like that, the judge would throw him out for contempt of court. He told him that with a mouth like his, he would be better off keeping it shut and letting a lawyer do the talking. Amen. I will, if I can, make just one exemption: I will retain for myself my new moniker: Rangerchick.

2. Rangers

When the question of occupation comes up, and I respond, "park ranger," I can expect to hear, "That's so cool! How did you get your job? I always wanted to be a park ranger." I understand the sentiment of such enthusiastic comments yet, despite a childhood of hiking, camping and backpacking, I never set out to be a ranger. It wasn't until my nebulous dreams of other more prestigious occupations had disintegrated that the allure of a career writing dog-off-leash tickets suddenly hit me: I could be working outside! It's not the intellectual or academic profession of those youthful aspirations, but it suits me quite well. I wish I'd come to this realization a lot sooner.

Obviously the greatest thing about a ranger job, whether working for the National Park Service, the Forest Service, the State Parks, the County Parks or some other land management agency, is that one gets to work outdoors. Office drudges of all stripes can justifiably envy a ranger's days in the sunshine. Other enviable perks include wearing a uniform that instantly makes the ranger appear an expert in all things from emergency medicine to natural history and solves the problem of what to wear to work. I get to drive a patrol truck that allows me to park in red zones and under "No Parking" signs and I have keys to all those "dead end" gated back roads, and I can travel with impunity where only scofflaws dare to tread. I spend my days riding and hiking through redwood forests, serpentine meadows, tidal mudflats, and vast stretches of chaparral, and get paid for it.

One of the less-great things about the job is working all weekends, evenings, and holidays. If I want a weekend off next month for an impromptu trip to climb Half Dome with friends, I better have applied for it last December when I submitted my request for my two weeks of "guaranteed vacation," contingent upon seniority, and being first in line to ask for those particular days. For the last ten years, my days off have been Thursdays and Fridays. My co-workers, who work those Thursdays and Fridays, get Mondays and Tuesdays off. Weekend and holiday vacation time with one's spouse is particularly special and precious because there are minimum staffing requirements— minimum of one early ranger (7:00 am to 3:00 pm) and two late rangers (eight hours shift ending about an hour and a half after sundown) per field office.

Rangers are also near the bottom of the pecking order of the bureaucratic, hierarchical, protocol-bound, decision-making machine of the Midpeninsula Regional Open Space District, my employer, so it can feel like my every decision and every utterance is being dictated, monitored and critiqued by policy-pushing micro-managers. Can't do that; must do it this way; did that wrong, again. The day they install a GPS tracking device on my hat—supposedly for my safety—I'm outta here.

Mind you, I'm not complaining. I fully appreciate the financial security of being a "lazy government worker." I know full well that plenty of shop clerks, fast food workers, and people working two part-time jobs don't even get two days off in a row. Like me, they work nights, weekends and holidays, but certainly get no special recognition for their efforts, much less shift differential, holiday pay or overtime. District Rangers are unionized and operate under a "Memorandum of Agreement" with the District (one more layer of bureaucracy!) and I thank the leaders of the labor movement every time I fill in my time card for a week of paid vacation or a day of sick leave. I was 43, after all, before I landed this, my first "real" job, and had been a seasonal, hourly, or minimum wage worker up until then.

I was primed for this job by the time I reached middle age and my pie-in-the-sky, served-up-on-a-silver-platter dream job hadn't fallen into my lap. I had a husband, a ten-year-old son, a house in suburban Menlo Park and a part-time English as a Second Language tutoring job, all of which left me feeling un-fulfilled. Was this it? Was this all I was ever going to do with my life? I had been looking for adventure, something fun, new, interesting and exciting. I hadn't been looking for a job. I had thought that maybe I'd go hike the Pacific Crest Trail or go ride my bike across the country now that my son was finally old enough to manage in my absence. I'd given up actual job-hunting because I'd never figured out what a good job for me would look like. I had worked as a seasonal on the District trail crew years before and loved it. I had enjoyed the hard physical labor, the acquisition of new maintenance and construction skills, and the camaraderie of the rest of the seasonal and permanent OSTs (Open Space Technicians.) Were it not for my total lack of interest in engines and machines, I would even have considered applying for a permanent OST job, but I never saw myself as a ranger.

I had toyed with the idea of a fire department job and had even taken a wildland firefighting course and gotten my

EMT (Emergency Medical Technician) certificate, but I wasn't impressed by the firefighters' job on the couple of ride-alongs I went on. Way too urban for me, and too much down time. I knew that my real interest lay in natural history and my real strength in teaching, but paid "interpretation" jobs were few, hard to get, and, honestly, sounded boring. I didn't enjoy making interpretive displays and didn't relish being stuck leading the same nature hikes and campfire programs over and over again. I had applied for several "seasonal interpretive ranger" jobs anyway and never even got an interview, probably because I didn't have a degree in anything remotely resembling biology, ecology, geology, or any other "-ology."

I was not interested studying administration of justice, doing law enforcement or being a cop, that is, a ranger. At least that's what I told myself. I saw myself as an educator, an interpreter, not as the cold, hard fist of the law. Perhaps I was trying very hard not to see the big elephant in the room of my personality: like most happy rangers I do have an affinity for doing the "right" thing, for doing what I am told, for complying with the social norms, and following the rules. But in this regard, I honestly don't think I am any different than 90 percent of the rest of humanity, and certainly very much in keeping with the attitude of my co-workers. Don't we all try to keep ourselves out of trouble? Don't most people want to be helpful, kind and compassionate toward others? Can't we all avoid stress and trouble and just get along? Can't we all just follow the rules?

Rangers, especially un-armed law enforcement rangers like me, lean heavily upon this world view every time we stop someone for an infraction of the rules. People comply with peace officers because they have been trained since early childhood that they should, and must submit to the authority of the law as embodied in my badge and uniform. Strict and blind obedience to the law can also be a problem, (Yes, I've been called a Nazi more times than I can count) but rangers, and cops, have discretion about enforcement matters, and often they err on the side of leniency and compassion.

We are a pretty social bunch, the rangers of the Open Space District, the kind of folks who are comfortable making small talk with strangers while waiting in line, or are the first to introduce ourselves to others at the start of a trip. We like inclusiveness, joking around, telling funny stories and playing practical jokes on each other. We value teamwork and being good team players, everyone doing their bit, and doing their duty (which doesn't include hanging around telling stories!). We all have small but important roles to play, like good little cogs on the outer rim of the wheel of the District. At least we get to actually contact the earth.

At the same time, rangers are self-sufficient loners, often crowd-averse, lovers of wide-open spaces with only wild nature for company. Our heroes are explorers, and fossil hunters and naturalists and Native Americans. Out in the field, far from help, we carry on the fading mantle of frontier justice. When I say "Stop," and when I say, "You're free to go," my word is law, at least for the time being. Out in the field, I am powerful. The wheel rests on my cog. The lawyers and judges can poke holes in everything later.

Rangering provides me with a perfect mix of sociability and solitary reflection. I can feel stifled and suffocated indoors at parties, trainings and meetings. I get antsy and fidgety and can't get comfortable. I'm often happiest alone out on the back roads with my truck, Dumbo, or on foot away from all vestiges of 21st century life, except the duty belt, of course, and the duty that goes with it. But after several quiet days with barely a nod to a co-worker or a visitor, I start to feel lonely and sad and need some human contact to cheer myself up. Easy enough: just head to one of the more populated preserves.

The District doesn't tell the rangers the results of the psychiatric tests we have to take as part of being hired. In fact, we have to sign wavers saying we will never know our scores, but I'd bet District rangers' scores converge on some key personality traits—a desire for justice and fairness, mixed with compassion and a sense of humor.

So now, when the subject of my career choice comes up in conversation with friends, strangers, preserve visitors, and even suspects, I respond with enthusiasm. I reassure curious wanna-be rangers that they are not too old, or too unqualified, or too compromised by their past to be eligible. There are lots of doors into the rarified world of rangering. Follow my example. Send in an application. You never know.

SANTA ROSA JUNIOR COLLEGE
104th Ranger Academy
9/23/02-11/14/02   Bill Orr, Director

3. Application and Academy

I really did ultimately luck into this job. I was out hiking, which I did a lot since I was only working part time, and happened to meet Daniel, one of the supervising rangers, who remembered me favorably from the couple of seasons I had worked for the District as a seasonal on the trail crew. Daniel said I should apply for the open ranger position, and he was serious even though I just kept laughing him off. However, that evening in bed as I was trying to get to sleep, the thought kept popping into my head: R-a-n-g-e-r. That would be fun, new, different, and challenging. Why not? I should at least apply. I realized then that I would never forgive myself if I didn't at least apply.

So I did, the next day. I drove down to the District office, got an application and sat there in the lobby filling it out in pencil, just so I couldn't be mad at myself for not "at least trying." I didn't think I had much of a chance at my age, and with no appropriate education and very little experience in the field, so I didn't want to get too emotionally invested in this application process. But I kept making the cut: the first interview, then the second interview, and even the practical tests with the scary scenarios. One question that kept cropping up was whether I was tough enough to deal with disrespectful and even violent suspects. Having no experience or education in law enforcement, I could only assert that I felt I could put on a brave face, even if inside I was quaking in my boots. I said if I could summon the grit, as a substitute teacher, to maintain order in a classroom of surly adolescents, how much worse could a couple of overgrown brats on bicycles be?

I survived the physical exam, the fitness test, the background check, (where your friends and neighbors are encouraged to say nasty things about you) and, finally, two rounds of psychological tests. Round one was about four solid hours of filling in bubbles on Scantron cards answering permutations of the same questions over and over again. Have you ever smoked pot? Have you ever stolen anything from an employer? Have you ever cheated on a test? Round two was three months later. They bring you back and have you do it all over again. Apparently lies are really hard to remember, and being squeaky clean (at least in some key categories) didn't hurt either, I'm sure. After a while, as the months of the hiring process passed, I secretly started to get my hopes up.

I had a consolation prize all lined up for myself: the cross-country bike ride. I had the maps, was looking at dates, and had my mom enlisted to drive sag wagon. Perhaps I was really making myself look forward to this ride in a desperate effort to avoid tears when the dreaded "skinny envelope" arrived. It was one of the happiest moments of my life when I got the call that I had gotten the job. I was the only person hired out of the 100 and whatever who had applied, not an unusual statistic, I learned later. Other rounds of hiring have produced no ranger candidates at all. Most, I hear, fall prey to the background check or the psychological exam. So, against all odds, I was in. Now I had to prove I could do it, both to my new employer and to myself. I had to pass the academy and pass probation.

There was just one week left from the day I was hired before I was to report for eight weeks of law enforcement training at the National Park Service Law Enforcement Training Academy in Santa Rosa. I think my first day of work was the day after my acceptance phone call, and I spent that week riding around with each of the four District supervising rangers, driving through the 60,000 acres of Open Space District land. We may as well have been driving in circles. There were so many preserves and so many gates and un-marked access roads. I had hiked through a good many of the preserves and figured that would stand me in good stead in learning my way around, but getting someplace in a giant Ford F-350 pickup with a fire pumper mounted on the rear was an entirely different matter. Not everything marked as a road on the patrol maps was actually drivable and many were incredibly steep and rocky with almost no place to turn around. I remember my supervisor, Tony (although I wasn't yet assigned to his team) driving me up through Loma Prieta Ranch in Sierra Azul Open Space Preserve. It seemed almost unbelievable that this hugely rutted, rock-studded, precipitous gully should even be regarded as drivable. A mere passenger at this point, my palms were sweaty with anxiety, already intimidated by the prospect of having to navigate these roads myself.

A good part of one day was spent at the uniform store followed by the Westco boot shop. The District bought me a really cool jacket, three pairs of green pants, hemmed and pressed, three long-sleeve and three short-sleeve tan shirts with cuffs and epaulettes and badge grommets and District patches sewn on the shoulders, and a pair of $300 fire boots. I also got the duty belt with all the various holders: radio holder, handcuffs holder, pepper-spray holder, baton holder, key holder, cell phone holder, etc. We ordered the ranger hat and the body armor and I was issued raingear and coveralls and leather gloves and a District baseball cap. Altogether I figured this amounted to a couple thousand dollars worth of personalized clothing and gear, and I had yet to do a lick of work. That evening I couldn't resist putting on my new duds and strutting around in front of the full-length mirror feeling silly and excited and rather embarrassed about the investment the District was making in me. I had a growing sense of commitment brought on by this outrageous outpouring of funds. I was being shown a lot of faith and support; I wouldn't let them down.

The academy was only eight weeks long, which seemed an awfully short time to teach a bunch of average Joes like me anything much about detentions and arrests, and searches and seizures, and officer safety and defensive tactics, much less allowing enough time to get everyone qualified in the use of a handgun, rifle and shotgun. District rangers are not armed, but, to pass the academy and get the job, ranger candidates have to qualify with the firearms. It's crazy, but true. I wasn't too worried about it; I assumed it wouldn't be that hard, but I'd never had a gun in my hands in my life.

As I packed the car and headed north for the Golden Gate and the four-hour drive to Santa Rosa, I was more thrilled about the upcoming adventure than worried about passing any sort of exam. I had been a good student, an excellent student actually. I knew how to drill and practice and study. I wasn't worried about making the grade either mentally or physically, even though I knew I would likely be a good bit older than the others. I was looking forward to eight weeks of fun and excitement. The District was paying for the whole thing—mileage to and from, including one trip home per week, tuition, housing, and food. It looked like a vacation compared to my humdrum wife and mother, part-time English teacher suburban existence.

The Training Academy campus in Santa Rosa was established to train seasonal park rangers for the National Park Service, and the curriculum assumes that this is the destiny of all the graduates. In reality, at least half of my class of 50 or so ranger wannabes were probably headed for jobs with local land management agencies right here in northern California, mostly county park districts. None of the county park rangers would ultimately be armed either, but we all had to qualify. We had to memorize a slew of federal regulations and lots of historical information about the National Park Service so that we could dutifully regurgitate it onto tests. I certainly don't remember much of it. Those lucky few who actually had seasonal jobs lined up with the NPS got to politely lord it over the rest of us. They were headed for really cool-sounding places like Acadia National Park in Maine and Isle Royal National Park in Michigan. They would be the real park rangers, packing heat, doing their own felony crime-scene investigations, single-handedly catching murderers, smugglers, poachers, and pedophiles, like fictional Ann Pigeons incarnate. No dog-off-leash tickets for them, surely. I was in a different happy minority: those who had already been hired, and were on an all-expenses-paid ride. Most of the others were paying their own way hoping to pad their resumes to land a job. There were a couple of ex-Marines, lots of young people who had worked summers for concessionaires in Yosemite or Grand Canyon, or had had recreation-oriented jobs at summer camps. One was an ex-seasonal-smokejumper for CDF. Most were bored and restless salespeople, technicians, handymen and teachers. I was the second oldest and one of only eight women.

As I had suspected, the classroom part of the program was not an issue for me, and the defensive tactics training was decidedly fun, even though I had no hope of being the top student in either case. I remember when the first quiz result was posted, with our names disguised as numbers, and I had ranked somewhere in the middle, just barely passing. I was disgusted and frustrated with myself, and resolved to study even harder. How could I, a college graduate with a master's degree, not have out-competed more than half of my class? I refused to settle for such mediocrity, and I scored much higher on subsequent tests. Others did not, and after each quiz another two or three aspirants would throw in the towel and head home. Sadly, many of the dropouts were some of the few people in the pool who were not native speakers of English, or were ethnic minorities, or people with limited formal education. The loss of these classmates lead to a whiter and more affluent student body and ultimately to a similarly skewed demographic in the ranger profession, as I assume this culling happened with every class.

In defensive tactics class, I also soon sank to the level of my age-induced incompetence, which I clearly demonstrated when I had to take down and handcuff 20-something males. It really only happened when they let me. My poor 20-year-old classmate Josh, who was renting the other room in the same off-campus house as I, suffered endless hours of my practicing taking him down, only to easily pin me when I told him not to go easy on me. I was in good shape, having been a competitive Masters swimmer all my life, and I am taller than most women, pretty muscular, and no shrinking violet, but age and gender were against me.

I did pretty well in the physical strength and agility tests required by the NPS, scoring in the middle of the pack in most tests—climbing over walls, running obstacle courses, etc. The only woman who always beat me was the ex-Marine. All the same, my younger male classmates really impressed me with the effectiveness of their all-out, aggressive, physical response when dealing with un-cooperative, violent "offenders." If one is bigger and stronger than the bad guy, just grab him, throw him on the ground, and cuff him. Standing back, yelling, and ordering people around only works some of the time; then you are screwed. Of course, in all these scenarios we had our orange plastic "guns." At the academy, it is assumed that rangers will be armed, so all the training and all the scenarios are built around guns. By the time we were doing such scenarios, of course, we had either qualified, or gone home.

The guns almost did me in, although firearms training didn't start out that badly. We had had to read and complete a study guide about the 9 mm Glock handgun we would be using, learning the names of the various parts and how they worked. No problem. Sort of interesting, actually. Then came day one at the firing range, where we met the instructor, who seemed a reasonable fellow, and got a long lecture about all the safety rules and precautions. Seemed easy enough. Then we got empty guns and practiced holding them and squeezing the trigger smoothly without jerking and aiming at the targets through the sights. This was a bit tougher. The real guns were heavier than I expected and the sights were just these two tiny blips not an eighth of an inch tall on the top of the barrel, not really user-friendly. We practiced loading and unloading the guns and snapping on and off the safety, and finally we got to shoot a bullet. Even with the earmuffs on, I was astonished at the horrible, noisy explosion as my neighbor's gun went off. I couldn't believe that that awful noise was the correct and expected result of firing one very small bullet. I nearly swung around to check, but stopped myself. Directing the muzzle of a gun, loaded or unloaded, anywhere other than down range, is a safety no-no. Good thing the instructor had been pounding that into our heads for the last hour.

I was not happy about the target, the human torso with the concentric circles around the heart. I didn't want to think about the broader implications of what I was learning to do: kill people. Shoot to kill. One aims at the center of the chest, not the head, which is smaller and harder to hit, or the arms or legs. The only reason for firing that gun is to take another person's life. Didn't that bother anybody else? Were they better able than I was to distance themselves from this reality and just see this deadly weapon as a clever toy for punching holes in pieces of paper? It made the exercise more palatable if I thought about it that way. After all, I would never actually be carrying one of these things, and would never bear the responsibility of deciding whether to use it. How could these young men and women be so cocksure of themselves? As we were now a week or so into the academy and I had gotten to know the other students a bit, it was scary to think of some of them with a badge on their chest and a gun on their hip. As I fired my first bullet, heard the terrible noise, felt the gun recoil and punched my first hole in a paper torso, I realized that this wasn't going to be so easy after all.

I came to really hate the firing range. The noise, the smell of gunpowder, the cavernous yet claustrophobic darkness and, of course, above all, my on-going failure as a marksman: I seemed to get worse and worse rather than better. As qualifying drew nearer, I started to panic. I spent every spare minute I was allowed on the range, but bullets are expensive and the academy range was solidly booked with other classes from the police academy. There was a private range an hour's drive away and a number of us under-achievers would carpool down there and spend our time and money. The problem was that, at the private range, unless one hired a private instructor, one couldn't draw and fire from a line out on the floor, but rather only point and shot from inside the booth, which was a really different skill. So I hired a private instructor, Mr. Sam. He was a Godsend, for my sorely flagging self esteem, if nothing else. He was an older Asian man, very cheerful, kind, forgiving and friendly. His encouragement and his enthusiasm for pistol shooting as a sport helped me to overcome some of my loathing of this entire activity. Mr. Sam really enjoyed accurately punching holes in pieces of paper. We practiced and practiced, but I still couldn't qualify, couldn't get enough bullet holes inside the target area, and the dreaded test was only days away. I always wondered if I wouldn't have done better if the range had been out of doors. When I think back to those awful weeks, it is that oppressive, noisy, smelly darkness that haunts me. I just wanted to bolt. But I stayed on, kept trying, hoping for a miracle. And now came the moment of truth and it was do or die, well, not really die, but that's what it felt like.

The night before qualifying was one of sleepless misery. We had done two practice qualifyings during the previous week and I hadn't passed either one, although I was close. How could this be happening? How could this be this hard? I tossed and turned and agonized. I agonized that all the time and effort and, above all, money that had been invested just in getting me this far, was all for naught. The faith and trust that the District had bestowed upon me was clearly misplaced. I was going to fail. A couple of bullet holes a couple of centimeters outside the lines and my exciting new career would be all over. It would be all over in a couple of hours, and then I would have to crawl home in shame. I was a wreck by the time I was called to line up with the nine others in my group to face the firing squad, I mean firing line. We stood in the dark, quivering with adrenalin, and waited for the by now familiar buzz and snap as the targets whipped around.

My heart was pounding and my grip was so very sweaty, but I was trying so hard to think positive thoughts. Keep trying. Don't give up. You can do it. Don't look at the holes and try to count as you go along, just concentrate on shooting. Think of nothing else. In the ringing silence after it was finally over and we had holstered our weapons, we waited while the instructors counted up the holes. Every hole inside the torso or head counted, no bonus points for a bull's eye. I knew that I had failed again, but it's not over until it's over, and I was faintly holding out hope for a miracle. Maybe the instructor would miscount. I would take it. I just needed to pass. As the numbers came in, I saw the crack shots strutting around and comparing scores. Then I noticed Kathy, our class president (by popular vote, but without much of a role, or any actual authority) who had the spot next to mine on the floor, was standing stock-still with tears sliding silently down her cheeks. Uh-oh. This would never do. Kathy was our Golden Girl, our role model, and the favorite of the range instructor. She and I had both failed. My heart felt like a stone in my chest. As the jubilant qualifiers filed out, the instructor called us over, presumably to give us our walking papers. But no, we were to wait outside for the rest of the groups to finish. We were to be given another chance. Another chance. It wasn't over. The icy grip of despair settling in my bones would have to hold off a few more minutes. I would have to endure the tension and stress yet again, but where there is life, there is hope. In the final round of qualifying that day, Kathy and Virginia (one of my under-achieving carpool buddies) and I faced the targets one last time. Kathy and I passed. Virginia went home.

That is, everyone assumed she would go home. There is no point in continuing once failing to qualify, and yet, there she was Monday morning in her seat. She'd paid for it and she was going to stick it out. What a brave woman, to suffer all the pitying and condescending looks. My heart went out to her. I wonder what happened to her, if she ended up as a ranger.

What a relief it was to qualify! What a weight off my shoulders! I felt like I could fly. In exaltation, I called my husband and my parents and Mr. Sam, who were also very relieved. I was home free having qualified, somehow, against all odds, and would never have to qualify again, ever. Oh happy day! True, there were still some scary tests ahead, like the final scenarios and the final exam, but the worst was behind me and the night before those tests I actually slept. I wasn't a nervous wreck. I knew now that there were second chances and that the instructors actually did want us to pass. They were just enjoying scaring the hell out of us.

We spent one horrible, cold, wet, evening in the dark and driving rain practicing felony car stops. We got to take turns playing the bad guy, crawling backwards on our knees with our hands in the air, being handcuffed on our bellies in the mud and getting rolled around and stripped during the concealed weapons search. I was freezing and miserable, but happy. We spent a whole day out at a deserted airport driving Crown Vics around an obstacle course at breakneck speeds with the code three sirens blaring. I was beside myself with fear, but I was happy. I had qualified and the world was my oyster. Everyone was sure we would be doing car chases and felony stops for our final scenarios, but, in general, they were a lot tamer. They just liked to keep us scared.

My lead role scenario was a domestic dispute, a husband and wife screaming their lungs out at one another, disturbing the peace, but not hitting each other. Damn! Domestic disputes are tricky. The police officer, or ranger, is supposed to figure out which disputant is "the aggressor" and arrest them. In a husband-versus-wife fight, this is usually the husband, but not always. Statistically domestic disputes are the most deadly calls for law enforcement, because emotions are running so high. What was I supposed to do now, with no actual physical aggression at all? There was no right answer. If I took one of them outside, then my partner and I couldn't see one another any more, couldn't watch each other's backs. That would be bad. But as long as they were within sight of one another, they continued to carry on so loudly that I couldn't think. Just shut up, would you? It was like those first aid scenarios where I always seemed to be assigned the screamer patient. How come I couldn't have the unconscious guy? Of course, my main concern was the instructor standing in the background with his clipboard watching me flounder. While I was floundering one of the suspects brought out an orange plastic gun and shot me. Why would anyone want to be a cop?

Graduation was on a Friday. Thank God it was finally graduation Friday after eight very long, hard weeks of training, including most weekends. I had only made it home once in those two months. Various agencies that regularly sent students to the Academy sent representatives mostly as spectators, some to take part in the ceremony. Supervisor Murray came for the District and took me out to lunch afterward, Chinese I think. Some people's families even came. It seemed incongruous seeing these guys with wives and small children, who, just the day before, had been screaming profanities at me and shoving me onto the ground. The Academy was weird, a very strange and artificial place, where nothing was as it seemed. The bad guys were good guys, just play-acting. The instructors were actually human, despite the evidence to the contrary. The scenario village was a mock-up, and the scenarios in them were pretend. The finals of defensive tactics and defensive driving and felony car stops were not really do or die after all. The scenario guns were made of orange plastic. About the only real things were the real guns, and those real guns just about killed off my new dream job.

4. Training

Finally home again from the academy, I was exhausted, and scared. What had I gotten myself into? I wasn't ready to be a park police officer, a "pine pig." I no longer felt so ready to put on a brave face when confronted with real-life criminals; I really understood now how quickly I could become dead meat as soon as some bad guy had opportunity, and a gun. If I proved to be as lousy at my actual job as I had been at many of the skills at the academy, I wouldn't last a week. How long could I maintain a façade of competence and bluff my way along? No, that wouldn't work, and I couldn't do it. I would just have to admit to my stupidity, incompetence, ignorance, clumsiness, forgetfulness, and every other failing, and ask for help. I would try harder, and be exceedingly conscientious and hardworking. Above all else, I wouldn't give up, no matter how many times I might have to swallow my pride or face embarrassment or reprimand. As I discovered at the Academy, sometimes there were second chances, after all. I also felt some reassurance when remembering back to my experiences while on the District trail crew years before, and also to my many years volunteering for the District as a Nature Center Guide, that I surely wouldn't be facing any critical situations any time soon. First there would be a lot more on the job training and, with any luck, this ranger job just might work out.

In the first couple of weeks after returning from the academy, I really was intensely focused on learning the basics of the job, doing everything I was told as "by the book" as possible, and not screwing up. As expected, I had about four months of hands-on training still ahead of me, mostly riding around with my supervisor, as well as with the other rangers, at lot of it simply learning my way around. I remember sitting shotgun next to my new supervisor, Tony, feeling completely stunned to find myself in this calm, quiet, safe, green preserve after all the stress of the academy. He must have sensed that I was a bit overwhelmed because he asked if I had any questions or concerns. I told him that I was worried that I couldn't do it, that I wouldn't make it if my job was going to be anything like the scenarios I had been dealing with. He didn't laugh or deny the serious nature of my concern. He said not to worry, that I would be okay, that the job I was headed for wasn't very much like that at all. He assured me that when serious incidents occurred I would have the means to handle them, both with my own skills and with the support of the other rangers and supervisors. It began to dawn on me that I had lucked into a superior supervisor, not a bully or a nag, not a mother hen or a worrywart, but a truly skilled supervisor who trusted the rangers to do our jobs to the best of our abilities. Part of the credit for my success as a ranger, and my enjoyment of this job, was certainly my fortuitous assignment to Tony's team.

The District is a public agency, a "special district" as allowed by state law, supported by local property taxes, and its tax base happens to cover a couple of the richest sections of the richest counties of California. If you own property inside the boundaries, you're helping pay my salary. Most other "special districts" are school districts, water districts, sewer districts, or fire districts. The Midpeninsula Regional Open Space District is almost unique. The East Bay Regional Park District across San Francisco Bay from us is very similar as far as their funding is concerned, but they have a very different mission, being primarily focused on human recreation. And over there armed "park police" do most of the law enforcement, not unarmed rangers.

Most park visitors have only a general notion of the jurisdiction of the land they are visiting; they assume District rangers must somehow work for the state or the county. I'm glad I don't. In years past, the District ranger position served as a springboard to launch a career with state parks, but since the great recession and the huge California state budget deficit, state parks have seen better days. They are certainly not stealing District rangers anymore. As for the county parks, well, no thank you, not for me. Why would I chose to spend my days cooped up in just a couple county parks patrolling the picnic areas, barbeque pits, car campgrounds, restrooms, garbage cans, sports fields, drive-up vista points and inevitable toll booth? Boring. County park rangers who work at the reservoirs also get to deal with drunken boaters and illegal fishing and all the other trouble that a body of water invites. I'm spoiled, I know, but the District's clientele are mostly hikers, runners, equestrians, mountain bikers and dog walkers, with a goodly sprinkling of birdwatchers, photographers and other tree-hugging nature lovers.

We do have one campground, but it is a backpack camp and a two-mile walk in, uphill. There are a few scattered picnic tables and "memorial benches," but no picnic areas, car campgrounds, garbage cans or restrooms, except a few port-a-potties and pit toilets. The District's lands are called preserves, not parks, and the District's stated primary mission is not recreation, but rather the preservation of a "greenbelt" of undeveloped land in the Santa Cruz Mountains above the urban mega-city of the San

Francisco Peninsula. There are 26 separate preserves--ranging from tiny Pichetti Ranch to enormous Sierra Azul-- comprising a total of more than 60,000 acres. This is not wilderness land; it's urban interface, and shows the scars of centuries of human use such as invasive weeds, mine tailings, grazing terracettes, skid roads, and the stumps of former giant redwoods. Along with other local land management agencies, the District is helping to preserve, and possibly even to restore, at least a remnant of what was once an amazingly bio-diverse and beautiful region of the earth.

Okay, I lied when I said there were no amenities like picnic grounds and BBQs and flush potties and playing fields. We do have all those things, but they are not really ours. For better or for worse, the District wholly manages Rancho San Antonio County Park, which abuts highly upscale, suburban Cupertino, CA. This county park is mostly a giant parking lot serving visitors to the many miles of hilly trails in Rancho San Antonio Open Space Preserve. There are exactly eight flush toilets, four picnic tables with accompanying raised barbeque thingies and an un-mowed, un-watered ex-playing field and abandoned tennis courts. And yet the place is gridlocked with vehicles every sunny weekend. A good half of all those weekend visitors are families who are going no farther than the pampered pigs and sheep at Deer Hollow Farm (managed by the city of Mountain View with financial support from the District), on a level, one-mile, stroller and tricycle friendly paved path. There is nothing else like Rancho in the whole District, thank goodness. I don't understand why anyone would spend half an hour circling for a parking place just so they can hike the same trails week after week. Why not go check out one of the other preserves? Like it or not, my assigned duty station, the Foothills Field Office, sat smack in the middle of Rancho.

In those days, there was no training manual, and training new rangers was pretty much left up to the individual supervisors. Tony and I gradually worked our way through the Ranger Operations Manual, discussing disciplinary procedures, use of force, officer safety, vehicle accident protocols, working with volunteers, fire fighting expectations, fitness requirements, and patrol procedures. All pretty much what you would expect from a bunch of dry words on paper with everything reduced to black and white, the right and wrong ways to do anything, with hardly a mention of the enormous murky gray gulf between these two easy extremes, that damned-if-you-do and damned-if-you-don't spot where discretion and judgment make all the difference. My take on the greater part of the Ops Manual was simply that if I were honest and hardworking I needn't worry about remembering any of it. It was almost true, as I later found out.

Of much more interest and value was the time spent learning the land, learning how to get from one preserve to the next—often through a bewildering matrix of back roads—and how to get around within the preserves without getting stuck in the mud or having to make a 36-point turn on a steep, narrow dead-end road or, worse yet, back out. Again, it didn't seem so hard when I had time to stop and consult the map, but when suddenly called upon to get to a specific location Code Three (urgent; use the lights and siren), I had to know by heart the absolute shortest and fastest way to get there from wherever I happened to be.

Before I could be of any use, I also had to get comfortable using the radio, and using "10-codes" and "phonetic alphabet" jargon. "10 Codes" are supposed to make radio communication clearer and quicker for us, and, at the same time, somewhat obtuse to outsiders—like suspects—who might be listening in. Officially, District rangers are discouraged from using 10 codes, because, in a critical situation if someone were to use a little-known, lesser-used code, this might, in fact, hamper communication. Rangers are encouraged to use "plain speech." Naturally, it turns out that even "plain speech" isn't just any old way of saying something, but has its own special set of terms. For example, let's say I am headed for a reported fallen bicyclist in Sierra Azul Preserve. When I get there, I am supposed to let the dispatcher know that I have arrived. Remembering that I am supposed to use "plain speech," I could say, "Okay, I'm here now with all the other emergency vehicles, with the guy who fell off his bike on the Kennedy Trail." No, no, no! I would sound like an idiot to all those experienced speakers of Ranger Radio Jargon who are listening in. At this point, I must say, "I'm On Scene," or just use the 10-code, "I'm 10-97." Every 10-code has its prescribed plain speech equivalent so that, in fact, there are two sets of new vocabulary to learn, the 10-codes and their plain speech equivalents. There is also a funny sub-set of codes, like "Code 3," that describe the urgency of a situation or what the officer is doing. One might thus say either, "It's 10-6 here but Code 4; I'll give you a 10-21 when I finish my Code 7," or, in so-called plain speech, "It's busy here but situation normal; I'll telephone you when I finish my lunch." There is a cheat sheet provided and rubber banded to the sun visor of most patrol trucks, but in the thick of the moment there will be no time to refer to it, and I wouldn't want to broadcast my 10-Code ignorance by having a suspicious pause, while I peruse the sun visor, before replying to an inquiry such as, "Are you 10-36?" (Ready to copy confidential information)

And then there is the so-called "phonetic alphabet." As a former student of linguistics, I shake my head at this misnomer. To a linguist, a phone is a speech sound, and phonetics is the study of speech sounds. Some phones function as phonemes, in that they can change the meaning of words. All these terms have precise and exhaustively detailed meanings, which some small part of me still seems to care about, because it irks me that the system of assigning special names to the letters of the alphabet (A is Adam; B is Boy; C is Charles; D is David; E is Edward, etc) is called the phonetic alphabet! This silly system has nothing to do with phonetics, unless I'm missing something. How did it ever acquire this name?

The "phonetic alphabet" is used when spelling out names over the radio. So, for example, if I had detained Barack Obama and wanted to check to see if he had any wants or warrants outstanding, I would say "Mt. View (our dispatcher) 9L15 (my call sign) 10-29a on one, verbal information." "Go ahead" says Mt. View. "Male, last of Obama, Ocean, Boy, Adam, Mary, Adam, first of Barak, Boy, Adam, Robert, Adam, Charles, King." The logic of using this system is supposed to be that just saying the regular names of the letters, can be confusing over the potentially scratchy, staticky radio. The names of most letters are very short, just two phonemes in most cases, (B is / bi/, C is /si/). If all English letters had nice long names like W, (du/bul/yoo), maybe no "phonetic" system would ever have been devised. I wonder if this all started 50 years ago when radio communication was always scratchy and staticky, and has now become standard practice. I find it anything but helpful. Although I have gotten better at fluently spelling out suspects' names, I still routinely struggle when I am on the receiving end. If I have called in a car's license plate and the dispatcher says she doesn't know how to pronounce the name of the registered owner, but she is going to spell it for me, my heart sinks. Ready to copy? Sam-Charles-Henry-Adam-Robert-Tom-Zebra-Edward-Nora-Edward-George-George-Edward-Robert. More often than not, I have to ask her to repeat it, and more slowly please. German names (Schwartzenegger) aren't so bad for me, but the

Rangerchick

super-long Hindu names, Armenian names, and Slavic names are tough. My brain just can't quickly visualize the letters under their new names. I could never be a dispatcher, if for only this reason alone.

The most interesting, worthwhile, and fun part of this training period was simply riding around with Supervisor Tony as well as various experienced rangers getting to know them, to learn their style, and to watch them perform when confronted with various situations. I sensed no machismo or condescension from any of my new co-workers, just a sincere interest in their jobs, serving both the visitors and the land. I was impressed by their consistent kindness and thoughtfulness and their serious devotion to the profession. A great sense of humor never hurt either. When I would lament getting lost, or getting the truck stuck in the mud, they would just laugh and tell some funny story of their own initiation trials.

Most rangers didn't just fall into rangering like me, but had been actively pursuing the job for years. For instance, a good many of the other District rangers, like my new teammate Cory had attended the Parks Management program at West Valley College and had then worked five years as a seasonal for Santa Clara County Parks. Matt had attended Humboldt State, majoring in forestry, and had done a couple summers of seasonal maintenance for Humboldt Redwoods State Parks up in northern California. I felt sort of silly admitting to myself how ill-prepared I was by comparison.

Like about half of the patrol staff, both Matt and Cory were "resident rangers," meaning that they lived on one of the preserves in houses rented from the District, at half the going market rate. This is not a bad deal price-wise, if you don't mind putting up with visitors tramping past your door, being first in line to get called out in the middle of the night, having marijuana gardeners fleeing through your backyard, and having deranged District-haters accosting your wife on your driveway. As a resident ranger, you are more of a full-time ranger because you never do fully escape from your job; it is all around you, all the time, on duty and off.

It seems funny now, but one concern I had as a complete novice in the law enforcement field was about how embarrassed I felt confronting people about their misdeeds. As a frequent hiker, I had seen many dogs in prohibited areas and many dog-off -leash violations, and had usually felt too uncomfortable about correcting other people to actually talk to them. How righteously rude of me that would seem! Who did I think I was? I was sure the violators already knew they were in the wrong and didn't need me to tell them. But when walking around in a park ranger uniform, even without a badge yet, it was clear that the game had entirely changed. Now it would be strange and confusing if I were to do anything but confront the offender. Imagine a park ranger just casually strolling past someone obviously and blatantly misbehaving, even turning their head to look the other way, as an embarrassed visitor might!

It took a good many more years before I really lost all sense of discomfort, not just about initially stopping people, but about intensely questioning them about their doings, scrutinizing their responses and pointing out inconsistencies. As a new trainee, when a visitor said they didn't see the signs and didn't know the rules, I wondered why Cory continued to harass them with questions, and why Matt was asking them where they were parked and how they entered the preserve. I was not used to people lying to me, and I still don't enjoy making suspects squirm by pointing out inconsistencies in their replies. I don't enjoy extracting information from them this way, but it does help to reveal a dishonest person.

I had thought perhaps my knowledge of natural history and volunteer work as a docent, naturalist, and outdoor education leader would have been seen as an asset when applying for a ranger job, but in fact, maybe not. District rangers lead no interpretive programs, and aside from an optional annual wildflower identification walk, receive no on-the-job natural history training. Many rangers are hired not knowing the name of a single wildflower or native songbird. Some newly hired rangers don't know a bluebird from a blue jay, an Indian Warrior from an Indian paintbrush, or a damselfly from a dragonfly. This paucity of a thorough grounding in local natural history seems to me a glaring deficiency in the job requirements and in our training. I would expect that these young men and women who have obviously been raised with an appreciation of the out-of-doors and an enjoyment of outdoor recreation would have learned the names of the flora and fauna.

I feel incredibly lucky to have been raised by a family of nature lovers, which ingrained my affinity for natural history in early childhood. Certainly my most important teachers were my parents, who took me on innumerable weekend outings: camping in the Mojave desert, rock-climbing at Joshua Tree, snowshoeing at Big Bear, and peak-bagging in the San Gabriel, San Jacinto and San Gorgonio Mountains. My mother was also my Camp Fire Girls leader, and while we did our share of making sit-upons, and baking cookies we spent more time camping and hiking. I was 11 when I went on my first of many weeklong backpack trips: to the High Sierra, out of Glen Aulin in Yosemite National Park. I learned not just the names of the flowers, but also a mindset of wonder and appreciation for all the tiny living things, the miniature belly flowers, the lichens and mosses, and the multitudes of tadpoles and copulating "double frogs." Mom's friend Mary, our leader, would be distraught to see me muddying the waters of a still pond or putting big brown footprints across a soft green meadow. She had a very sharp tongue in such cases, but also a very big heart. She saw the little budding naturalist in me and delighted in showing me things, like the little white wormy grubs inside the bright red galls on the willow leaves.

I went from appreciation to interpretation when my own friend Mary, who rescued me from a kindergarten-student-teaching induced acute depression, got me a job as a "naturalist" teaching for San Mateo Outdoor Education. We worked at Camp Jones Gulch, nestled deep in the second-growth redwoods of the Santa Cruz Mountains. We lived in a trailer with four other women and got paid $75 a week. There I slowly regained my self-confidence, learned a bunch of silly kid tricks, camp songs, and natural history trivia, and I adopted the Santa Cruz Mountains as my home. That job had a tremendous influence on the course of my life; it is thanks to that job that I ended up as a ranger. Living at the camp, without a car or a television--and in those days there were no computers or Internet--I spent all my free time hiking the trails, old logging roads, ridges and creeks. Workdays were spent much the same way, but with a gaggle of fifth and sixth-graders behind me. Each week we lead "survival hikes" and "alone walks" and night hikes, and we had a beach day exploring the tide pools and the marsh. After two years of this peaceful, predictable life, my mental health gradually resumed its former stability and I knew that I had finally found myself. The classroom and I had parted ways for good. I knew I needed a land-based job, something that kept me in my sweet spot, safe in the loving embrace of Mother Nature, vis-à-vis the Santa Cruz Mountains.

My enthusiasm for local natural history did land me at least one fun assignment early on in my ranger career, I think even before I was badged. I was asked to escort a class of Stanford students on a walk at Windy Hill Preserve, just west of Portola Valley. This class was focusing on innovative methods of land preservation and had taken various field trips to visit land conservancies, conservation easements, and wildlife refuges around the San Francisco Bay Area. I was to lead them on a short hike and discuss not just the nature of the Open Space District and its inception (which they had already studied) but also the local scenery—the geography and history of the preserve and the species that lived there. It was great fun; the students were lively and interested and full of questions, a real mix of young people from around the world.

After the walk, the professor took me to dinner and we talked and talked. She was from the South and had grown up on a farm. She was as pleased with her bright, enthusiastic students as I was, but she made one interesting observation, which stuck with me: these kids had no sense of place. A good many of them had lived all over the world, but seldom more than a few years in any one place. They had visited exotic parks on all five continents, had climbed Kilamanjaro, walked with penguins, swum with dolphins, explored ancient ruins, but now they had no roots, no homeland, no sacred ground.

While I would love to see more of the Earth, I do know without a doubt that when I go into the mountains of my mind in search of John Muir's good tidings, I see myself high in a serpentine meadow ringed with ancient oaks and with the sun setting red far out over the Pacific and long tendrils of cottony fog bulging through the gaps in the Santa Cruz Mountains. It is the forever scenery of home, the way the world is "supposed" to look to my primordial, Neanderthal brain. Having lived my whole life in California, no other place feels quite right. When I return to some small canyon or creek which I haven't visited in years and years and find it just as I remember in my mind's eye, I feel immense satisfaction. Yes, one can return to the past! Sweet youth is not forever lost, but is waiting for me in every dewy morning meadow. Unlike returning to one's home town or to some city last visited 30 years ago, where everything seems to have changed, and there is a feeling of loss and disorientation, re-visiting a by-gone mountain top or sandy beach is very comforting. The pace of change in the natural world is so slow that, to our puny brains, nothing at all seems to have changed.

Eventually, after months of training in policies and procedures, and riding double with others, I got badged, got my own assigned truck, and starting patrolling on my own. (The badging "ceremony" is just a short interlude during a regular Wednesday night meeting of the Board of Directors. I stood up to be introduced to the Board and Superintendent Bernie pinned my badge to my uniform. No swearing in, which means I was "appointed" as a peace officer.) I was still on probation for my first two years, meaning I could be more easily fired if I screwed up, but now I was free to patrol where and how I wanted. I wasn't just following my trainers around. For me this meant spending as much time as I could out of the truck, on foot, exploring not just the official trails, but the unofficial ones as well—the creek beds and ridgelines, the disc lines and deer trails. Nine months after I turned in my application, here I was on the job. There were struggles ahead and difficulties I could not have imagined, but having a job I loved, working in and for the land I loved, would sustained me. And should I meet with further stumbling blocks in the future, should I find myself ashamed, with my head hanging low and my ego dragging in the dust, I would know the surest route to recovering my equilibrium: go for a hike, a long one, off trail and alone. My cares would drop off like autumn leaves; my soul would be restored.

5. Dumbo

In complete juxtaposition to my love of the land is my ambivalence about how I get there. Visitors to the preserves may walk or run or ride their bikes, but I drive. I spend most of my working days driving my truck. My image of the ideal ranger does not allow for this cheater, this loafer sitting behind a steering wheel. A true ranger ought to be on foot, alone, and self-contained with everything she truly needs on her back. On the other hand, I love having 60,000 acres to explore, and reluctantly acknowledge that I would never see a tenth of it without my truck. Rangers are stuck behind the steering wheel, often against their own inclination, because of the need to respond immediately to emergency calls anywhere in the District. The care and feeding of the truck thus becomes an important, even critical, part of the job. I have reconciled myself to this, but just barely. My truck, Dumbo (named for its huge side mirrors), a Ford F-350 extended cab pick-up, and I have a love-hate relationship.

One of the things I hate most about Dumbo is that she is huge. She barely fits on many of the steep, narrow mountain roads, especially if there are visitors whom I must squeeze past, and she's so tall that I cannot easily get in and out. I struggle to climb in, and then heave the heavy door closed when unavoidably parked sideways on a steep hill, or, conversely, I have to keep myself from falling out when I open the door! My first truck, some sort of Chevy, was smaller and shorter, and even then most elderly people getting a "courtesy transport" back to the parking lot, had trouble getting into the cab. Sometimes a boost to the rear end was needed, producing embarrassment all the way round. Frail, ill and elderly people cannot even begin to get into Dumbo. I need to get a stool. An escalator would be better!

Dumbo is also a gas hog. Even without the fire pumper and its 125 gallons of water, she only gets about eight miles to the gallon. That's outrageous, and shameful for an agency that is supposed to be in the conservation business. The terrible gas mileage combined with the teeny weenie 25-gallon gas tank means that nearly every other shift starts with a trip to the gas pump, and another $100 down the drain. Are you beginning to understand the hate part of this relationship?

Then there are the quarterly vehicle inspections, wherein every three months I have to check the complete inventory of Dumbo's tools and equipment—the lights, the tires, the Code 3 equipment, the fire gear and pumper, and on and on. Time consuming and boring, but not incomprehensible, except for the part under the hood. I have only the most superficial understanding of how an internal combustion engine works and used to really dread seeing that inspection form in my intra-office mailbox (That's an actual mailbox, not an electronic one.) I could never remember which of the dipsticks was for which fluid, and whether you were supposed to add more fluid through that same orifice or a different one, and how you were supposed to get the stuff into that tiny hole way down in there without spilling it all over the place. I finally made a cheat sheet for myself, which helped a lot, but no cheat sheet can equal in ease my usual strategy, which is to try to schedule Dumbo's 5,000 mile tune-ups and oil changes to immediately precede the quarterly vehicle inspection due dates. Chuck, the kindly mechanic, has then taken care of all those pesky fluid things for me, as well as irritating, time-consuming, frustrating jobs such as replacing burned out taillights. (Yes, we rangers also spend lots of work time just shuttling trucks to and from the mechanic, and the radio shop, and the Code 3 lights and siren place!)

Some rangers delight in tricking out their trucks' cabs with mounted GPS devices, rechargeable flashlight holders, spring-loaded Smokey Bear hat holders, radio battery chargers and so forth. Their panel boxes are cleverly outfitted with wooden map holders and tool holders. They actually enjoy doing this. I'll take the bare bones model myself. There is less stuff to break, less stuff to keep track of and less stuff to clean: yes, I'm a minimalist. I do take pride in keeping Dumbo clean, organized, and fully stocked with maps, garbage bags, staples, fencing materials, sunscreen, drinking water, paper towels, junior ranger stickers and a bunch of other necessities that aren't on any quarterly inspection check sheet. I hate it when my truck in is the shop and I have to use someone else's truck. Although major items such as the first aid kit have prescribed locations, many miscellaneous things do not. Thus I can't find where other rangers may have hidden an extra "Area Closed" sign, can't find the Bandaids in their first aid kit, and they don't seem to have any garbage bags at all. I'm sure my compatriots, when using my truck, feel the same way. Many agencies simply have a vehicle pool and no one has their "own" vehicle. As much as I may complain about my issues with my truck, I do appreciate that it is "mine." When I return from vacation, or from my days off, and hop into my truck, I sense immediately if someone else has been in there. The seat and side mirrors are wrong. The AM/FM radio comes blaring on to some country western station. Things are missing. Trash is where it is not supposed to be. Someone has been sleeping in baby bear's bed.

Unlike inspecting Dumbo, I don't mind washing her. Elephants like baths, after all. One advantage of a Spartan cab is that I can dust it out with the air compressor and can clean the muddy foot wells with the pressure washer. As far as washing one's truck is concerned, there are only two seasons, the mud season and the dust season, and the dust season is far worse. After five or six months without rain, the fine-grained clay soil of the meadows has been beaten into a thick bed of fine powder by the pounding of thousands of feet. No matter how slowly I drive, I am going to raise a choking cloud, smothering the outraged visitors and coating my freshly washed truck in a new layer of grime. On a hot summer's day, there is nothing better than washing your truck as an excuse to get soaking wet.

Driving this giant, heavy, awkward vehicle safely along narrow dirt roads and through crowds of visitors, many with small children, is a dangerous business. The District knows this and has set very high standards for drivers of District vehicles. My own slow learning curve just about got me fired. Somehow, in all the time going through the Ranger Operations Manual, I hadn't savvied to just how serious the District considers moving vehicle accidents, even very minor ones. While I was still on probation, and in the space of my first several months of solo patrol, I managed to pull off a spate of minor fender benders. In my defence, I had never driven a truck before in my life, and had very limited experience driving dirt roads, much less using four-wheel drive, after dark, on disc lines, and cross-country. Throw in talking on the radio and fumbling with the map book, and there are all the makings of an accident waiting to happen. It was like being stuck in a bad dream, helplessly watching as the dents and scratches piled up, a treadmill of disaster.

It was midwinter when I began patrolling alone. (Memorably, my first day on solo patrol was Christmas Day!) One of my more memorable "fender benders," although not the first, therefore involved not just damaging the truck, but getting stuck in the mud at the same time. New field staff, rangers and Open Space Technicians (OST's) alike, get stuck in the mud a lot. I certainly did. In this case, I was driving the perimeter of the meadow at Bear Creek Redwoods, finding the dirt road to be surprisingly firm and drivable, when, in the lower meadow, I came upon a small creek crossing not more than three feet wide and bright green with aquatic vegetation in contrast with the surrounding dead brown of late December grass. Driving across it looked like a non-issue. In I went. My front tires somehow made it across, but the rear tires plunged into the wet ground as though there were no bottom and my rear bumper dropped onto the firm, rocky far bank with a bone-jarring smack. Oops! (Not my exact words.) At least the truck didn't seem to be damaged, but I did have to get on the radio and admit to all listeners that I need to be pulled out of the mud. I later learned that most people use their cell phones for this purpose.

Matt came to the rescue but, in driving the other way around the meadow, and, for some reason, cutting across part of it, he hit something and blew out a tire and got stuck himself. Tony arrived but he didn't have a winch on his supervisor's SUV, so then Cory had to come to pull both Matt and me out of the mud. I guess you could view it as good practice for winching out stuck visitors or visiting scientists or something but, in ten years the only vehicles I have ever removed from the mud have been patrol trucks. At any rate, when the streambed released its death grip on my rear axle, and I was once again on dry ground, it turned out that the electrical socket, intended for plugging in trailer lights, which was mounted sticking below the bumper, had gotten badly bent. Supervisor Tony was already on scene to inspect the damage and start me on the vehicle accident paperwork. The

Safety Committee, on the basis of this and another employee's similar accident, later decided to change the location where these sockets were mounted, and to instead have them sit in the middle of the bumper where they would be more protected. Probably I should have tried to get this accident off my record because I could argue that it was a stupid place to mount the socket and wasn't entirely my fault, but I was quite chagrined about my accident record and didn't feel like I had the standing to argue. Besides, what difference did it make how many minor boo-boos were on your record? The important thing was just to report them all promptly to your supervisor, and you would be covered, right? I was still green behind the ears.

The next accident was only weeks away. No mud, no long story, nothing to explain away my culpability when I backed up into a boulder in an embankment while making a multi-point turn at the top of a dead end road. No story that is, aside from the giant truck and the steep, narrow road and my ignorance of the fact that there was no good place to turn around up there. Now I know I should always walk up to the top of such dogleg roads first before driving them and that I should get in and out of the truck at every forward and back when making a tight turn, that I should call for help when turning in a tight spot, or that I should just back down to a better turn-around. I know it all now and I knew it all then, but not so profoundly and sincerely. I had to have the lesson pounded in good and hard. As I felt the sickening impact of the back bumper against the rock, I knew I was doomed, but when I got out and looked at the damage, I couldn't believe how bad it was. How could the bumper be that badly dented when the truck had only gone a foot or so and had been moving at much less than five miles per hour? How could this have happened to me again? How could I have been so stupid? I sat lamenting my fate for a good quarter hour before calling Tony. I just couldn't imagine how I could possibly face him again, after all his advice, his concern, and his understanding dealing with my previous incidents. I just wanted to fast-forward through all the painful parts—the part where I try to explain what happened without "justifying," the part where Tony asks me what I should have done differently, and, above all, the part where I have to have the same conversation all over again with Superintendent Bernie, which I had no doubt was coming.

The reality proved to be every bit as bad as my imagination. There were no ameliorating circumstances and no more second chances. I had to sign off on the accident report wherein Tony described me as "careless," and as possessed of "poor judgment." That really hurt but, in this case, it was inescapably true. The next couple days at work were torture. My self-esteem seemed already to be scraping bottom, but I knew there was still one more painful ordeal coming and it was almost a relief when Bernie called me into his office and closed the door. The punishment he imposed seemed mighty stiff. My yearlong probationary period would be starting over, beginning with the day of the accident, and if I had any further vehicle accidents, I would be fired. Additionally, a letter of reprimand would go into my permanent record. One whole year without so much as a scratch? The odds of my accomplishing this task seemed ridiculously slim, but I had no choice. At least I still had my job and, really, nothing else mattered; nothing else had actually changed.

Eventually both my truck and my psyche got patched up and life went on. It wasn't a big deal, at least not to anyone else but me. If anything, my relationship with my co-workers grew stronger as a result of my being disciplined. As I shared my grief, frustration and guilt with the other rangers and OSTs, and expressed my doubts about making it through the next year without an accident, I felt a lot of camaraderie and support. It seemed some of them had also faced reprimand, discipline and punishment. What had changed was the starry-eyed naiveté and unconditional trust with which I viewed my employer. Having been sharply criticized, strictly punished and even threatened with termination, I suddenly realized why the field staff was unionized. The District and I might often share the same mission and sometimes even the same ideals, but we were not friends. As my employer, the District wielded great power over me and should I fail to please, I could be swiftly eliminated and replaced. Dumbo, it seemed, might well outlive me at the District, being clearly the more valued of the two of us. It did seem incredible that I might so easily be fired after all the time and money and effort that had been invested in getting me hired and trained. It made no sense, yet somehow it was true, and I now had to get through the next year living with this fear in the pit of my stomach. What might I do wrong next? Would my next stupid decision be my last? What other combination of trivial errors might be grounds for termination?

To get me through my extended probation, I made a few self-imposed self-help resolutions: face each day one at a time; don't think about all the days left to go; drive as little as possible and spend as much time as possible on foot; no distractions while driving, no eating, drinking or listening to the radio and, most important, do anything to avoid backing up. As a result of this unfortunate series of events, I learned that driving is not only the most dangerous thing rangers do, it is also the easiest way of getting in trouble.

Many years later, another new ranger had a nearly identical sequence of minor accidents during her probationary period. Several of us happened to be in the office when, with trembling voice, she called in her third accident in as many months. I heard no blame or criticism from my co-workers, only commiseration for the censure she was now sure to face. As we sat discussing her probable fate, we re-hashed all the tales of accidents past, including my own, and we agreed that we would all far rather damage our bodies than damage our trucks. You still have to fill out an accident report, which, like the vehicle accident report, goes to the Safety Committee for review, but you would never be called up on the carpet for cutting, bruising, spraining, or otherwise damaging you own body, no matter how stupid the manner in which you did it. So, when new hires ask me for the single most important piece of advice I can give them, I say, "Don't scratch the truck."

6. Lions and Tigers and Bears

There are no bears in the Santa Cruz Mountains, not anymore anyway. The closest bears are in the Los Padres National Forest south of Monterey. With any luck someday those bears will wander north and fill the empty niche here waiting for them. The last California grizzly bear was shot nearly 100 years ago, in 1922; the last Santa Cruz Mountains black bear was probably shot about the same time. The amazing thing is that the last few mountain lions escaped this massacre, despite a bounty on their heads here in California from 1907 to 1963 and overt government campaigns to exterminate them. I find it astonishing that these large predators still survive this close to a major metropolitan area. Being solitary, stealthy and nocturnal probably helps, as does having the locally exploding deer herd as their primary foodstuff, and, of course, being protected by state law since 1990 as a "specially protected species." Would-be hunters first have to go get a depredation permit before they can shoot one. But as the metropolis swells and the trophy mansions mount the unprotected ridges, the lions find their hunting grounds morphed into lawns, rosebushes, and vanity vineyards. Residents of these wealthy urban interface communities, as well as visitors to parks and preserves, sometimes catch glimpses of these elusive cats, which often strikes fear into their civilized hearts. Mountain lions, after all, are known to kill humans. Not very many humans (about six in the last 100 years), and not very often, but even so, sometimes primordial fear prevails.

As a ranger working late shift, I just know that a large and dangerous animal is out there with me, possibly not far away, possibly watching me, when I go for a walk, alone, at dusk. I don't really hear anything or see anything, but the hair starts crawling on the back of my neck with the sound of a slight rustling in the bushes, and I start to imagine that my next breath may be my last. I break out in a sweat as the adrenalin kicks in. Any second now I will feel the 200-pound impact as three-inch-long claws pierce my spine and, almost instantaneously, it will all be over, as the equally long canines pierce my neck and skull. Not a bad way to go, actually, nice and quick. But thinking about it can sure ruin a nice moonlit walk.

Certainly visitors are worried about the lions. One of the almost-daily questions I am asked is whether we have any mountain lions in the area. I try to explain that yes, there are mountain lions in the area, because this is their home. They live here; we are just visiting. But an individual mountain lion has a huge home territory, with male lions covering as much as ten square miles and females somewhat less than that. They roam around picking off the low-hanging fruit, i.e. the old, sick, and injured deer and the young fawns, and then they move on. I try to reassure visitors that lions eat deer, not people, and that, in fact, if our local lions had had me on their menu, they would have eaten me a long time ago. The lions, after all, must be pretty used to seeing me, even if I almost never see them. This leads naturally to the next question: how often do I see mountain lions? Many folks are surprised when I explain that I've had only a few glimpses over the course of the last ten years. Maybe they have watched too many nature documentaries, by which they are led to believe that wild animals are just sitting around in plain view waiting to be ogled and photographed. While the once-in-a-blue-moon visitor may get a sustained, up-close look at a lion, most "sightings" are very quick, lasting only seconds: the lion that jumped across the Chamise Trail and up the road embankment right in front of me at Rancho, or the lion that took off up the hill and into the bushes at Sierra Azul. By far my best glimpse was the following (taken from my journal):

1/20/07: My sister, Margaret, is along for a ride-along today. She's just visiting for a couple of days, mostly to celebrate our father's 70th birthday yesterday, so, since I couldn't get today off work, I though we would go for this. Gives us lots of time for yakking, anyway. Most exciting event of the day, undoubtedly, was seeing my first ever mountain lion. Wow! The awful thing was that it was—it really was—a goddamn "baby mountain lion." Arrgh! That's right, a juvenile, and yes, it was right about the size of a bobcat. I will have to file an "Animal Observation Report," and I'm sure there will be many doubters given how many reports of "baby mountain lions" we get all the time, which are, of course, bobcats. We had gotten a report of a "baby mountain lion" from a bicyclist just five minutes before our sighting, which we had pooh-poohed, and then there it was, right where the guy had said, sitting only some ten feet off the road! I couldn't believe it! We both got a really good look. Then, as it wasn't moving away, I decided to go get my camera out of my daypack, which usually lives next to me on the passenger seat, but which today (as I had a passenger) was in the side box of the truck. By the time I got it out and tiptoed around the truck, the cat had moved off a good ways into the dappled shade of the bay trees, and I was quite eager to get back into the truck since I was beginning to wonder where this kitty's mother was.

My pictures came out terribly, just silhouettes of light and shadow under the trees. If you know where to look, you can see the lion, including the characteristic long, long tail, but it's a stretch, one my co-workers weren't willing to make. As expected, there was a lot of teasing about "Nessie, the baby mountain lion," widely believed to be a bobcat. So much skepticism might seem a bit harsh, but after investigating many mountain lion sighting calls and having found everything from deer to coyotes to bobcats, we have all come to expect anything but the real thing. I hate these calls, and we get them once a week or so. We end up interviewing the reporting party at some length, either in person or on the phone, and, at least for the sake of common courtesy, we are obliged to take them seriously and treat them as a credible witness, as they very well could be. It's just that most of the calls run more like this one:

1/5/10: I was at El Sereno happily pulling more evil, invasive, weedy scotch broom when a call came in from Ray at Deer Hollow Farm of an injured mountain lion on the Wildcat Loop Trail, so I and all the other rangers came scurrying back to Rancho. As I was a good 45 minutes away and therefore last to arrive, I'm stuck as the fifth wheel here in the county parking lot, while Matt and Zack get to go and see what we actually have. Might as well have stayed at El Sereno. Most likely a bobcat. Probably will have wandered off altogether.

A few weeks ago we had a reported sighting of a mama lion and three kittens on the Limekiln Trail. It came in as an email to Bernie saying, "pictures to follow," which had us all laughing until, sure enough, here came a whole series of photos. Never all three kits and mom visible in the same shot, but very likely three, which is really unusual. Two is the standard max. Some other interesting mountain lion photos recently came from Foothills Park. They found a gut pile on the front lawn in front of the visitor center and a long bloody trail where the deer was dragged across to the creek. They set up a wildlife camera on the carcass and got pictures of mom and kittens.

Report from the hill is: there is a large and very healthy bobcat sitting near the trail.

While investigating mountain lion sighting can be exasperating, investigating deer kills is kind of interesting. The idea is that, if rangers, or other field staff, can get to the body while it is still fresh and largely un-eaten, we can determine if the deer was likely killed by a lion. There might be visible canine punctures to the head and neck. There might be long bloody claw marks down the back. Quite often there is a pile of guts and drag marks where, after evisceration, the cat pulled the offending offal away from her entree. The heart, lungs, and liver are lip-smacking full of fresh blood and are eaten first, before starting in on the steaks and chops. If the deer is too big to be eaten in one serving, the lion caches the leftovers in the brush and scratches some leaves over the top. Supposedly they also drag half-eaten animals into trees to try to protect their booty from those rascally scavengers, the coyotes, but I have never seen an aerial remains.

Coyote kills look different. They hunt in packs, like wolves or hyenas. They take turns chasing the victim until it is exhausted. Then the predator can grab onto and rip off a chunk of flesh from around the anus, then another chunk, and another until Bambi gradually bleeds to death while still running. The kill is dismembered by the pack, drawn and quartered so to speak, with bits spread all around the kill site, a leg here and a leg there. I've found leg bones 100 yards away where an individual coyote has run off with his chunk, trying to have it to himself, or herself. There aren't any leftovers, except the lower gut track, and maybe not even that.

I like examining deer kills, both because I always learn something new about the natural history of the animals involved, and because seeing and smelling and feeling a bloodied, partially dismembered carcass is a gruesome sight, not in and of itself, but in the reconstructed video of the victim's death replaying inside my head. The terror of the pursuit and the suffering of the prey are awful to contemplate. Not being a hunter myself, this is as close as I am going to get to the reality of predation.

1/18/11: This morning we got numerous reports of a dead deer by the pedestrian bridge leading into the back side of the shop. A doe, and pretty obviously a mountain lion kill. It was about 20 feet off the trail down in the poison oak by the creek. The whole right flank was wide open, all the ribs sheared off as though cut with a saw, and all sorts of big pale swollen organs on view. Sort of curious to guess what was what. As the least susceptible to poison oak, I volunteered to crawl into the thicket to put a noose around the legs to pull it out. Zack got detailed to haul it up to our usual deer dumping grounds off the Chamise Trail. He told us later that when the doe slid out of the truck, the uterus slid out, clearly containing a fetus. Wow.

A couple years ago, the District starting sponsoring the research of a University of California Santa Cruz professor who has been photo-trapping as well as collaring lions in the Santa Cruz Mountains. Although I have found the cameras, strategically positioned near deer carcasses, and have come upon the collaring crew out in Sierra Azul, I have never gotten to participate in a collaring. As something I've never done and have only seen on wildlife shows on television, I imagine it would be very interesting, but I would feel sorry for the lion. The researcher works with a professional trapper and his team of hunting dogs. When the dogs sniff out a lion, they follow the scent track and chase the lion until it takes refuge in a tree. Then the wildlife biologist shoots it with a tranquilizer and it falls to the ground to be examined and collared. (At least this is the process in a documentary film I saw about monitoring mountain lions in the endangered big horn sheep area of the Sierra Nevada.) The collar then "pings" to a satellite every 15 minutes or so, producing a very accurate picture of the range of an individual cat. The collar is supposedly designed to break off if subjected to sufficient stress--presumably more than that produced by the lion scratching at it with its hind foot--so the lion cannot accidentally hang itself. The collar drops off automatically after two years.

I don't know how else I expect a lion to be collared, but the whole chasing, treeing, shooting thing bothers me. It's something about the exhilaration and indulgent pleasure of the human participants, contrasting with the mortal fear of the cat. Putting GPS collars on lions, the only remaining large carnivores in California, and thus icons and relics of our lost wilderness, also strikes me as incredibly sad. The king of beasts reduced to wearing a collar, like a house cat, and his every meal, his every nap, his every trip to the restroom now a data point for some land manager's political agenda. Is nothing sacred? Nothing now can be truly wild, not in California.

I have seen only a little bit of the data—a map showing the trails of several cats in the Sierra Azul Open Space Preserve south of Los Gatos—and found it amazing and fascinating. One intriguing piece of information to come out of this study so far is the clear evidence that many lions spend their evenings prowling around the back alleys of Los Gatos. They clearly regard the urban interface as part of their hunting territory, and why not? Those leafy green suburbs backing right up into the mountains are totally over-populated with deer. If you have deer eating your roses, then you have mountain lions eating your deer. So how come, for the most part, we never see them? Mostly, I'd guess, because the cats don't want to be seen. After all, look what happens when they get caught out in daylight in urban places like Portola Valley, Palo Alto or Los Altos Hills: they get shot, as a threat to public safety. And yet, at seems, they are there all the time, every night. And now we can prove it with our collared-kitty research. But does that change the "public safety" call? Will it ever?

9/5/11: Rhus Ridge parking lot. I am guarding the lot and waiting, hoping for the CA Fish and Game guy to show up. We have the lot barricaded and the trail from here up to the Black Mountain Trail closed. Two days ago Warren (former long-time Scoutmaster of BSA Troop 206, of which my husband is now Scoutmaster) saw a live mountain lion lying beside the trail about halfway up. He later showed me how close he had gotten—ten feet? Pretty stupid. He said he was checking for the long tail. Anyway, Roy, the Rhus Ridge "caretaker" went up and found the lion near the same spot although further from the trail, and that resulted in our closing everything down and monitoring the lion the rest of the day. I never got to be part of it, or see the lion, despite being on Rancho duty all morning. Then yesterday Ranger Chantal and I came and checked the trail and, finding no lion, pulled the closure. I had made it halfway to Ravenswood when we got the call, "Any ranger near Rhus Ridge." Turns out that the neighbor here, Alvin, had seen a mountain lion (maybe) right in the parking lot. We then have the usual problem of determining whether Alvin is a reliable witness, because he claims the mountain lion was—what else? —a baby mountain lion! So, if it was a lion, what is the relationship to the sitting lion of yesterday? What's going on? What to do? Chantal and I ended up re-closing the lot and the trail. Sheriff showed up. CA Fish and Game came out. Rose, the District's resource management boss, came in too and it turned into quite a cluster. I escaped for the afternoon, but had to stop by with my Wildlife Observation Report on my way south.

So today I am here again, turning around people who can't read our "Area Closed" signs. Both Alvin and Warren put in appearances. Sheriff deputy is here too, waiting. They reportedly put out a "reverse 911" call to all the neighbors last night saying that Fish and Game was sending in a trapper this morning. I'm surprised we don't have media here as well. Everybody waiting for Fish and Game to say we can open the lot. Also met

"Charlie," this local wildlife conservation guy who sat on the trail and shot pictures for a couple hours yesterday. This saga ain't over.

9/10/11: To finish up the mountain lion story of five days ago…On Tuesday morning I met Tony and Conan (subordinate to Rose in resource management, but in charge of most wildlife issues, in addition to the District's beef grazing program) at the Rhus Ridge lot. Fish and Game not coming. Discussion. Drive the trail. More discussion. Okay, open the trail, but first, post every entrance to Rancho with the additional "Caution Mt. Lion" signs. Okay, I have quite a few signs in my truck. I can handle it and then will return and open the trail. I get Olive Tree, Stonebrook, Ravensbury and Mora entrances done before I realize I need more signs. Call Tony. "Oh well, those are the wrong signs. The new Mt. Lion Encounter *signs are on your desk." What? Shit. Go get new signs. Start over. Only good aspect is practicing how best to get through Los Altos Hills to the various entrances. I replace all the yellow signs with red ones, getting most of the County Park done before, at Deer Hollow Farm, as I am stapling the sign to the pedestrian stile, I finally notice it says, "Caution* Coyote Encounter." *Double Shit. I imagine everyone listening in got a good laugh as I explained the latest goof-up to Tony. He was coming up from the Admin Office with more signs. I got to start again. Although it turned out that about half the Encounter signs had indeed been lions, I still had to go check. By the time I had made the rounds again, it was almost 1500, but I was granted overtime to walk out the mile and a half to post the two Hidden Villa junctions. Of course, when I got there, I found I was out of staples and had to dig through my first aid kit for medical tape with which to stick up the signs. Finally finished and sauntering back, now late afternoon with dusk approaching, I had to chuckle when thinking of the top line of the signs I had spent the day posting:* Don't hike alone.

While we are on the subject of cats, I'll put in a word or two about the bobcat, the smaller, less worrisome feline of our local hills. These are not large animals. While a mountain lion is about the size and weight of a large human, about 150 to 200 pounds, a bobcat is only about twice the size of a housecat, maybe 20 to 30 pounds. Their fur is spotted, like a "baby" mountain lion, and their tail is nowhere near as long as their bodies. They used to be an incredibly common sight at Rancho San Antonio. Any casual visitor strolling in to Deer Hollow Farm could expect to see one, since their preferred lounging spot was right in the front meadow near the signboard and the maps. These fat cats—the bobcats--belied any hint of nocturnalism by exhibiting themselves there constantly, in broad daylight.

Certain supervisors fretted that some ignoramus would start feeding our "pet" bobcats, which would lead to someone getting hurt, but I thought it was a fantastic opportunity to educate visitors about mountain lions, one of their biggest fears. Back in the "pet" bobcat days, we would get call after call to respond to "a mountain lion seen in the front meadow near the signboard." Sure enough, there would be our reported kitty, lying in the long grass sunning itself. I could spend an hour standing there talking to groups of visitors with a museum quality specimen bobcat dutifully exhibiting herself.

Then, about four years ago, the bobcats all died. It was awful. We started getting reports of emaciated, mangy, sick bobcats in the front meadow and out in the county parking lots. They were clearly diseased, and the contagion was clearly spreading. I participated in one of the futile efforts to capture one of these poor beasts. It could barely stand up and was all skin and bones, but could still summon enough strength to dash into the bushes as soon as we could creep within reach of its head with the catchpole. A day or two later it was found dead. We did send in two fairly fresh corpses for testing. They both had mange, but that shouldn't have killed them. The first one came back positive for anticoagulant rat poison, which raised concerns that the epidemic might be of our own making as Deer Hollow Farm had occasionally used rodent bait, but that was considered confidential information. Very hush-hush. Then the second dead guy came back negative for rat poison. So now what? What was it if it wasn't rat poison? We never found out, and the bobcats continued to die until they were all gone.

The weird, and equally sad thing is that I now often forget that they are missing. Everything else still looks about the same, and most of the time, I just don't think about their absence. Like the all-but extinct frogs and toads of the High Sierra, killed by pesticides blowing in from the Central Valley, the bobcats' disappearance has passed mostly un-remarked, and un-mourned. Only in those quiet, contemplative moments of sunshine through the long grass, or across the silent sunset-lit tarn, does their lack suddenly hit me. Where are the frogs? Where are the bobcats? The frogs may disappear for good. Their remaining range is too small, their numbers too few. The bobcats will be back; they are already returning, although I have yet to see a healthy one anywhere near the front meadow of Rancho. It is rather startling to see one now. Wow! That was a bobcat! Cool.

At all preserve entrances, observant visitors will notice a familiar oblong brown sign, the regulation sign, with little stylized pictures of a car, a cigarette, a gun and a fish, each with a red slash diagonally across it to indicate that the activities pictured are not allowed. Then there is some text spelling out some further "thou shalt nots," and then more little pictures, of a bike, a dog (which looks like a Great Dane, leading to the thought that perhaps small dogs might be okay), and a horse, each with or without the red slash depending upon the preserve. Finally, visitors are specifically warned about some of the most prevalent dangers that await them in the preserves: ticks, poison oak, and rattlesnakes.

(Three or four years ago mountain lions got added to the list of common dangers, but not just as another picture next to the snake. Oh no. They got their own special bright yellow sign with text and pictures telling visitors to wave their arms, pick up their children and fight back if they got attacked. These were appended under every single regulation sign.)

I have non-outdoorsy friends who are so terrified of snakes that they absolutely will not go for a walk in the woods. I have seen and spoken to visitors who, having parked their car and made it out of the parking lot as far as the reg sign, have turned around and gone back upon seeing the picture of the snake. They are that scared. Of what? It's that primordial fear thing again. Even some of the rangers will not handle our captive gopher snake, first Snickers and now Twix, up at our Daniels Nature Center at Skyline Ridge, much less a wild snake. Luckily for me, in this case, I suffer from no such phobia.

The sighting of a snake, lizard, toad, or salamander is enough to make my day, especially if there is a cluster of visitors already gathered around the mysterious creature, usually at a safe distance. A ready-made audience! These impromptu interpretive sessions are one of my favorite parts of the job. I love the simultaneous shocked intake of breath as I casually lean over and pick up the terrified common king snake or ringneck snake who often promptly voids its stinky excrement all over my hand—a defence mechanism. I love seeing the people draw nearer as they realize they are safe. I love answering their excited questions. Many visitors to Rancho are recent immigrants or travellers from foreign countries where many or most of the reptiles and amphibians are venomous and even aggressive. They are often surprised to hear that rattlesnakes are comparatively docile, and are not known for chasing people down the trail. Our California snakes just want to be left alone, (I am setting a bad example by picking them up?) and they will nearly always turn and flee if given a chance.

I have an old favorite story from way back when I was working as a naturalist at Jones Gulch YMCA camp one summer. While leading some kind of nature hike of maybe a dozen adults, we had come upon a garter snake, which I had promptly grabbed. I was holding up the snake, looking at my group, and blathering away, just as I have described above, when I saw all their faces take on looks of horror and revulsion. Glancing down at the snake, I too reacted with horror and revulsion, and quickly dropped the poor thing to the ground. An enormous yellow alien was bulging out of its mouth. I thought its guts were coming out. The snake writhed and twisted and eventually finished throwing up...a banana slug! I didn't know anything ate banana slugs. I had heard that snakes, and other creatures, will throw up in a last ditch effort to get a predator to drop them, and now I will never forget it.

The only poisonous snake in the Santa Cruz Mountains is the rattlesnake. The odds of being bitten by one are tiny, and the odds of dying of said bite even tinier. Given the large number of rattlesnake sighting reports we get, as many as one a week in the summertime, the number of bites is very small. I have first—or, at most second--hand knowledge of exactly four in my working life, and at least one of those was provoked. The first happened during the short period I worked as a Seasonal Park Aid for the City of Palo Alto, shortly after my stint at Jones Gulch and a decade before becoming a ranger.

I was at the Arastradero Preserve, picking up trash or cleaning the restroom or something, when this young man came speeding in on a bike yelling for help. He said he had been bitten by a rattlesnake. He said he had almost hit it with his bike and it had struck him on the ankle. I was pretty skeptical, especially when I looked at his ankle and saw no fang marks, no discoloration, no swelling, and no blood, just a tiny pink dot, the size of the head of a pin, but he swore it was a rattlesnake and said his ankle really hurt, so I called for the paramedics. They came, looked at his ankle, and started some pretty skeptical questioning of their own. He went to the hospital in the ambulance. It seems he really was envenomed, by just one fang. I remember the Operations Manager hounding me for "the whole story," and "more detail," but it was a simple story and quickly told, not nearly enough drama for an honest-to-God rattlesnake bite.

Here is bite number two:

5/1/05 Lars came upon a rattlesnake bite victim today while on foot on Zinfandel Trail in Stevens Creek County Park, adjoining Pichetti. She was bitten on the tip of the pinky finger. He said she had sat down to rest and had been sitting there for a while before putting her hand down—to push herself up-- on top of the rattlesnake. She ended up being airlifted to Stanford, which seems a little extreme given that from there to the hospital isn't far by ambulance, maybe ten miles. Lars said she "didn't look good," and "went downhill fast," which also seemed strange to me for a rattlesnake bite. I don't understand how she could be in such bad shape. The venom only does local tissue damage, supposedly. Could she be shocky just from pain? I don't know.

Prior to this incident, as you can see, I was firmly of the opinion that rattlesnake venom caused only local tissue damage, which is not to say to say that having a chunk of your flesh die and fall off isn't bad or doesn't hurt! Following this incident, I spent a little time reading up on the subject and found that, indeed, about five percent of victims suffer a systemic reaction such as numbness and tingling in other parts of their bodies and drops in their blood pressure. I should have completely welcomed my new medical insight, but it was more than usually difficult to admit to others, especially Lars--with whom I had been having a polite debate about whether his victim had truly been in mortal danger or had simply been over-reacting to the fear and excitement of the situation--that I had most likely been mistaken, and that it was entirely possible that his victim was suffering a systemic reaction to the venom. This woman's reaction was a classic example of the comparatively rare systemic reaction given in the text. However, so intense is the innate human fear and loathing of venomous snakes, that I shouldn't wonder if many listeners--including many of my co-workers-- would look upon this woman's story as justification for their own convictions. I could just envision other rangers gloating in glee as I was forced to admit that this woman's systemic reaction was not so abnormal, without apparently hearing the part where I try to emphasize that 95% of bite victims really do have only local reactions. A little humility is a good thing.

The second rattlesnake bite story also comes from Pichetti.

8/1/09: When I got on scene at the winery, the guy was already on the gurney being stuffed into the ambulance. On the ground was a decapitated rattlesnake in a one-gallon Ziplock bag. "Who killed the snake?" I asked. "I did," the victim growled. "With what?" "With my hands." Good grief. What an idiot! He said the snake was under the picnic table and was "attacking my family." I guess he was trying to step on the head and then pull on the body--which might explain the two or three inches of skin missing on the snake's neck-- when, surprise, surprise, it bit him. You might say poetic justice, but really the snake was the way bigger looser. I was tempted to cite him for harassing wildlife.

It's a good story because it is really hard to believe that anyone would be stupid enough to try to kill a rattler with his or her bare hands. How about just quickly vacating the picnic table and alerting the winery staff? The drama evaporates. This bozo ended up with a bite on the leg, which he more than deserved. I hope he got some pain and suffering out of it because, from his report, I doubt he learned a damn thing.

Most rattlesnake bites are to the extremities, the hands and lower legs, and a good many of the bites to the hands I might say are the victim's own fault for behaving stupidly, as in the above example. A goodly proportion of victims are young men, and a goodly proportion of those young men are drunk and showing off their imagined snake handling abilities. But, like the young woman in my other story who found out she'd been sitting next to a rattler, sometimes snakebites are no more than bad luck, and a little lack of attention. Last year District Ranger Wanda was bitten on the tip of the index finger of her right hand. She didn't see the snake when she bent over to pick up some litter. She didn't even see the snake bite her, just felt a sudden prick, like being stabbed with a sharp needle, then saw the snake slithering away and realized she must have been bitten. Wanda somehow then had the presence of mind to get out her camera and get a photo of her attacker before driving herself to the nearest Cal Fire station. She spent two days in the hospital and was given antivenin when the pain started spreading up her hand and arm, but she didn't lose her finger, not even the tip, and she went on her scheduled vacation the day she left the hospital! Antivenin is made from "horse serum" and is not routinely given to all rattlesnake bite victims because it is extremely allergenic, and might send a victim, who would have survived a dose of rattlesnake venom. into life-threatening anaphylactic shock. Bite victims who suffer relatively little pain and swelling and are judged to have received only a small amount of venom are not, in general, given antivenin.

A final rather amazing rattlesnake story, speaking of those young men with a lot of bravado and not much sense: Matt was at the office when one of the OSTs came driving in saying that there was a guy walking along the service road carrying a enormous rattlesnake. Sure that the OST was exaggerating or mistaken, and that the creature in question was most likely a big gopher snake, but not willing to take the chance, Matt threw the snake can into his truck and headed down the driveway. Strolling through permit parking lot he saw a small crowd following a man proudly holding aloft one of the largest rattlers Matt had ever seen, and encouraging visitors to come over and touch it. This guy claimed he had been specially trained, knew what he was doing, and had been catching rattlers all his life. He was, however, completely compliant when Matt insisted he put the snake in the can. I missed the whole thing but can't help thinking that, like most show-offs who flirt with danger, this guy is eventually going to get what is coming to him.

That's it. In all my life of hiking, camping and backpacking, mostly here in California, I have never heard of another friend or acquaintance being bitten. I have certainly nearly stepped on or nearly sat on or nearly picked up a great number of rattlesnakes. Unfortunately, rattlers like to sit in the sun, which often means on the side of a cleared path or dirt roadway, where they are likely to encounter humans. Fortunately, they don't like humans, and they quickly coil up and rattle menacingly if anyone steps within a few feet of them. My otherwise dormant quick-twitch muscles and youthful semi-automatic reflexes spring suddenly back to life at that well-known and hair-raising sound, and I find myself ten feet farther away looking around for the snake. Sometimes the snake decides on its own to slither away and hide in the bushes, which is nice if I need to get past it, but often it sits there stubbornly buzzing away, giving the impression that it is too scared to turn around, for fear that the threatening human will attack it the minute it looks away. You can usually go around the snake, staying out of striking distance, or you can go back the way you came: you can wait, or you can gently encourage the snake to leave. I favor going around, but have been known to rain twigs and pebbles on immobile rattlesnakes who need encouragement.

At Rancho we have a designated garbage can used for moving rattlesnakes. It comes with a bungle cord strung between the handles and over the lid just to make extra sure the lid stays on during transport. We probably move five to ten snakes a year from the main drag between the parking lot and Deer Hollow Farm to one of our remote dumping grounds in the hinterlands. We would probably also move rattlers at other heavily used preserves, but by the time we round up the garbage can and drive over there, the snake has disappeared. Moving rattlers is easier and safer with two people. One person operates the catchpole, the same implement used to catch stray dogs, (although I don't think I have ever managed to actually catch one) or you can use a special snake grabber that works rather like a litter stick. The catchpole feels more secure than the snake grabber since, with a big snake, you have to squeeze the grabber grip very tightly to keep the snake from muscling itself free. With the catchpole I just worry that I am strangling the poor thing as I lift them up with a noose around their neck and their body dangling down.

I especially remember one of the many calls for a rattlesnake removal near the signboard at Rancho. I had been on bike patrol all morning and was still wearing the uniform bike shorts and shoes and short-sleeved shirt, but I wasn't far from the office, so I rode back and collected my truck and the snake can.

At the sizeable crowd gathered around our quarry at the signboard, I met another ranger, Jen. She was one of those exceptionally snake-shy rangers and wanted nothing to do with this assignment, so I agreed to take the slightly scarier job of the catchpole, while she got to slam the lid closed on the can the minute the snake was inside. But I was in bicycling shorts, bicycling shoes and a short-sleeved shirt, meaning that I was exposing a lot of flesh on my more-likely-to-be-bitten extremities, should some sort of mishap occur, and my pants and boots were back at the office. Thinking fast, I pulled on my bright yellow Nomex fire pants and jacket and Westco fire boots, part of our fire gear which lives in our "fire bags" in our trucks all fire season. Jen, seeing me do this, thought it was a great idea and did the same. Rounding out our costumes, we pulled on heavy fire gloves, since we already had the fire gear duffels open, and we grabbed the snake catching equipment. The crowd loved it. We were stars! Our protagonist, a very large black snake, also put on quite a show, buzzing and hissing and thrashing around trying to evade the snake grabber tongs. I barely got it in the can before my hand strength gave out; the stiff fire gloves were not a good idea. The crowd clapped and cheered. It was pretty silly. I'm sure they thought those yellow suits were standard issue snake catching duds!

That's about it for "dangerous" wildlife. While you are not likely to be eaten by a lion or bitten by a rattlesnake or attacked by bobcats or coyotes, you do have a slight chance of getting rabies from a skunk, raccoon or bat (all of which also live in my suburban neighborhood, and probably yours too) but you have a one in 100 chance of being bitten by a tick carrying Lyme Disease, pretty good odds. Yes, possibly the most dangerous creature in our local hills is less than an eighth of an inch long and doesn't even have teeth.

Lyme Disease is caused by a bacterium for which western blacklegged ticks are the carrier. It causes a progressive neurological disorder and is painful and debilitating, and you can catch it by being bitten just once, by one infected tick. Of course, you have a one in 100 chance that your eight-legged friend is a carrier, and, if you do find one with its head buried in your flesh, you can reduce the chances of disease transmission by pulling it out immediately. Just pinch its flat, slippery little body and stubby wiggly legs and pull it straight out, no need for any special apparatus. You can wash your hands if you want. Disposal is either down the drain or out the car window. Quite often I feel the little monster when it bites me. It hurts, like a deer fly bite or a needle prick. Before that happens though, I will usually I feel it crawling on me, zeroing in on its favorite spot, the hairline behind my ears. Even more often, I will see a parade of these little guys climbing slowly and steadily up my pant legs, especially during an off-trail hike in the warm, wet days of early spring, their favorite season. I brush them off, pick them off and pull them out. But I am not totally blasé about the danger of Lyme disease. Every couple years one little sucker evades detection and I find it embedded, with the skin right around it sore and red. It may require tweezers to get a hold of the bugger at this point. I send the tick in for disease testing and go get myself a round of antibiotics.

Last year I found one embedded in a most embarrassing spot, just below the bikini line, just inside the pubic hair. Worse, when I attacked it with the tweezers, I couldn't see it very well, being at an awkward angle and right at the juncture between the distance and the close-up parts of my glasses, and I ended up ripping it apart leaving a chunk still embedded. Now what? I couldn't just leave it; that would be asking for trouble. No, I would have to go to the doctor, and since I was at work, that would mean the Workers' Compensation doctor. That poor guy; I think he was more embarrassed than I was. There he was, digging away in my public hair, and no more able to get the bit of tick out than I had been! I really felt sorry for him. He ended up cutting out a tiny little bite of skin and stitching the wound closed. Of course that meant I had to come back a week later to get the stitch out! Same guy, can you believe it? So, yes, the frequent attacks by dangerous wild animals are one of the hazards of this job, but only if you count ticks.

7. Marijuana

My job is much the same today as it was the year I was hired: I mostly spend my time patrolling. However, two big, District-wide changes with similar negative impacts have effected just how and where I may patrol. The first big change was the opening of the District's South Area Outpost a few years ago, which halved my patrol area. More on that later. The other big change was the Off Trail Patrol Policy, which again decimated my freedom of movement. The policy was meant to address the danger to District rangers posed by marijuana gardens in our preserves. It all started with one tragic incident. By way of contrast, the following log comes from long before the incident.

10/2004: First nice day after a week of overcast and drear. Yesterday, Tony, and Matt and I went for an exploratory hike down in Sierra Azul. We were traversing cross-country between the upper reaches of the two main branches of Rincon Creek looking for a pot garden. Last week Tony found a sleeping platform with abandoned camping gear near the northern fork, but could find no trail leading from it to a garden. The country we traversed was nice—tanbark, nutmeg, madrone and bay going to scrub oak and elderberry on the little ridges—with steep and rocky stretches alternating with flatter areas. The rocks on the exposed ridges were covered with dried up lichen, which is probably really beautiful in the spring. Great views, of course, looking down to Rancho de Guadalupe and

Almaden Quicksilver County Park. We did eventually find an abandoned pot garden, a huge one, somewhat above the platform and not far below Woods Road. Looked like maybe they ran out of water. They had cleared all the underbrush and cut down all the smaller trees from a huge area, maybe a quarter-football-field size. Some of the cuts looked to be from previous years. Tons of garbage: tubing, stoves, sleeping bags, clothes, fertilizer, and empty soup cans.

The sheer amount of material in a garden with residential laborers is astounding when you consider that it all has to be hauled in on the backs of human workers, usually Mexican immigrants illegally smuggled in specifically for this task. There are miles and miles of black plastic tubing for bringing the irrigation water from some remote perennial creek. There are hundreds of pounds of high-nitrogen fertilizer and a seemingly equal amount of rat poison. Rats seem to appreciate pot buds as much as humans do. There are saws and axes and shovels and picks for creating the clearing and, of course, all the camping equipment. Food has to come in on a regular basis, involving a risky weekly rendezvous with a support vehicle. Getting caught hauling garbage, however, is not a problem, as it is never removed. All of this has to happen secretly, quietly, and in the dead of night, under the very noses of District rangers, county park rangers, county sheriffs, and California Fish and Game Wardens, some of whom, like the sheriffs, work 24/7, and all of whom are on the lookout for the suspicious and peculiar circumstances that indicate a possible grow.

Pot gardens are often on or near ridgelines and generally on the sunnier, south-facing slopes. Growers need a spot that is remote enough, or little used enough, that the comings and goings of the workers will not be noticed. High-tension power lines are growers' friends, as the Sheriff's Marijuana Interdiction

Task Force helicopters can't fly too close to the lines. Lands closed to the public are ready-made for pot farming; there are no observant visitors to stumble across caches of food and equipment, or to notice the check dam in the creek with the black plastic tubing heading away downstream, no visitors hiking the dirt roads to find and report a rickety bicycle stashed behind a tree, or a filthy, ragged man they saw nervously waiting beside some back road. The most common indicator that there may be a garden nearby is a suspicious vehicle frequently parked in the same spot, especially in an area where there are no back roads or trails and the land is closed to the public. Suspicious vehicles are not necessarily beat-up old pick-ups, although pick-ups are nice for transporting all the endless stuff. Workers also need to be transported, and they cannot ride in the bed of a pick-up without attracting a lot of unwanted attention. Extended cab pick-ups are good, especially ones with baby seats in the back to give the impression of innocence. Vans, especially ones with no back windows or with the windows blacked out, are the best.

In the good old days when we discovered a suspicious vehicle or black plastic tubing, or, as in the case in the log I quote above, some other indication of a garden, we would actually go hunting for it! At that time, rangers were encouraged to hike cross-country, to scout up the creeks and down the ridges, to follow deer trails and un-designated use trails of all kinds, just as a matter of course. This broad license to explore was simply viewed as a routine aspect of patrol, of thoroughly knowing the land we serve. This policy, of course, also led to the discovery of at least a few illegally built bike trails and other "social trails" as well as encroachments from neighboring properties, archeological and historic artifacts, and possible future trail alignments. Going off-trail was rewarding even if you found nothing at all worthy of report, just knowing what was out there and what the land was like, not to mention that the ranger thereby became a better and more confident route finder. Of course, it was always way cooler to actually find something and, given how few official roads and trails traverse the District's wide lands, off-trail travel is a must if one is truly to patrol all the land. Yet, even before "the incident," off-trail travel was not exactly a daily occurrence.

3/3/2005: Sparky and I had a great hike. The faded orange flagging seems to have been no more than marking a route to get down into Trout Creek—something I have been trying to find for a year or so. So now I am excited to get back there and hike it through. The trouble is trying to find an opportunity. The supervisors seem to be cracking down on foot patrol time, and on cross-country foot patrol in particular. I felt sort of put-upon at the patrol meeting, because they were going on about how you shouldn't be going out on foot when you are the only one on duty, or when someone else is already out on foot, or on weekends or holidays—as though we didn't already all know and abide by these guidelines! All these restrictions do make it pretty hard to actually get out on foot. No weekends means, for me, that only Monday, Tuesday and Wednesday remain as possibilities. But, on those days, there are usually only two earlies and two lates, (if everyone is at work) meaning the only good time is during the two to five hour overlap during midday. Wednesday, when everyone is on, is usually booked with meetings and trainings. So, there are some potential times, but it is amazing how frequently these evaporate. Bernie also made clear that he preferred us to stay on trail, "where the visitors are." I understand that they want us monitoring visitors and being "visible," but I really do think the backcountry is getting short-changed and ignored. Isn't my job supposed to include knowing the land and the state of its inhabitants? I'd bet that if I added up all the foot patrol time I have done, with the off-trail time singled out, I've spent less than 5% of my time off trail, and I know that others spend almost none at all, so asking me to spend even less time off trail seems crazy.

Looking for and eliminating marijuana gardens was considered part of our jobs, and there were accolades for those who found them. So, while out hiking these obscure use trails and trying to figure out who built them, how long ago, who's using them, and to what purpose, in the back of one's mind at all times was the thought that this trail could be leading to a marijuana garden. Usually deer trails proved to be just that, and, while better than no trail at all, deer trails were usually not worth following. I ended up crawling under brush that a deer could walk under and scrambling across gullies that the deer could jump across. Trails to marijuana gardens were not much easier, but they bore the tracks of boot rather than of cloven hoof, and, while the tunnel through the chaparral was cut so low that I could not stand upright and had to proceed in a hunched over position, at least I didn't usually have to crawl. It was hard going, but exciting, with the prospect of finding something.

It is hard to believe now, but the presumption used to be that any gardeners actually present would scatter if a uniformed ranger were to step into their grow. We were dramatically disabused of this idea by the following incident:

In late July 2005, Ranger Joe lead the Sheriff's Marijuana Eradication Task Force to the site of a garden he had found the previous year high in the hills of Sierra Azul Open Space Preserve, but instead of just the expected denuded area and mounds of garbage, they found that a new garden was up and growing on the same site. They took pictures and left with plans to return soon with enough personnel to cut and carry out all the plants. Joe could see only one 50-by-25-yard area covered with four-foot tall plants, but often gardens contain several different plots, and they expected they would find more on their next visit.

A week later Joe accompanied armed law enforcement personnel back to the same spot, three Sheriff's Deputies from the Taskforce and three California Fish and Game wardens. The plan was to cut and carry out all the plants. It might seem like it would be easier to destroy them on site, but the Task Force is paid by the plant, so each plant is carefully carried out and then counted! Sometimes this involves giant bundles carried out by helicopter, but in this case I think there was no plan for a helicopter, initially. Joe reported later that officers had "cleared" the first garden plot of potential hazards, like armed guards, while he hung back waiting in a safer position. They had moved on to a second plot, when suddenly gunfire erupted, directed at the officers. Joe dropped to the safety of the ground and then heard one of the Fish and Game officers call out that he had been hit in the thigh. Law enforcement officers immediately returned fire, and one of the growers was hit and killed; the others fled and escaped. Joe told us that the wait seemed interminable for the helicopter to evacuate the wounded officer. He had lost a lot of blood, was in terrible pain, and the helicopter just would not come in because of uncertainty about whether the scene was truly secure. The wounded man as well as the dead man were eventually evacuated and Joe walked out with the rest, severely shaken. Here is part of my log from the next day.

8/6/05: Joe is off today, so I got just some second-hand details. I actually first heard about this incident when I read the article on the front page of the Mercury News *this morning. I was pretty surprised to realize that I knew exactly where the "remote area" was, and more shocked and alarmed to realize that I knew the officer who got shot. Pretty scary stuff. I like to poke fun at the Marijuana Task Force guys sometimes, their sneaking around the woods in camo like boys playing at war, but now I guess I will have to back off.*

The repercussions of these gunshots were both swift and long lasting. At least that is how it seems from my present vantage point, but, in looking back at my log from 12 days after the incident, it seems the arrival of the Off Trail Patrol Policy may, in fact have been a more gradual affair:

8/17/05: Staff meeting today was pretty uneventful. I was worried about some sort of drastic new policy from the Operations Manager relating to the shooting in Sierra Azul, but the "new policy" really isn't much different than what we are already doing. We can't participate in "raids" of marijuana gardens, but we can go in and assist with removing plants once the area has been declared safe. There is going to be another debriefing next Wednesday for the patrol staff, but what they could possibly add to what's already been said, I don't know.

The wounded Fish and Game Warden recovered, but it took a year before he was back to full duty. Ranger Joe just about got fired. He was grilled at length by the District brass about his role in the "raid," and he ended up leaving the District a few months later for a park police job with the East Bay Regional Parks. He definitely seemed to feel that he had violated no policy, and had not behaved in an unduly risky manner, yet here he was in the hot seat being censured for poor judgement. Some of the criticism surrounded his agreeing to change into the camouflage fatigues provided by the Task Force. Why did he need camouflage fatigues unless the proposed operation was inherently dangerous? He said he hadn't questioned it at the time; he was just doing as he was asked while going along for the ride. Only in 20/20 hindsight did it seem questionable. It was simply Joe's misfortune to be "caught" doing something any one of us might have been doing.

Times were changing, and the days of "White Boy Grows"—small plots of five to ten plants tended by ex-hippies or starving college students for their own and their friends' use—were over. This incident finally forced us all to acknowledge that we were now dealing with the big boys, the professional drug traffickers, the Mexican mafia. The drug cartels had been moving their operations north of the border as border security tightened and the relative risks of losing their crop to the Border Patrol vs. losing it to the Marijuana Task Force had tipped in our direction; we were just slow to acknowledge it, and Joe happened to be the fall guy.

I think this was my last "find:"

4/2/06: My last good foot patrol, last week on Tuesday, I went up a side creek off Stevens Canyon toward Monte Bello Ridge. Very quiet and clean, no garbage or other signs of use. I tried to cut up to a side ridge for the trip back down, and ended up running into some garbage cans and rolls of black plastic piping. My heart was beating like a drum and had to take a deep breath and summon courage before investigating. One garbage can was full of baggies of various soil amendments (?) and the other of fertilizer. Time to skedaddle. I gave up on following the ridge and hightailed it straight downhill to the creek. I tried to place it on a map, but not sure. I did leave a giant boot heel mark and a three-stone duck where I reached the creek. Need to alert Task Force, if hasn't been done already. Don't know what good it does. Now we can't ever go back in there.

I didn't seem to be too concerned about losing my job by being obviously and repeatedly off trail nine months after the shooting. Here is another log from a month later still talking about visiting old gardens:

3/07: Maintenance Supervisor Sean, Ranger Matt and I get to go out tomorrow with some of the Task Force guys and check on some of the old garden sites. We're meeting them at the Bear Meadow trailhead at 800 to do the one at Pichetti, then down to Bald Mountain, Reynolds, Woods Road. The map Superintendent Bernie gave us shows about eight sites! So should be fun--unless it is still raining. Sounds like the belief is that these sites are not in use this year and can get cleaned up. Sean is along to assess how much cleanup is needed. I'm just wondering if, once they are cleaned up, we will be allowed back into those drainages. We also are posting placards in the gardens in both English and Spanish warning that they are being watched.

I'm disappointed that I don't have a journal entry describing that next day crawling around behind the SO deputies. It was raining and the ground was muddy, steep and brushy, the trip gruelling and exhausting. We walked miles in an almost doubled over hunched position or crawled on hands and knees, which was sometimes preferable. I was glad it was Sean and not I who had to remember how to get back to all the various gardens. My brain was as much toasted as my body by the end of that day—but fun! No bad guys, no live gardens, just mountains and mountains of garbage despoiling the beautiful wild country. I had my daypack, of course, with various bits of survival gear, but each of the three sheriffs carried a side arm on their duty belt as well as a rifle and cartridges, probably an extra 20 pounds over what I had. They had brought along a new guy that day, his first day on the Task Force, straight off the street. He was not a happy camper come sundown.

In all the years since, I have never been allowed back to any of the garden sites mentioned above, (so much for the signs saying they were being monitored!) and no field staff ever went out with Marijuana Task Force again. I'm not sure those sites even got cleaned up. The interpretation of the "keep the rangers safe from marijuana growers" policy became ever stricter to the point that, as hinted at in the above logs, we could never again enter an area where once a marijuana garden had been found. Eventually, about a year after "the incident," management came out with the Off Trail Patrol Policy which prohibits rangers not just from entering former garden sites, but from being anywhere at all off trail, except in groups of two or more rangers and with prior permission from a supervisor. Given all the existing difficulties of actually getting out on foot, this policy has effectively stopped all off trail exploration, orientation and patrol. The most bizarre aspect of this safety policy is that it only applies to rangers, meaning that I am prohibited from entering areas where anyone else—visitors, scientists, contractors and even OSTs--are free to explore. The policy certainly has severely hindered our ability to protect the land from the ravages of marijuana gardeners.

I believe the policy is too extreme. Rangers need to be allowed to patrol as widely and thoroughly as possible so that we serve and protect not just the visitors, but also the natural world, the remaining wild lands of the Santa Cruz Mountains. Are satellite images and aerial surveys sufficient when it comes to really knowing our own lands? Shouldn't someone actually be out there checking? Can you truly know what plants grow and what creatures live in those far canyons if you never go and look? Yes, I know there is a degree of danger, but, minute for minute, is hiking cross-country any more dangerous than driving my patrol truck down the highway? Driving may well be the more dangerous activity, but it is just a far more familiar activity to the District's policy makers. Like 99 percent of District visitors, like nearly all the District staff, and even, unfortunately, a like goodly percentage of the rangers, the managers and directors of the District, who are the policy makers, are not themselves comfortable traveling off trail. I doubt some of them have ever been off trail. I do wonder if some of their rational concern about the threat posed by armed desperados isn't also tinged with an irrational paranoia of the unknown, of the boogieman in the bushes, the unknown dangers of the deep, dark forest of their imagination. An even more cynical part of me contrasts the visitors' unlimited freedom to explore against my restricted freedom to patrol, and this part believes that, in fact, my employer cares only about limiting the District's liability. But are they any less liable if a visitor gets shot than if I do? I don't know. I'm not a lawyer, just a lowly ranger who wants to do her whole job.

There are some pristinely beautiful spots that I found years ago while out wandering and which are now in prohibited zones. I'm thinking in particular of a magical little grove of redwood trees in Loma Prieta Ranch, Sierra Azul, which I found on 11/15/04 and visited many times after that because it was, *"like a little piece of paradise, a redwood flat with some pretty old trees, though not very big with no evidence of prior logging. Easy walking across fallen needles, and tanbark oak and madrone leaves, and, once you get above the creek, silence."*

On my last visit, sometime pre-incident and pre-anti-foot policy, I came as close as I ever have to walking right into a guarded garden high on the ridge above this special grove. I stepped into a clearing not ten feet from an open tent in which someone was sleeping. I had been following a trail of yellow flagging tape thinking I was going to find an illegal bike trail. I had never seen a garden trail marked with yellow flagging before. When I saw the booted feet sticking out of the tent, I was almost paralyzed with an adrenalin rush of fear. Those first 20 or 30 feet of carefully backing up, trying not to step on a single dry twig or fallen leaf, were some of the scariest moments of my life. As soon as I thought I was out of earshot I ran out of there as fast as I could. I had no illusions about what would happen to me if the guards caught me. I will never make the mistake again of following a tape trail with such blithe unconcern; I learned that lesson. Now, of course, I will never have the opportunity to apply that kind of hard-won knowledge because I will never again be out patrolling like that, and I realize with profound sadness that I will never see my special redwood grove, or any number of other remote areas, ever again. It may just be too dangerous.

8. Doggie-Do

My usual workday does not involve running away from marijuana growers. A usual day doesn't even involve writing a single citation, even a parking ticket, since I write an average of only one citation per week. The vast majority of ranger time is spent patrolling, that is, driving around the preserves looking for trouble and waiting for calls. Sometimes a whole week can go by without a single call, usually a winter week with rain, and temperatures in the forties, and sunset at five o'clock. Such days are good for maintenance projects or long foot patrols, but they are not what we rangers signed up for. We want some action, and most of our action comes from dogs and bikes.

Without dogs and bikes, rangers would have nothing to do. That is an exaggeration, but with a big dollop of truth to it. We write lots of tickets for Dogs Prohibited, Dog Leash Required, Bikes Prohibited and Bike Helmet Required. These are all really low-level infraction citations, like glorified parking tickets. You sign your citation, I give you a copy and you're out of there. That's not to say they are not expensive. An infraction citation is going to run you somewhere between 150 and 350 dollars! Maybe it wouldn't be so bad if the violator could believe that the money is going to support the Open Space District, but no. The District gets around 50 bucks out of those several hundred. The rest all goes to pay the salaries of the data entry clerks who process the paperwork, and the bailiffs and commissioners who staff the traffic courts, just in case you wish to protest your ever-so-unfair Leash Required ticket.

The violators whom I'm citing are not heinous criminals but doctors, lawyers, and business executives. And that's where the action comes in, you see, because many of the well-heeled recipients of these piddling little citations are not used to getting called out for misbehavior. Some of my favorite comments, recorded in the "statements" sections of incident reports, involve not just their excuses, but also their derisive views of my law-enforcement job. "Don't you have anything better to do? There are real criminals out here selling drugs, stealing cars, vandalizing property. Why don't you go bust them?" "You've got to be kidding? You actually write tickets for unleashed dogs and you can sleep with yourself at night? How stupid. What an asinine job." "You are just a meter maid in the woods." I love this last one, because, of course, we have all heard it so many times before: the righteous indignation of someone who has long ago justified his or her own exemption from the rules. What's more, it is absolutely true. They are absolutely right. Their dog really isn't doing any major harm in the grand scheme of things, and, in that sense, it is a stupid job. Many of these violators are way too upset to really listen to me, however, and wouldn't hear a word I said if I tried to explain why I continue to do my job. Most of the time I say as little as possible and just try to get the detention over with quickly. Sometimes I just can't help being a little bit naughty. I can't help letting escape a little smile as I hear the familiar refrain (which annoys the heck out of angry violators, and is not such a good idea, better to restrain myself) and I have even said, "Yep, That is a very good description of my job. That is very true," which leaves them standing flat-footed. They can't believe that I would agree (wholeheartedly in fact) that my job is similar to that of a meter maid. They thought they were insulting me, but, in fact, that is the exact level of my law enforcement training. By using it as an insult, my detractor reveals that he had pegged me somewhere higher up the stratified rungs of law enforcement, where being compared to a meter maid would be a blow to an officer's prestige.

I don't absolutely have to write anyone a ticket. I have discretion; I can decide if I think they deserve one or not, given the totality of the circumstances. There are no quotas, or tallies, or any itemized competition with the other rangers. (There is the in-joke that she who writes the most cites wins the Toaster Award.) I will not be disciplined or have my pay docked if I write fewer cites than others. It's not easy playing the "bad cop;" so much easier to play the "good cop," and just give the violator a warning. Some violators have really nailed the ticket avoidance routine: "I'm so sorry. I didn't know. I'm just visiting and this is my elderly mother's dog and I am just walking it for her. I'm from out of town. I didn't see the signs. I'm really sorry. I will always keep him on leash in the future." The violator is so friendly, so compliant, so understanding, how could I possibly cite him? This type is not making it easy for me. Why can't he help me out, be nasty and rude, make up silly excuses, and say derogatory things about my person? Then I don't have to feel so bad about ruining his day. For nasty and manipulative violators with amazing improvisational skills and little desire to take responsibility for their own actions, check out these two:

From Terry's Incident Report:

Mr. D stated that I had made him fall in the mud. He was hoping to go to church, but now could not. He comes here from time to time, and says his dog does not need to be on a leash. Mr. D said he had lost his job and if he had my job, he would not write a citation. He asked if he were to let his dog back off leash, if I would then write him a second ticket and I said I would, to which he replied, "Of course you would because that is the kind of guy you are." He repeatedly refused to sign the citation, and when he finally did, he said I was an asshole and he would see me in court. He told me that because of Karma, something bad was going to happen to me now, maybe when I was off duty.

From Chantal's Incident Report:

Mr. K told me that his dog is old and runs behind him. Last year he was ticketed for running with his dog off leash, so he started running with his dog on leash. He tripped and was unable to break his fall due to the dog being on leash. He landed on his chin and broke his jaw. He will continue to run with his dog off leash to prevent another fall. He will risk getting another ticket. Soon his dog will be too old to run with him.

No, I don't hate dogs. I love dogs. I grew up with dogs although regretfully I don't have one now. I have to get all my doggie love at work, where I will happily climb out of my truck to greet the canine as well as human visitors. I am a sucker for a wet doggie kiss. Dogs are wonderful human companions, especially for people who otherwise have little companionship. Dogs and humans have been wedded to each other through thousands of years of breeding and conditioning. It is no wonder most people see the dog as part of the family and love the dog as dearly as they would a child. I acknowledge and respect all of that and believe that there is a place for dogs in the preserves. However I also see the counter-argument: dogs are pets. The modern dog is not a working dog, herding and guarding our flocks, or aiding us in the hunt. It is a lap dog: sheltered, pampered and spoiled. It is very much a first-world luxury to own a dog, to have enough disposable income to maintain a healthy, happy dog. The dog is a plaything, an accoutrement that adds joy and fun to our lives, rather like a bicycle. As such, the rest of the world should not have to go out of their way to accommodate other people's dogs. And dog owners should not expect their pets to be universally welcome, and should expect to take full responsibility for all ramifications of dog ownership.

As I said, I appreciate both these viewpoints, and somewhere in the intersection between them must lay the happy medium, the baby bear solution. This is what the District is trying to do by having some preserves open to dogs and others not, and requiring the dogs, for the most part, to be on leash. The District Board of Directors makes the decisions about which preserves allow dogs, (or bikes, or horses) hopefully based on some criterion having to do with the impact dogs might have on the preservation of native plants, animals, and other natural features of the preserve, and not just on the demands of the multitude of dog owners for more space.

Visitors often ask me why the District is so strict about the leash laws, and why it disallows dogs from many preserves. I usually start with reasons that have to do with the dogs' and the visitors' own safety: off leash dogs will leave the trail and get into the poison oak and into the long grass where they could pick up ticks or meet up with a rattlesnake, or get coated with burrs and stickers. Off leash dogs are more likely to get into fights with other dogs. Off leash dogs are more likely to injure another visitor or another dog. Finally, my showstopper, many people, especially children and developmentally disabled people, are terrified of dogs. A big stupid mutt running at them all googly-eyed, with its tongue lolling out and its tail wagging its whole backside is a terrifying sight to someone with an intense fear of dogs. Such a dog once sent 12 inner-city kids trying to climb onto my shoulders at once, screaming in terror.

For those few visitors who are still listening, whose eyes haven't glazed over, and who are still sure they haven't heard a good reason for keeping Fluffy on leash, I bring out those reasons that aren't about visitor safety, but rather about the well-being of the organisms who live in the preserve. This is their home. They have nowhere else to go. These creatures are already relegated to living in a preserve, an isolated island of nature surrounded on all sides by human metropolis. The competition for living space is already intense, but with Fluffy running around off leash, 100 or more yards off-trail in any given direction, the "footprint" of man has just increased many fold. Our dogs leave scent on the ground with every step they take; they leave scented fur behind when they crash through the weeds, and, most obviously, they leave poop, lots and lots of poop.

The District has a major dog poop problem at every preserve open to dogs and most especially at Pulgas Ridge Open Space Preserve in San Carlos. A mile up the Blue Oak Trail you reach doggie heaven: the District's only dog-off-leash area. The off-leash area encompasses the entire grounds of the City of San Francisco's former tuberculosis sanatorium. When the District acquired the property in 1983, we demolished the old buildings and landscaping in the hope of eventually returning the land to something of its former self. Vestiges of infrastructure remain, and, despite an all-out effort to get rid of non-native plants, invasive species such as broom, acacia, and eucalyptus continue to plague us. This is not pristine land and never again will be. It became the perfect place to turn into a monster dog-off-leash area.

Predictably, this has turned into too much of a good thing. Every dog from Palo Alto to San Mateo must now visit this place on a weekly basis, and its popularity only grew after we finally put in an actual parking lot and a (human) bathroom. As word spread, doggie overload slowly escalated.

Since its inception, the District's official dog poop policy has simply been that you couldn't leave dog poop sitting on the trail. You could either collect it and carry it out, or simply "golf" it off the trail using a stick. As long as it was not on the trail, where someone might step in it or a bicyclist might squish through it, you were in compliance. I always wondered at those dutiful folks who carefully picked up all deposits and carried them out. Were they even bigger environmental Nazis then I, totally into the Leave No Trace ethic? Or were they so conditioned to doggie-do collection from their long-practiced suburban ritual of not fouling their neighbor's lawn that they just accepted as the norm the encasing of biodegradable material in little blue plastic bags for transport to the landfill? I should note here that District "staging areas," (i.e. parking lots) do not have garbage cans. Even the pit toilets, which are stocked with hand sanitizer and t.p., have no trash cans, only laminated signs reminding visitors not to put trash into the pit as it clogs the pumping mechanism. Whatever the case, the dog poop issue was simmering along without much notice, despite the ever-increasing number of dogs, until a couple of incidents at Pulgas Ridge suddenly raised the issue to a crisis.

8/2010: We spent a good part of the patrol meeting today discussing dog shit. Long time volunteer, Carol, has pulled her garbage cans from next to the restroom at the Pulgas Ridge parking lot. She has resigned as a District volunteer in protest of our continuing removal of the "majestic" eucalyptus trees in the off leash area. For years and years she has maintained those cans, weekly carting off and throwing out hundreds of pounds of plastic-bagged poop, an unbelievable amount of work. So now, naturally, people are depositing their poop bags right where the cans used to be, despite the new signs explaining their disappearance and telling folks to either take it home or golf it off the trail. So this afternoon Lars and I spent two hours hiding in the bushes, staking out the Pulgas parking lot hoping to catch a poop regulation violator! Pretty funny, and no takers.

Lars, a long-time ranger second in seniority only to Sandy, has long had Pulgas Ridge as his assigned preserve. All rangers have assigned preserves at which they are expected to spend more time, and for which they have more responsibly for dealing with issues that arise. Downed trees, vandalized signs, volunteer projects, and visiting researchers needing assistance all get routed to the person assigned to that preserve. Lucky Lars was sitting square on the doggie-do problem with no easy answers in sight. He spent more than that one day in the bushes outside the parking lot. And we spent many more of our monthly patrol meetings talking about almost nothing other than dog poop. No dog owner, it seems, wants to put that smelly little blue bag in his or her car. Pickup truck owners might just toss it in the bed, and, if one's sedan had a trunk, the poop bag might manage to make it home in there before stinking up the whole vehicle, but for the ubiquitous suburban soccer moms' mini-vans and hatchbacks, there really wasn't a pleasant poop cargo option. As the pile of poop bags continued to mount up outside the restroom, the patrol meeting discussions continued, with rangers falling into the pro-garbage can or anti-garbage can camps.

9/09: I hope we don't go to providing the plastic poop bags like they have at municipal dog parks. Let the dog owners take on at least that level of responsibility. Heaven forbid that we install garbage cans and bag dispensers. That would only set precedent, and pretty soon we would have dog shit service at all trailheads. Guess I better move on.

Like usual I am guilty of hypocrisy. Encasing waste, human or canine, in plastic and carrying it out to the landfill seems incredibly silly, whereas golfing it off into the trees or burying it for decomposition seem so obviously easy. Yet wasn't I just ranting about the off-leash dogs spreading their "footprint" over too wide a space? If there were fewer dogs and thus less poop, this would be a non- issue, but through sheer number of visitors, we have arrived at the Mount Whitney predicament—too damn many people loving the park to death.

Everybody wants to climb Mt. Whitney, the highest mountain in the lower 48 states. Even for people who have never climbed a mountain in their lives and never will again, there seems to be a magnetic attraction. The demand for permits has resulted in a permit quota system, which is strictly enforced by rangers whose primary job is to punch the hiker's ticket (not literally) at the trailhead and at the summit. With your permit, you are also issued WAAG (Waste Alleviation and Gelling) bags for all members of your party. That's right, you squat into the bag, the same bag, multiple times. All human waste, liquid as well as solid, comes off the mountain. And it seems to be working: the stench of third world village or seedy city street no longer pervades the trail camp. Compliance is not perfect and one now finds WAAG bags, empty and otherwise, stuffed between rocks in the talus fields, but the National Park Service has done a good job explaining the problem, as well as enforcing the solution. If people can be convinced of the need to carry their own pee and poop around for two or three days, surely we can do equally well at getting them to carry eight ounces or so of dog waste for an hour. Easy for me to say; after all, I don't own a dog.

With doggie-do brouhaha in full swing and no resolution in sight, a policy decision was finally reached with a gentle nudge from the San Mateo County Health Department. On a mid-winter day following several days of wet weather, an inspector walked slowly up the Blue Oak Trail from the parking lot to the off-leash-area and, with no difficulty at all, counted the piles o' poop. It looked like it had snowed. When dog poop stays moist, rather than quickly drying out and crumbling apart, it grows a two-inch tall furry white beard of fungus. Looking out through the winter forest of mostly deciduous trees and shrubs, now dormant and barren of leaves, the hundreds of fuzzy white mounds would be hard to miss. Hundreds is not an exaggeration because, as any dog owner knows, if Lassie really has to go, that urge, plus the excitement of the outing, usually results in a doggie dump during the first couple hundred yards up the trail. Some observant and enlightened owners have told me that they just wait in the parking lot until the duty is done so they don't have to carry the loaded bag the whole time, or join the ranks of the indolent idiots who just leave bagfuls of dog poop along the trail for Good Samaritans to clean up.

Not long thereafter, an injunction from the Health Department arrived on the Operations Manager's desk stating that our preserve was a public health hazard and we needed to do something. The outcome? New signs at every trailhead of every preserve open to dogs, "Dog Waste Regulations. Dog Owners must Bag and Remove Dog Waste." No more golfing it off the trail option, and no garbage cans. Dog owners are now forced by law to bear the full brunt of dog ownership, including the stinky and unpleasant part. Volunteer Carol is not going to do it for you. District field staff is not going to do it for you. It's your dog. The poop goes in your car and your garbage can.

My parents have a dog, Ginger, who enjoys the freedom of romping across the 30 acres of their place in central California. Ginger goes everywhere with my mother, as most errand runs also include a trip to the dog park, or over to the coast to the dog friendly beach. Naturally when they come up to visit me, Ginger comes too. We take her down to the local city dog park, only a block away, and, of course, up to Pulgas Ridge. We dutifully bag and carry poop. Then Mom wanted to take Ginger to the beach. That is, I wanted to go to the beach, but, of course, the dog had to come too, so where to go? Dogs were prohibited at every beach I could think of. Did that deter Mom? Heck no, I got that stubborn streak from somewhere. We put on our shorts, for wading in the waves, and our fleeces and windbreakers, for the invariably windy, foggy coastal weather, and hopped in the car with Ginger.

Every beach had clear signs—the dog silhouette with the red slash through it—at the entrance to the parking lot, on the signboards and at the start of every trail down the bluff to the sand, showing that dogs were prohibited. It was a quiet weekday morning; there was no one around, and we had driven all this way. I knew this would happen and inside I was thinking, "I told you so." But Mom has other ideas, "Just pull in here. We'll just go for a little while. We're not hurting anything." As we sauntered past the signs with Ginger long gone ahead of us (off-leash of course) charging up and down the strand frolicking and rolling in the mats of rotting kelp, I was cringing with guilt and disgust at myself for being unable to get my own family to abide by the rules. Particularly here at the inter-tidal zone with its plethora of endangered habitats and wildlife, the reasons for prohibiting dogs seemed so very obvious and important. I was upset enough about our arrogant and selfish rule breaking that I was not even enjoying watching Ginger enjoy the beach—chasing her ball, wading in the waves and sniffing at the occasional piles of doggie-do. (Gosh, where did those come from?)

Finally Mom had had enough of ignoring my silence and my disapproving looks and we returned to the car. Rats! I was kind of hoping we would meet a ranger. But I guess Mom got the point because we have never tried to take Ginger to the San

Mateo Coast again. Then again, the point she got may not have been the one I intended. She no longer even brings Ginger to visit at my house, even though I assure her that it is fine and that my two cats will recover from the stress and horror in a few days. No, I think she has decided that I am just an incurable, uncompromising, narrow-minded, dog-hating meter maid in the woods.

9. Fire!

It was June, 2006, one day before the annual joint wildland fire training at the District's Rancho de Guadalupe property off Hicks Road outside San Jose, in the Sierra Azul Open Space Preserve. The Santa Clara County Fire Department was running the show, as usual, as wildland fire training for their new recruits and, as the "hosts," District field staff got to participate as well. County Fire probably had 50 guys there, both recruits and trainers, plus another 12 or so District field staff. Everyone was suited up in thick, fire-resistant yellow Nomex pants and jackets, worn over cotton pants and long sleeved shirts. Bright, clean Nomex marked the newbies and was to be avoided, even if it meant surreptitiously scrubbing some dirt into your pants while donning them. Well-worn, wrinkled, faded, soot-blackened Nomex was worn like a badge of honor.

That June day we were prepping the meadow for the actual training--which would come the following day--by "blacklining" around the edge, following the disc line, thereby practicing our "mobile attack" skills. (The District "discs," essentially plows, around the edges of all large meadows, so that if a fire starts in the volatile grass, it will have difficulty spreading across the 20-foot wide disced strip into the trees.) I found myself on the nozzle with Mitt, now a Lead OST and formerly a CDF firefighter, right behind me helping to drag the inch-and-a-half diameter hose, which was stiff and heavy with water. Mitt was also busy keeping up communication with OST Brad who was driving Dumbo slowly along the disc line behind us. Mitt, Brad, and I, plus Dumbo with her pumper unit in the back, formed a classic mobile attack unit. Meanwhile, I was wishing I were Brad sitting there safely in the cab with the windows rolled up and the air-conditioning blasting. I was struggling, even with Mitt's help, to keep up with the pace of the county fire guy ahead of me with the drip-torch who was lighting fire off the side of the disc line. I was supposed to let the fire burn out about five or ten feet into the dry grass and then douse it with water. Essentially we were just doubling the width of the disc line, doubling the insurance that during the various practice exercises tomorrow, no fire would escape the meadow.

Put the wet stuff on the red stuff. Sounded easy enough, but the County Fire supervisor who was running along somewhere behind me and Mitt in the "black" (the burned part of the grass) kept shouting directions to the effect that I hadn't quite got it right. I was either not letting it burn out enough, or I was putting it out too soon. I was going too slowly. My pattern of bursts of long sprays extending in front of us some 30 or 40 feet, which took the heat out of the fire and mostly killed it, alternating with furious little zigzags close up, intended to drown the embers, were not to the liking of my trainer, either. I was doing it wrong, and changing what I was doing didn't seem to make it right. I didn't even know what I was doing there, and I was more than kind of scared.

Despite the novelty and the excitement and the challenge, I was not having a good time. I was so incredibly hot. My body felt like it was radiating nearly as much heat as the five-foot tall wall of flames in front of me. As well as the Nomex suit and under-clothing, I was swathed in a broad helmet with its accompanying shroud and goggles, thick gloves, tall boots, and a web-gear harness with two full water bottles and my fire shelter. The very tip of my nose, which stuck out below the goggles and above the shroud, and through which I might have been able to actually breathe, was covered with a double thickness of bandana. Otherwise it would be burned and my already-less-than-favorite facial feature would tomorrow sport a giant burn blister. Also, although I was breathing hard, I felt light-headed from lack of air.

Behind Dumbo came a second District patrol truck with its 125 gallons of water, so when Dumbo's tank ran dry, the second truck could pull ahead of us and take our place. For now, they just caught all the stuff I missed, all the embers and little spot fires that escaped me. There was a second crew "blacklining" away on the other side of the meadow and we were supposed to meet up top somewhere. We were progressing at an amazing pace. Couldn't we slow down?

Then a patch of coyote bush came looming out of the smoke and the thick condensation of sweat inside my goggles, but it was on the "wrong" side of the disc line, that is, the meadow side. Part of the point in burning this meadow was to try to stop its being taken over by coyote bush and other bushes and trees, to maintain the meadow as a meadow, in this case using fire as a tool of vegetation management. (The other point was to give District field staff some live fire training!) So this patch of coyote bushes should get torched when we burned out the meadow the next day. But this particular patch, just a couple bushes, was right next to the disc-line, within the five or ten feet we were black-lining, lying directly in our path.

But the drip-torch guy in front of me had already lit the grass, which was growing really tall and strong up underneath the looming coyote brush. I tried to raise my hose in one of those long cooling sprays, but it was too late and the coyote bush had already burst into flame, now just five feet away from me and I couldn't back up because suddenly the truck was right behind me. Brad couldn't see me because suddenly there was so much thick smoke. I couldn't see either and, even worse, I couldn't breathe. The air wasn't air at all, just thick gray smoke. No air. I panicked but I don't think anyone noticed, since, after all, running like hell would also seem like the sensible thing to do, and, a second later when I cleared the coyote bush and its panic-inducing smoke and insufferable heat, I realized that we had been in a tight spot for a second there. One good, deep breath of only slightly smoky air, and I was okay, and calm again.

That little incident helped me to understand the behavior of many a panicked firefighter under much worse circumstances. I've had only a taste of the gruelling physical labor of working on a fire crew, but I'm certainly convinced that the front line of a fire is no place for me!

Despite appearances—the fire pumpers in the beds of the patrol trucks all summer long, the fire gear, the fire training— District rangers and OSTs are not experienced firefighters. We go to training burns and prescribed burns, and we help Cal Fire with "mop up" sometimes, (going around after the fire is mostly out, digging up burning roots and squirting them) but on a real fire, most of us would be out of our element, and I would be all but useless. We have an annual one-day in-house fire training in the spring at the start of "fire season," when we practice progressive hose lays (adding lengths of hose to a live water line), fire line construction (using hand tools to scrape away all the vegetation along a line around the fire to keep it from spreading) and fire shelter deployment. Fire shelters, facetiously called "Shake and Bakes," are little aluminium and fabric tents, which wildland firefighters can quickly deploy and crawl into in a last-ditch effort to save their lives if they are being overrun by fire. We watch scary firestorm videos and recite the LCES acronym (Look-outs, Communications, Escape Route and Safety Zones), and the 10 Standard Fire Fighting Orders and the 18 Look-out Situations. These are moribund lists of danger situations and safety no-nos when firefighting, such as napping on the fireline or failing to post lookouts. Memorizing and regurgitating lists never seemed to me a very worthwhile method of learning and understanding information. Nonetheless, it's a fun day, teaming up with OSTs to do the hose lays, competing for the fastest fire shelter deployment times, and having work time to socialize over breaks and lunch.

But only going to real fires will truly prepare District field staff to fight real fires, and we are not prepared. We know just enough to get ourselves in trouble. The smarter-than-your-average-bear ranger realizes this, and realizes that there is no real expectation of our partaking in much actual frontline firefighting. It's a farce that we continue to stage because, well, because that's what we've always done. We have all the equipment; the program is all set up, and change is so difficult. There is also a line in the District's charter from the State of California requiring the District to have a fire program. The huge expense of maintaining all the vehicles and equipment and paying for all the training may eventually force a change, but the love of the fire program runs deep. It has been around since our inception, and ditching it would mean the loss of all that tradition.

Some rangers love responding to fires because they are dramatic and spectacular and exciting. With our fire gear on, we can get admitted right up close to the front lines and really see some wildfire. Usually one gets only as far as staging and is stuck there yakking with other curious extras. I only want to go if I actually get to participate, which is usually the case on prescribed burns, (such as the one described above, when I had my mini-panic attack) which are carefully planned and staged and often used to train beginners and novices. Prescribed burns are usually done for vegetation management—keeping meadows clear of brush, or burning out the brushy understory below the tree canopy. Prescribed burns only take place when the weather cooperates, when the weather "prescription" is met. Wind, air temperature, fuel moisture, slope and aspect of the burn site, and a dozen other factors must all be in alignment before the weeks of planning can culminate in a fire.

Here is another journal entry from a prescribed burn. I was fortunate to get to go since it was a State Parks prescribed burn and only two District trucks got to participate.

11-2-04: The prescribed burn yesterday at Ano Nuevo State Park down on the coast was really fun. We were burning the northern half of that big meadow you cross when you walk out to meet the docents to go on elephant seal walks. It seems that one of the last wild populations of San Francisco garter snakes lives in this meadow, which is being taken over by coyote brush, so the fire was supposed to improve their habitat by burning out the brush. We actually got a little training from a state park biologist about San Francisco Garter Snakes, what they look like and what to do if we should actually see one. Call her. Mostly the coyote brush didn't burn, but the grass and the thick clumps of reeds did. Some of the more low-lying coyote brush burned. Terry and Mitt and I were working with CDF firefighters, Portia and Cindy, lighting fire off a service road, walking along with the drip torches, which was really fun. The fire was moving really slowly and wasn't very hot, so you could wander out into the meadow a ways and re-light bits that had gone out. Our fire was burning against the wind, so the smoke all blew back on us, but it wasn't too bad. My truck still stinks. The coast was beautiful. I was tempted to stop at the beach. A very fun day altogether.

Many larger land management agencies, such as the National Park Service and the National Forest Service, have become more fire friendly over the last 50 years, as science has discovered more about fire's role in maintaining a healthy ecosystem. The District has not. In Yosemite's backcountry, lightening strike fires are nearly always allowed to simply burn themselves out, or are put out naturally by the onset of winter. In driving through the Sierra it is not unusual to smell smoke and see large areas of landscape blackened by prescribed burns. Not on District land, and not in the Santa Cruz Mountains with their patchwork quilt of private estates in the midst of what is now mostly public land. We are in total fire suppression mode.

It's too bad because many of these hills could really stand to burn. It would open up the thick canopy of trees and dense stands of chaparral and create more meadows. Every time a little fire starts in the grass when a model airplane crashes in the remote control airplane field at Rancho, I think how cool it would be if the little fire were to become a big fire and spread into the trees, and all the way up the ridge. There are no houses up there. In fact, I think the next structure for a fire spreading due west would be our own Skyline Field Office. But all the telecommunication antennas on Black Mountain would burn up and that wouldn't be so good. Even prescription burns are almost non-existent. There is just too much risk of the fire escaping onto private property in a giant firestorm. Of course, as the scientists are now telling us, if we keep suppressing all these fires, when one does really get going, it is going to be a doozie because of all the dead material that has been piling up for the last century.

The closest we have recently come to having real fire on District land were the two fires in the Loma Prieta area of Sierra Azul, one in 2008, and one in 2009. One was started by a local who was illegally burning a brush pile.

5/24/08: Cool, overcast, even a few sprinkles, which is very weird weather, considering that last week we had temperatures in the 90s. This should help to get the fire out at any rate. We have been following this fire pretty closely because it started very close to Loma Prieta Ranch. In fact, the first I heard of it, on the radio on Thursday morning, was that there was a brush fire in the Sierra Azul Open Space Preserve. I don't think it is out, but conditions are a lot better now than Thursday when it was awfully windy all day. At last report—in the Mercury News *this morning—it had reached 3,000 acres and burned 17 houses. Here at work, with (finally!) a real map of the fire, it is clearly not on our property at all, but just slightly south. Looking at patrol logs, it seems various rangers have managed to find some excuse to get down to the fire zone and see what was going on, but not to really do anything. I'm disappointed that Loma Prieta Ranch didn't get hit. It could use burning, especially a sort of cool, slow burn you might get on a day like today. Of course, we couldn't just let it burn. We have to come in with huge bulldozers and make a gigantic mess putting in a triple wide firebreak around the whole thing, or should I say, an invasive weed corridor.*

I was feeling sorry for the owners of the 17 burned houses, many of which were hand-crafted by the owners themselves, until I read that nearly all of them were built entirely without permits. No fire safe construction there, I'd guess. Also, having just forked over a several hundred bucks to local government for permits to re-roof my own house and install double-paned windows, I was in no mood to feel sorry for such cheaters. They have to pay just like the rest of us. Of course, many of these houses were also uninsured, so if they want to rebuild, they will be paying. Schadenfreude! My bad.

I can't remember what started fire number two, about a year later in more or less the same area, but it did indeed manage to make it into Loma Prieta Ranch this time, burning right down into the little canyon which cradles my "secret" baby redwood grove. Having now driven back through there, (on the formerly awful patrol road now massively improved by Cal Fire as a fire break) I couldn't tell from the road if "my" grove had burned or not, nor is it clear on Google Earth. I'm going to have to sneak back there sometime.

10-25-09: Tony, Henry and Cory are down at Loma Prieta Ranch representing the District on another wildfire. It sounds like it may indeed be on our property, but unclear. Supervisor Daniel called in all the late shifts (like me) early and notified the Area Sups and OM. He made it sound like we would all be going to the fire as firefighters, but, after I got all suited up and was heading south, Bernie came on and said no, all rangers would be staying on patrol and monitoring. We are not really useful in a real fire, which nowadays is largely fought with aircraft and bulldozers, backed up by convict crews doing fire lines and mop-up. The most we might end up doing is clearing visitors if the fire spreads into Sierra Azul proper. The radio traffic between those on the scene has come to a complete halt in the last hour, so I'm thinking things must be under control. I can still hear planes buzzing around, probably getting water out of Lexington Reservoir.

He didn't say as much over the air, but by calling us off, Bernie was tacitly acknowledging my point about the actual role of the rangers and OSTs on a fire. We are not real firefighters and Bernie knows it, and he wasn't going to endanger his staff by sending us in where we don't belong, where we would be in completely over our heads. It is a funny balancing act. On the one hand, he supports the fire program with all its accoutrements and he fully supported the purchase of larger, more powerful trucks when it was clear that the old ones weren't up to the job of lugging around the fire pumpers, and he recently endorsed the purchase of a second enormously expensive water tender truck (mostly loaned out, with its driver, to Cal Fire!) On the other hand, he has, by his actions, acknowledged the weak link in our fire program. We have all the greatest equipment, but our staff is not adequately trained, and we are a danger to ourselves and to others on anything but a prescribed burn. As much as Bernie may wish to fix this problem by getting each of us annually to enough live fires to bring us, and keep us, up to snuff with our skills, it's not going to happen. Devoting that huge chunk of time and cash to the fire program would cut too deeply into all the other duties and tasks. That's why there is Cal Fire and County Fire. Fire is their first priority. As they attend every wildfire in the area, they have no trouble keeping up their live fire experience. That's their job. It really should not be ours.

10. Umunhum

One of the District's proudest accomplishments during my brief tenure is—or will be—the oh-so-very-imminent opening of the summit of Mt Umunhum. The District constantly buys new lands, we steadily build new trails, and, in 2003, we even doubled our sphere of influence by annexing into the District boundaries the coastal lands of San Mateo County, but I would judge the opening of Umunhum to outshine any previous acquisition or annexation. This spectacular 3,489" peak sits directly west of downtown San Jose and is close to the tallest peak in Santa Clara County. It's rugged, rocky summit towers high over the valley floor and is an unmistakable landmark when flying in or out of the San Jose airport. Given its prominent place in the public eye, how can it have taken nearly 30 years (!) to get it open to the public? Here's why:

Dec. 20, 2004, Top of Mt Umunhum: Sitting just inside the bottom of a blowing fog bank, with occasional breaks when I can see the blue sky above the East Bay hills beyond downtown San Jose. The old Air Force Station up here is a mess. There is this huge, four story high, square, concrete building called the monolith, which can be seen from all over Santa Clara Valley and which acts as a beacon to troublemakers. All the old buildings up here—offices, barracks, gymnasium, garage, apartments, etc—need to be demolished, but the federal government is supposed to pay for it, and it's not going to happen any time soon, unfortunately. It is going to cost a fortune to tear this all down, haul it down the mountain, and restore the area. I doubt I'll see it in my lifetime. However, it would be really cool to have Mt. Umunhum as part of the Bay Area Ridge Trail. I wouldn't even have a problem allowing the public to drive up here. We could have dioramas and interpretive displays, like Mt. Tam or Mt. Diablo. Looking around me now, that seems like a very far away notion.

The District acquired Mt. Umunhum from the federal government in 1986. The package deal included, along with highest peak on the San Francisco Peninsula and the spectacular wild lands around it, the remains of a full-scale Air Force Station built right on the summit. At the tippy top is the monolith, which used to hold up an enormous parabolic radio antenna. From this height it could scan 20 miles out across the Pacific Ocean looking for telltale signs of enemy ships and submarines. This was the 1950s, at the apogee of the Cold War, and before the advent of satellite spying systems. If the Ruskies were coming to get us, we wanted some prior notice so we could Duck and Cover. Of course, Sputnik launched in 1959 and United States satellites weren't far behind, so the base only had a working life of a decade or so before it was mothballed.

Across from the monolith, still on the highest of the terraced flats, is the former operations building with its double-thick blast walls on the ocean side and (formerly) fully provisioned underground bomb shelter. The next terrace down is the generator building with five truck-sized diesel generators, and across the way are the offices of the base commander and senior officers. Keep coming down the hill, past a former security checkpoint and now the top-most gate, and you arrive at the garage, the gym, the swimming pool and the bowling alley. The lowest couple of flats hold the remains of the housing units and the PX (grocery store). The old base is ringed with a chain-link fence topped with barbed wire and is three miles, two thousand feet of elevation, and four locked gates away from the closest public access. It has never been open to the public; it is plastered with "Area Closed" signs, and yet it has probably been visited by thousands of adventure seekers, vandals, graffiti artists, copper thieves, nostalgic military brats and plain old curious lookie-loos. It is an attractive nuisance on a grand scale.

In my earliest memories of the base--which I had never heard of before being hired by the District--all the buildings were secured, doors padlocked or boarded shut, windows intact, and roads and walkways relatively free of debris. This was in the early 1990s when I was a seasonal OST on the trail crew. At that point, there was actually a ranger living in the old base commander's house, which had been fixed up at least a little bit. I'm not sure why they stationed someone up there or why they pulled him out a few years later, but it must have been an even more isolated spot for him and his wife than it was for the military families who at least had each other for company. It is an hour's drive to the closest town and, with four gates to open and close, you get to climb in and out of your truck eight times each direction. The summit is nearly always windy with gusts that threaten to rip the truck doors clean off. It snows up to a foot deep in the winter and freezes regularly, turning the steep, one-lane mountain road to ice. But on a warm summer's evening sitting out on your porch, surveying the California coast from the Monterey Peninsula to the Farallon Islands, it might all have seemed worth it.

(As a Seasonal OST I had no business reason for being up there. I guess we were taking a break from one of the most memorably gruelling tasks I recall from those days: crack-sealing Umunhum Road with this hot, black, smelly, sticky, tarry stuff.

My rubber boots and cover-alls became glued together, forming a single item of clothing. It was mid-summer and unbelievably hot and the work was taxing, monotonous and slow. It took several weeks. We might have been up at the ranger residence recovering from heat exhaustion.)

By the time I returned as a ranger in 2002, the infrastructure was decaying. The cracks had widened in roads and sidewalks with bushes and even trees growing through. The swimming pool had turned into a little wetland with sedges and reeds and frogs. The thick gray paint on the buildings' exteriors was coming unstuck, cracking and peeling like the bark of a madrone tree, and, most importantly from a ranger's perspective, the base had become a destination for bored, adventure-seeking teenagers and young adults. I didn't understand the attraction, myself. Yes, I regularly unlocked the padlocked door on the monolith and ascended the spooky dank stairwell and out through the heavy trapdoor onto the roof, but that was for the sake of the better view and better breeze to be had up there. Yes, I poked around in most of the old buildings, but there really wasn't much left. What there was, control panels and electrical circuits and plumbing fixtures and such, didn't interest me. It wasn't until I spent a day exploring the old housing units and discovered that several of them had been broken open so you could now wander around inside, that I found something to spark my interest in an old military base. Standing on the buckling linoleum, leaning on the Formica countertop in a tiny kitchen, I could see the children's playground outside below me with some of the exact same climbing structures I remembered from my own childhood, the giraffe with the swinging handles hanging off its backbone and the jungle gym shaped like a turtle. I could easily picture a young military wife standing at this same window, years before, making dinner, waiting for her husband to come home, listening to the shouts of the children on the playground. This base was a part of her life. Maybe she raised her kids here, shopped at the PX, sat on the porch with its magnificent view and gossiped with her friends. Now nature is reclaiming the mountain, and, with a little help from the District, all trace of her life--her kitchen, her kids' playground and her husband's workstation--will soon vanish forever.

As my months as a District ranger turned into years, the number of illicit visitors to the base continued to grow despite our on-going patrols and efforts to immediately repair or remediate cut fences, smashed windows, and vandalized signs. Most visitor-violators, having driven as close as possible and parked where Gate SA08 barred their way, just continued right up Umunhum Road on foot. They were, in fact, pretty safe from being busted, as most of the length of the road was not District property. Almost surrounding the old base was a large piece of private property, the high point of which, Tomita Hill, was leased out to various telecommunication companies, and covered with huge antennas, including the giant "golf ball" visible from San Jose. The private property was well posted with "Private Property No Trespassing" signs, as well as a large rectangular red and white sign painted on the road warning trespassers to go no farther which we rangers called the Line of Death. If a ranger contacted trespassers on the private section of the road, we could not cite them for being on the base, (a "Hazardous Closed Area" violation and a misdemeanor) even if the suspects admitted that they were up there. We had to actually see them in the closed area. Many adventurous young people also figured out that one might easily reach the summit by a cross-country route ascending the rocky east ridge of the mountain starting from Barlow Road. The chances of getting caught on this route were next to nil as rangers rarely leave their trucks, especially to go cross-country. Upon reaching the chain link fence, there was a convenient gap at the bottom to crawl through. I used to enjoy patrolling this ridgeline route, but I never caught anybody on it. Probably my most memorable "closed area" bonanza was the following:

1-18-05 Exciting day yesterday. I drove up to the Umunhum monolith and…what the heck? There was a white SUV-like vehicle parked inside the big, open lower doors! I crept up and got a look at the license plate (which I checked later) and saw a bunch of camping equipment. I heard footsteps approaching and made a quick exit. I called for the Sheriff and we met, along with Cory, at Jacques Ridge parking lot and drove back up together. When we got to the top gate, which I had closed and locked behind me, it was open. I went down into the rest of the base and Cory and the Sheriff went on up to the monolith. I spotted the car, and then the kids, down in the housing complex. I hadn't wanted to make contact alone, yet here I was. I had them all come out onto the road, raise their hands and do a 360. I felt better once they were complying with directions. When the SO and Cory got there, he had them all sit down on the ground for questioning. Five kids, two 16, two 15 and one 18. The 18-year-old had a copy not only of our 2C10 key, which opens all District gates (and which we quickly relieved him of) but also our neighbor's key to Tomita Hill. Kid said his grandfather gave him the keys, that grandpa owns property in the area and had given permission for him to be there. (Right!) We cited them all for the closed area violation and for camping without a permit. Could also have gotten them for lighting fires and possessing a weapon. I found the gun when I checked the car. It gave me quite a scare, as it was an Air Soft weapon designed to look exactly like an M16. I called the Sheriff over to check it before picking it up. (He was in the National Guard and just back from Iraq. He had checked the interior of the monolith with gun in hand!) I would really have been shaken had I seen the kids carrying that weapon when I stopped them earlier.

I had to call the parents of the four juveniles last night. They didn't seem like bad kids, just under-supervised. One mom told me that her son had been up there many times over the last few months with his friend, the one with the key. She was really angry to hear about the Air Soft gun, and she told me there had been an incident just the previous week at a McDonald's where the cops had been called because the boys were spraying ketchup and chasing each other with the gun. I still need to get a hold of the girl's mom. Girl told mom she was sleeping at a friend's house. We still don't know how this kid really got the key. No record of anyone by the grandfather's name. I have spent all day today up to now doing and re-doing paperwork. Fifteen minutes of excitement, 8 hours of paperwork.

Tony discovered a website called something like "vigilante" that was devoted to the very breed of youth we were finding on Umunhum. Some of our known suspects had in fact posted pictures (with their faces blacked out) of themselves posing inside of and on top of the monolith! The site solicited companions for ventures to abandoned buildings, vacant houses, and other places generally fenced, gated and marked "No Trespassing." Putting up "No Trespassing" signs is like inviting in every troublemaker of this ilk in the Bay Area. After his discovery, Tony checked this site religiously, even obsessively, and he rather enjoyed reporting to the rest of us when a "mission" to the mountain seemed to be in the offing. I don't know if we ever caught anyone using such information. The site users eventually got smart and created a password-secured access, depriving us of Tony's animated descriptions of their latest transgressions. The other ultimately useless technology was the hidden motion-detection camera we mounted near the top gate to try to get pictures of everyone and everything going through. Mostly we got pictures of ourselves checking the camera. And the problems just kept mounting up.

It seemed others, beyond just this one kid, must have had keys to the kingdom as well, because we started to have trouble with copper thieves. These old buildings were loaded with copper, which must have been a lot cheaper in the 1950s. There were copper wires everywhere, and even copper rain gutters, but by far the biggest copper prize on the hill, a treasure trove of thousands of pounds of copper, were the copper coils of the diesel generators. Somehow, in the space of about a year, every scrap of copper on the base grew legs and walked away. Tens of thousands of dollars worth? Even more? But management seemed totally uninterested in trying to catch the thieves! It was unbelievable. We found their tools, their clothes, their flashlights, and their tracks but, as far as I know, on only one occasion did anyone actually lay eyes on the thieves. They had our schedule down pat. They only operated in the dead of night, long after the late shift had gone home to bed. We asked several times to be allowed to stake out the base on all-night patrols to try to get these guys, but we were turned down. We even had a contract Sheriff's deputy working for us during this time, who loved staking out Umunhum and was eager to participate in the all-nighter, but the answer was still no. It was very, very frustrating.

Finally we thought we had gotten a huge break:

8/3/08: This morning, just as we were logging on, we got a call from this guy who said he had just seen two guys on motor scooters coming down through Gate SA08. We called for SO and I headed south, but UTL, of course. Met with SO, then headed uphill and found our neighbor and our reporting party, Sam, his employee, repainting the "Line of Death" boundary marker, which was defaced some time ago. It turned out that Sam had been waiting at the Gate SA08 for his boss and had captured several good pictures of these two guys, which he would email to us. Sam reported that a month ago a different neighbor intercepted probably these same two at the gate in the middle of the night and they were very evasive and suspicious.

(Later) Sam did email me the photos and we could clearly see by zooming in on the computer that they have folded up copper sheeting on the back and in the foot wells of the scooters. They were both wearing full helmets with face shields so it was not possible to get a good look at them, but in one photo you could see that the guy on the white bike had a significant scar across the bridge of his nose. Neither of them really looked like Ollie, who was, or who had been, our prime suspect. Pretty frustrating that these guys were getting away with this. Tony was convinced that the locals all knew who it was and were afraid to tell us for fear of retaliation.

No one ever saw the motor scooters again, but we certainly began to see a lot of Sam. He became as much a fixture on Umunhum as any local resident, perhaps more so, as he, in total contrast to most locals, was always eager to talk to District staff. I spent an entire day with him wandering around the base so he could take pictures. He had been in contact with some of the old Air Force servicemen who had worked on Umunhum, and he had copies of their old photos. He was trying to find the exact locations where the long-ago photographer had stood, and then he would take pictures of those same views today. I thought it was a fun idea and rather interesting, but the guy was certainly obsessive. Cory and Terry also spent days escorting Sam around the airbase to help him plan and organize his planned veterans' reunion. The District gave them a permit and there were several rangers assigned to the event, but not me, although it would have been fun. Perhaps it was when he started planning a second reunion, along the lines of an annual event, that the District suddenly soured on Sam's Umunhum fetish. No more shepherding him around. No more special access to the base. But hardly no more Sam.

A month or two later, Sam's boss called. He had installed a "web-cam" system to remotely monitor the telecommunication installations on his property, and these cameras could also be pointed at the airbase: the monolith, the generator building, the various gates, etc. Would we like the passwords to access the system? Would we ever. What a deal. All of a sudden we were omniscient. A few keystrokes, a few clicks and wiggles of the mouse, and we could check the entire base as well as the road leading up to it, right from the comfort of the Foothills Field Office. It was great. Arrive at work. Log on. Go check the web-cam. Of course, if you actually spotted someone up there, the chances were slim of his or her still being there an hour later when you finally arrived. If, however, there happened to be another ranger already in the area, the "eye-in-the-sky" was hard to beat. One rather amusing snag was that the office computer was in a separate room, at the other end of the field office from the base station radio, so, in trying to direct the on-scene ranger toward the moving target of the suspect, the office ranger was obliged to scurry back and forth multiple times with updated locations. But when it worked, it was like serving up suspects on a silver platter. "Okay, they are not quite on our property yet. Just stand by there a minute. Good. Now they are coming out over by the swimming pool heading for the generator building. Darn, I think they must have heard you. They are heading up into the bushes by the water tank. Keep going...okay, they are up in the bushes to your right about 20 feet off the road." Another amazing bust. Like shooting fish in a barrel. One real frustration of the web-cam assist was that our legal department decided that we couldn't use pictures from the camera to prove that suspects had indeed been up there, when they had escaped our grasp and made it back off the base before we could contact them. We still had to see them with our own eyes actually on the base.

If the rangers got rather hooked on monitoring the web-cam, our Sam became an absolute addict. The guy must not have had a job or anything else to do. He had acquired enough of the rangers' cell phone numbers to just call us directly, and he did, any time morning, noon or night. When Superintendent Bernie got wind of this, he again cracked down on Sam's access: no calling rangers directly. He needed to call Mt. View Dispatch like everybody else. Then he called the ranger directly, prohibition or no! Actually much more efficient than having Mt. View relay. The problem was that it was so sweet catching these guys, and Sam's help was so useful, that we just couldn't quit using him, even if we feel like maybe he was the one using us. We were as addicted as he was.

So at last we felt like we were finally making some headway in deterring illegal visitation to Umunhum, and the evidence of copper theft had slowed down now that the easy pickings were all gone, the generators stripped bare. There had always been talk about how wonderful it would be to get the airbase cleaned up, to get Umunhum open to the public, and to see it included as part of the Bay Area Ridge Trail. All pipe dreams, we assumed, and, as I said above, nothing we were likely to see in our lifetimes. But maybe we were wrong. Bring on the Great American Recession with failed banks, a broken economy, double digit unemployment and, six months later, in December 2009, federal stimulus dollars. Yes! Wonder of wonders. The District went to Washington D.C. as supplicants, claiming to have a "shovel ready" project and lo and behold: we got the money: $2.3 million dollars. Celebration time, right? Given our state of shock and befuddlement upon receiving this windfall, along with the requirement that it all be spent in the space of one year, I think our reaction was more like…panic! We were a comparatively tiny land management agency of some 70 employees, all told. We were not prepared to deal with this. Help!

There was a rapid and complete readjustment in the District's priorities, particularly in the Planning Department. Everyone got pulled off their projects in other preserves, (some of which still haven't made it back off the back burner) and dumped onto the Umunhum project. The District also hired a new, very experienced and very competent planner/project manager, devoted just to Umunhum, and the race was on. We didn't see any actual shovels until long after the year was up, but we did see a lot of frantic long hours down at the Administrative Office (the AO) as the District tried to figure out exactly what all was up there. Hazardous waste? Toxics? How we were going to get rid of it? Haul it out? Bury it on site? Level it? And what did we want the finished project to look like? No point in starting this journey pointing in the wrong direction. We needed to pin down the destination, at least temporarily. Starting thus at the end, the planning department solicited input both from staff and the public about every aspect of the operation and management of the mountain's future. What uses should be allowed? (The hang gliders turned out in large numbers at every public meeting.) What amenities should be provided? (Garbage cans and poop bag dispensers?) What sort of access should be allowed? (Unlimited free access by personal vehicles seven days a week?) And, most controversial, which, if any, of the existing buildings should remain?

It seems there was huge public interest in saving the monolith. Even a goodly smattering of District staff voted to save it. But not me, absolutely not. For those few law-abiding citizens who had never sneaked up to the base, who had never climbed the mountain and seen the view from the top, the one and only association they had with "Umunhum" was the monolith, visible from the valley floor, so naturally they wanted to save it. They saw the monolith as a landmark, a monument, a tribute. To what? Umunhum's short-lived military career? Their own nostalgic memories of seeing it up there "since I was a little kid?" How about a nice plaque and some interpretive signs? The monolith is a monstrosity, a huge, ugly, gray pimple marring the nose of "the resting place of the hummingbirds." Umunhum means something like that in the language of the local Native American tribe, the Amah Mutsun branch of the Ohlone. Think of the feelings of all those long gone Native Americans—as well as their descendents-- who lived in the presence of the mountain much longer than our current civilization. How would they feel to look up there and see this decaying gray incisor crowning the Sierra Azul? Get the public up on the mountain to experience its true glory: the heat, the snow, the wind, and the view north to Mount St. Helena, south to the Ventana Wilderness, and, on a clear day, east all the way to the Sierra Nevada. They'll see what I mean.

There is still a seemingly endless line-up of public meetings and public comment periods to be gone through and the fate of the monolith to be decided, but I do now have hope that public access to the summit will exist in my lifetime. The Bay Area Ridge Trail has promised the money to build a public trail as soon as the dust has settled and the paperwork has been signed. I think I speak for many District staff when I say that I will be very glad to see the end of the era of project Umunhum, and the advent of legitimate public access, whatever form it takes.

11. Modified Duty

El Sereno Open Space Preserve north of Los Gatos was for many years one of my assigned preserves and is definitely one of my favorites. There are no real trails, no parking lot, no official public map, and even the PG&E service roads that traverse the steep, south-facing slopes until recently had no names. It was an orphan preserve used mostly by mountain bikers (since they don't care so much about the lack of parking) and by the wealthy neighbors. The preserve encompasses the headwaters of Trout Creek, which flows down into Lexington Reservoir, and Tomas Aquinas Creek, which flows down through San Jose. The PG&E Road cutting through the middle of the preserve from Montevina Ridge in Saratoga to Overlook Drive in Monte Sereno is out on an exposed chaparral-covered slope. This road, now called the Aquinas Trail, is about five miles from bottom to top with a persistent grade which, back in my bike patrol days, was just unrelentingly steep enough to keep me panting and sweating the whole time, but not so steep that I ever had to get off and push.

If you never left this main drag, you might think that El Sereno had little to offer, being largely an impenetrable thicket of manzanita, chamise, and ceanothus. Due to this vegetation, it is hard to find places to get off the trail and down into the creeks and forested side slopes. That was partly why it was so fun and exciting for me to look for and find old, mostly overgrown roadbeds to take into this pleasant shady backcountry. I liked spending time at El Sereno because it was still so wild, so quiet and so natural. Yes, there were the usual weedy infestations along the roadside--yellow star thistle, Italian thistle, burr chervil, and French broom—but the thistle hadn't invaded the one little meadow too badly and the broom looked to have been attacked before. I hoped that if I committed myself to the task, I could get rid of the broom altogether. There were only a couple of really bad patches of 15-foot tall plants with four-inch thick trunks. One of these patches was alongside the Aquinas Trail at what I now call back injury corner.

Broom is native to the Mediterranean and how it got here I don't know, but maybe as an ornamental. It is vigorous, compact, easy-to-grow (obviously) and has attractive yellow flowers in the springtime. You still see versions of it in nurseries, supposedly sterile versions. After spending hours and hours pulling the stuff, I cannot abide it and can't imagine anyone planting it. It is in the pea family and the flowers turn into little peapods which, when ripe, burst open with an audible "pop," scattering hundreds of tiny seeds everywhere. On a hot day in a broom field you can hear a chorus of little explosions. The seeds are as tough and resilient as the plants; they can survive decades of stasis waiting for their chance to sprout, so when you "finish" weeding a broom patch, you will be greeted at your next visit by a mini-forest of foot-high seedlings thanking you for exposing them to the sunlight. To truly eliminate broom, you have to be really, really committed, that is to say, obsessed. Who, me?

December 2004: Raining all day and the preserves are consequently quiet. Major accomplishment of the day was three hours of broom pulling in El Sereno. I've been plugging away at this patch on and off for months, and today I finally finished the uphill section. It was wet, dirty, difficult work.

The road embankment where the broom is growing is really steep, and while the broom comes out pretty readily, the whole shaley, loose, hillside comes too! An erosion disaster, and, of course, since I have all my weight on the weed wrench, when the bush comes out, I go tumbling over backwards with bush and tool on top of me. I got so filthy, particularly since it was raining pretty hard the whole time, and I was sprayed with mud whenever the roots let loose. When the one visitor of the day rode up on his bike with his helmet on the handlebars, I just let him go with a warning. It was just too much trouble to get myself cleaned up to the point where I could write a citation and not have it soaked and muddy. Looking forward to a nice hot bath.

I not only don't mind pulling weeds; I actually rather enjoy it. Weeding is so peaceful and mindless and the results are so immediate and gratifying. I have also been working on eliminating Italian thistle from the Zinfandel Trail at Pichetti OSP. It is a great rainy day activity for when I can't get far away from my truck for a hike. Pulling mature broom plants, however, is a lot more physically challenging than pulling thistle. Broom plants have woody stalks, basically trunks, and long tap roots. Once they are more than a foot or so tall, you cannot hope to pull them out by hand, and breaking or cutting them off at the ground just encourages more vigorous growth. For pulling broom, you need a weed wrench. They come in four or five sizes; the biggest one can grab a stalk about four inches across. The handle of this big guy is as tall as my shoulder for major leverage and I have to use all my body weight to pull and jerk and wrestle each plant out of the ground. It is good aerobic exercise and easy for me to get carried away. I don't do this anymore. I learned my lesson, the hard way.

January 24, 2005: I went to attack my El Sereno broom patch this afternoon but had barely done a half hour when my back started killing me.

I forced myself to continue for another half hour because I was only a few monsters shy of finishing the part below the road. Big mistake. I lay down in the bed of the truck and took some Naproxen, then struggled into the cab. Even sitting here the pain is unbearable. What to do?

February 19, 2005: I just checked my last entry and see it's the day I did in my back. Today is my first day back to full duty. I've been out almost a month. I barely made it home that night, and then spent three days flat on my back mostly in the recliner. I couldn't stand up and was crawling to the toilet. I was sure I had done something really bad and would never work again. I had to have my husband drive me to the Workers' Compensation doctor because I was in too much pain to drive. She said it was just a "lumber strain" which I find hard to believe, although I am obviously relieved. I spent another week at home with the ice and the meds and then three weeks at the AO on modified duty. I was pretty bad at data entry, which seems to be the bread and butter of modified duty, but I also got to do some pressing of leaves from various species of oaks. I'd never learned to do that before, so that was fun. Then I got to do a bunch of reading about coyote attacks to follow up some aggressive coyote behavior at Fremont Older. I actually spent the bulk of today finishing that project, summarizing and writing up the coyote stuff. That was fun too.

After that episode, and over the next few years I became quite the regular visitor at the AO as I suffered remission after remission: the chair at the modified duty desk sometimes still bore the imprint of my derrière from my previous visit. One of the best parts of modified duty, aside from getting to work nine to five, Monday to Friday, like a normal person, was getting to know Lee, the Support Services Specialist, who serves as the boss for recuperating field employees. Lee is in charge of all the bits of my job in which I have little interest, all the "stuff," such as vehicles, uniforms, radios, code three equipment, and fire fighting gear. Most of the tasks he assigned me--vehicle inspections, vehicle shuttles, uniform item inventories and shopping errands—were hardly thrilling, but he was so patient and friendly that my days were at least pleasant.

My other "bosses" at the AO were the administrative assistants for the Operations Department, who were always happy to see me. There on my desk, in anticipation of my arrival, would be waiting two little pink piles of citations and warnings for some poor schmuck to enter into the database, and also stacks of the attendance logs at mandatory trainings, and logs of hours spent running radar, and record sheets of who had been checked out on which pieces of equipment...and so on. When and if I finished entering all those, then the paper copies had to be filed. Doing someone else's job for awhile is really not a bad idea; I came to appreciate how much more work I create for my cubicle co-worker when I screw up writing a citation and have to do an amendment.

After several stints down there, I had almost learned how to operate the complicated and finicky office machines. Faxing, scanning, collating--anything was better than data entry! Mostly I enjoyed socializing with the other clerical staff while stuffing envelopes, assembling map books, setting up for board meetings, and staffing the front desk. Working so closely with my counterparts in the other departments, I gained a better understanding of how the District functions, as well as a little better knowledge of just who all those people were down at the AO. And I had lots more opportunities:

1/7/06: Kind of funny that my last entry almost two months ago was written at this same spot. On 11/17/05 I threw my back out again. Damn! I actually did it at home raking leaves and I am still fighting with Workers' Comp to get it recognized as a continuation of my back injury of a year ago. Sadie, the Evil Human Resources Director, says no. I was in the AO for most of December. Finished up doing the revision of the Exposure

Control Manual. The best part of the deal was two whole weeks off over Christmas when the AO was closed. I went to Anza Borrego with my husband and the Boy Scouts.

5/31/06: Now almost a month since my last entry, I see. Makes sense because I think it was May 4th that my stupid back blew out again, at swim workout this time. I was out for a week with the ice and drugs and then spent two weeks in the AO. This is now the end of my first week back on full duty. Back is definitely not all better but good enough, I guess. I think it will be okay once I lie down and rest. The good news is that the judgment came yesterday from the QME (qualified medical examiner, whose judgment is called upon in a disputed Workers' Comp claim) saying that my second back injury (raking leaves at home) was indeed just an exacerbation of my first at-work injury (pulling broom). Still not clear whether this most recent injury will get included as well.

The QME experience was pretty disgusting. What a horrible system. The District's insurance carrier sent me a list of three names. The first two didn't have any appointments for the next six months, so I went to number three. His one room chiropractic office was wedged between the massage parlor and the nail salon in a strip mall in Oakland. I was worried even to leave my car on the street outside. When the favorable judgment finally arrived, months overdue, he referred to me throughout the document as "Mr. Reneau" even though I had been standing in front of him stark naked! Yet this was the "expert" whose judgment was being called upon. I know there are patients who are trying to scam the system and get time off and retirement benefits they do not deserve, but in my experience with Workers' Compensation, it seemed more likely the doctors were milking the system.

The best part of the Workers' Comp coverage for my back were the physical therapy appointments. The therapists seemed more knowledgeable, informed and helpful than the doctors. I discovered that although I was strong, and fit, and in good cardiovascular shape from swimming, I was pathetic when it came to the core strength exercises I needed to learn for my back. Thanks to my physical therapists, I gradually acquired a daily diet of crunches, bridges, and planks along with all the stretching, icing and drugs. It was time consuming and dull, but seemed to help, and pain is a great motivator. I thought perhaps I had seen the end of my bad back. Not quite.

9/2/07: My stupid back is still bothering me and keeping me from feeling motivated to get out and do my job. I re-injured it on the morning of the second day of our Sierra Club trip while pulling on a cinch strap. I limped along the rest of the trip with others carrying my commissary load and borrowing drugs from everyone. I considered calling in sick when I got back from the trip, but remembered what a huge hassle I ran into the last two times my back went out on my own time. Evil Human Resources Director Sadie sent me to my own doctor, who wanted nothing to do with a Workers' Comp case and, when I was running out of sick leave, the Human Resources Department kept rejecting my various doctors' notes trying to get me cleared to work. So now I'm just trying to lie low and do as little as possible, which isn't hard because my back hurts!

10-29-07: Finally back to full duty after six weeks in the AO. Yep, I shouldn't have gone back so quickly after the Sierra Club trip. What set it off this time was the three or four hours I spent up on the Twin Creeks fire digging out burning underground roots. So I'm back to work, but not really back to normal. Stupid back still hurts, not real bad, not all the time, but just enough to slow me down. Maybe I'm finally resigned to the fact that my back will be bad for the rest of my life and I have to be "good" and do my boring back exercises and still expect more attacks of pain. This whole thing really isn't going to just "go away."

The one good thing that came out of Sadie's refusal to recognize my on-going back issues as work related, was that, in the time I was seeing my own doctor, I managed to get an MRI, and see the neurosurgeon. So, yes, the bad news was I have significant degenerative disease in my lumber spine, particularly on the right side. The worse news was that there is nothing further to be done, beyond the boring regime of stretching, strengthening and drugs. "Lumber strain" indeed. I knew I hadn't just pulled a muscle, but, since the treatment is the same, I guess it really didn't make any difference. The disease eventually spread into my cervical spine as well and I added another drug and a phalanx of upper back, shoulder and neck strength exercises to my routine. Ironically, the more decrepit I became, the buffer I looked with all my exercises. I liked to say, "Abs of steel, buns of steel and a bad back," and "Looks good on the outside; crap on the inside." It was encouraging that each successive back attack episode seemed a little less severe. Maybe it was just not quite so scary now that I knew what to expect, and I knew that I would recover, albeit slowly.

Then, about when my back seemed to be slowly improving, my knees decided to give out and I had to have arthroscopic surgery to try to clean out some of the very painful arthritic cartilage. More sick leave, more ice, and drugs, more physical therapy and modified duty, this time actually working at the Foothills Field Office, probably because Sandy was still assigned to "my" desk at the AO.

(Sandy is probably the only ranger to have put in more modified duty time than I have. Having never once been out of uniform before, after 25 years on the job, he fell off the motorcycle, on duty, totally destroyed his shoulder, and was out for two years. He wasn't even moving very fast when it happened, and, in fact, the motorcycle wasn't even running. He was coasting it down the little hill from the Annex building trying to jumpstart it. He had found the battery dead when he went to do the vehicle inspection. He was off work completely at home for an entire year, then six months of modified duty. He too almost learned to use a computer! He had a running battle raging with human resources, to be allowed to return to his ranger job. His worker's comp doctor had long since cleared him to return to work, but the District was claiming that, because he couldn't raise his arm above his head on the affected side, he couldn't defend himself if he were attacked. There was even talk about a test he, and presumably others, would have to pass to be allowed back to full duty! Just what finally broke the impasse with human resources I don't know, but eventually there he was, back in uniform. It was great to have him back, both for his valuable contributions as a knowledgeable and committed long time employee, and because his spot had been held open for him for those whole two years making it harder than ever for the rest of us to get time off, given minimum staffing restrictions. Welcome back Sandy!)

10/12/10: After four years since the last remission of my back injury, I thought I was in the clear, as long as I kept up the boring back exercises. I'd gotten to be almost pain free. I feel like I am now being punished for being good because I have been so diligent, and the exercises really seemed to help. This happened at home following an hour or two or steady yard work when I bent down to pick up the pile of clippings. Horrible. I had to crawl into the house to lie on the kitchen floor next to the freezer with the ice pack. I was a week at home taking pills and icing, and two weeks scrounging for work at the AO. I'm so glad to be back in the field. Now if I can only make it another four years, or better yet, never again. I'm trying to be really, really careful, but I also don't want to short-change my job. This latest injury has really gotten me thinking about retirement. I have never intended to retire at 55, the youngest possible retirement date, but it looks like my body may have other plans. If I could make it to 58, that would be 15 years with the District. That sounds reasonable, and do-able.

How will I know when it is time to go? How little digging, lifting, pulling, and pounding can I do and still feel like I'm doing a reasonable part of the job, if not my full share? How long can I continue to justify (to myself as well as my boss) asking for a helper every time I have to dig a posthole or clean out a plugged culvert? I don't like being incompetent. I don't enjoy feeling inadequate, old and infirm. I know that I would not be eligible to be hired as a new ranger with my body in its present condition; I would not be judged as capable of doing this job. Not only is my back shot, but my knees are now so bad that I can no longer run. I can walk for miles given enough medication, but running is out. I'm trying to preserve what is left of that cartilage. So how can I justify staying on? I think the main thing is that I still love this job. In my mind, and in my heart, I am still the young, strong woman I was just a few short years ago, and I forget my infirmities while I am on patrol doing the 95 percent of the job that does not require a strong back or painless knees. I think I will know when it is time to go: when I can no longer smile about the inanities of low-level law enforcement, and laugh at the pickles I and my cohorts get ourselves into. When the party is over, I will go home, but not before.

12. Bikers

The District allows bicycle riding in most of the preserves, most of the year, on most of the trails. Biking is allowed both on what bicyclists call "road width" and "single track," or what I grew up calling "dirt roads" and "trails." This rather liberal and inclusive attitude toward bicycle access is controversial, especially with other user groups such as dog walkers, equestrians, slow-moving pedestrians, parents with strollers, or birders using binoculars. (This puts me in mind to misquote Tom Lear: "Oh, the bike folks hate the dog folks, and the dog folks hate the bike folks; the horse folks hate the running groups and everybody hates the poop, but during National Brotherhood Week, National Brotherhood Week…") I recall attending a District Board of Directors meeting about 20 years ago at which the District took public comment on a plan to close some of the smaller preserves to bikes entirely. The bikers and the anti-bikers both turned up en masse, and the name-calling and vitriol in the room made a field day for the local press. I'll let you guess on which side I stood.

The anti-bikers' main concern seems to be that bicycles are too fast and that consequently they, the pedestrians, are in danger of being run over. It is truly unpleasant to be passed by multiple speeding bicyclists. The contemplative peace and quiet for which many users visit the preserves cannot compatibly coexist with the challenge, thrills and excitement of downhill speeding that attract many younger cyclists. This conflict of interests, along with some concerns about the environmental damage caused by so many bikes, constitute my own main objection to bikes in the preserves. I'm not worried about actually being run over. I've never heard of an accident where the cyclist actually hit the pedestrian. Usually, I think, the cyclist sees the pedestrians too late (because the cyclist is speeding), swerves to miss them, and wipes out himself, going over the handlebars or into a tree. Of course then the lucky pedestrians get to be first on scene of a bloody mess!

While the pedestrian-versus-bike trail conflict usually results in an injured cyclist, equestrian-versus-bike more often results in an injured equestrian. The bicyclist comes suddenly upon a group of riders; the horses spook and rear or bolt, and the riders fall to the ground. I can think of only a handful of these accidents, probably because there just aren't that many equestrians on our trails.

The complaints about speeding bikes grew so vociferous that, about ten years ago, the District was compelled to initiate a radar-enforced trail speed limit of 15 mph, applicable to all visitors, not just bikes. I suppose a horse could be going that fast, but a human on foot going 15 mph would deserve an award, not a citation, so the trail speed limit really is aimed at the bicyclists. All District rangers spend three days getting POST (Peace Officers Standards and Training) certified to operate hand-held radar, and we each have to put in at least 50 hours a year running radar on the trails. This is not one of my favorite parts of the job because I am so obviously, and heavy-handedly, doing law enforcement. Fifty hours may not seem like a lot—only an hour a week—but I am chronically short of radar hours. I have good intentions. I check out the radar at the start of shift, drive straight over to Fremont Older or St. Joseph's Hill or some other biker hot spot, and head in to one of our usual radar spots, places where there is a nice, long, smooth, straight downhill with a nice shady spot at the bottom to park the truck and park myself on the bumper. While driving into the preserve, however, and while staked out at the selected spot for ten or 15 minutes, it becomes clear that there is not one single bike in the place, and that the next hour will be a waste of my time, and a waste of taxpayer money. All the same, I try to force myself to stay there and do it. Sometimes the apparently dead preserve is perfect for a speed cite because the cyclist also believes that he has the place to himself (or, less often, herself) and is free to really let loose.

The truer but more pathetic reason I don't just quit every time there seem to be no bikes is that I would end up with insufficient hours come evaluation time, and that would elicit an automatic "below standard," and no pay increase. Enough "below standards" and you get fired. I call it the "tyranny of the countable item," by which I mean that those activities which are tracked—radar hours, citations, parking tickets, written warnings, incident reports, sick leave, training attendance, committee participation—tend to outweigh other activities in the eyes of one's supervisor. (Resource management hours— pulling broom and thistles, wrangling rattlesnakes, and writing up Wildlife Observation Reports--are tracked as well, but only for the patrol staff as a whole, not individually, which is too bad because I would much rather pull broom than run radar. I would be the poster child of resource management hours.) Despite all the rhetoric about being "Ambassadors of the District," and about the importance of "making informational contacts," and "being available to the public," we all know that none of that stuff actually counts in the bean-counting, bureaucratic business of performance evaluations, so a happy ranger had better enjoy doing it for its own sake.

The best part of running radar is that we are allowed to do it together. That is, one third of the requisite 50 hours may be spent in the company of a second ranger. This contrasts with our status quo of maximal distance between rangers as we try to fulfil the prerogative of "coverage." This togetherness sweetens the pot a little bit. At least there is someone to talk to. It beats doing isometrics, counting airplanes passing overhead, or making mental lists of all the plants and animals seen or heard while stuck there, and daydreaming. The business reason for permitting what is otherwise frowned upon is that stopping and citing speeding bicyclists can be a formidable task. The vast majority of trail speed citations are given to very athletic young men. Like most other stops, for other infractions, most trail speed stops run smoothly. Most violators, that is, most of those young, strong, muscular, fit guys are completely cooperative, if not exactly happy. But when you end up with a 20-something miscreant to deal with, it is nice to have two of you. Mountain bikers are also a pretty tight-knit bunch. They regularly post and check web sites devoted to their sport, and news of a speed cite gets around quickly, especially once the offender gets his "courtesy notice" from the court with the "bail amount" of almost $400! That's right, it costs about as much to speed down the trail on your mountain bike as to speed down the freeway in your car. Most regular riders have probably heard from their friends just how expensive speeding tickets are, and, when they see, a little too late, the radar-wielding ranger trying to wave them down, it is understandable that the evil thought may cross their minds of just how easily they might simply slalom past and get away. This is harder to do with two rangers blocking the trail.

The official trail speed limit is 15 mph, but, just as you are unlikely to get a speed cite for driving 70 on the freeway, we don't necessarily ticket anyone for going 16 mph, or 17, or 18. As the court-imposed ticket price has crept up and up, patrol staffs' willingness to issue $400 tickets to cyclists going slightly over the speed limit has waned. Of course if the violator insists on behaving like a jackass when, in fact, you were just waving him down to talk to him and maybe issue a written warning, then it is easy enough to reward their rude behavior with an actual citation. It's not easy to cite the nice guy knowing what it is going to cost them. And they always ask. And I always say, "Oh, I don't really know. We operate in three county court systems, and they are all different, and I wouldn't want to get it wrong." It's all bullshit; we know the price, more or less. We just don't want to turn our nice compliant violator into an indignant, outraged, furious violator. Violators play dumb; we play dumb.

Another contributing factor to ranger speed cite reluctance is the near certainty that we will have to go to court. Court is always an option for anyone receiving a citation, but it is a giant hassle, and it may prove to be a complete waste of time. When there is $400 on the line, however, most people seem to think it may be worth a try. The commissioner may just say, "Guilty. Pay up." But the defendant can always hope that the officer will fail to show up, in which case the defendant wins by default-- and saves the $400. There is also an outside chance that the defendant will win their trial, although this doesn't happen very often. Commissioners also used to be willing to reduce the fines down to actually reasonable amounts, say $50 to $100 for an infraction, if the defendant showed up in court to plead unemployment, or poverty, or homelessness, or some other financial need, but no more. Now the courts themselves are so starved for funds that they depend on the exorbitant fees tacked onto minor infraction fines to keep the court system fed.

I have been to court frequently for all kinds of infraction citations and I think the only occasions I have lost have been for speed cites. Early in my career, there was a certain commissioner who really had it in for the Open Space District and in particular for our radar program, Commissioner Zane. A couple of rangers had lost cases with him presiding because he claimed we were operating "speed traps" because our trails had never been surveyed to determine what a "reasonable" speed would be. I believe District lawyers had to meet with Zane to clear up that confusion. All the same, I was nervous when I saw he was presiding over my trail speed violation trial, even though it wasn't my first such case. Sure enough, he raked me over the coals, quizzing me about the District's authority to write and enforce laws, and the sections of the California Penal Code which contained my authority as a Peace Officer. I was humiliated, red-faced and fumbling. He dismissed the case and I left the courtroom in shame. A few months later I ended up in Zane's courtroom again:

10/23/06: I'm feeling disgruntled, upset, wronged, beset, abased, cheated—something like that. I'm pissed off since losing in court again this morning to Commissioner Zane. I should look back and find the journal entry for the last time he cheated me out of a good speed cite. Court was this morning. Now 1400 and I've been digging a hole to put a new reg sign here by the restrooms. I'm pooped and sweaty, but still mad! I was so prepared this time. My schpeal went down perfectly. I got in the part about "Public Resources Code 5500 and 5561," etc. but then lost because the defendant claimed that Jen was holding the radar! True, she was there, but I think I must have been holding the radar because I know that this is an issue and that's how we've been doing it when I am out training her: (She is still doing

*her 40 hours and 100 estimations of training.) I hold and operate the radar;
she just gives estimations. But when good old Zane asked me if I could
remember for sure that I was holding it, I, of course, had to say no. I can't
swear to it under oath. And the defendant says Jen was, so he gets off—and
this is a guy with two previous speed cites! What difference does it make who
was holding the radar? I still saw him and made the estimation. Aargh!*

Between closing some small preserves to bikes and running
radar on bikes, the cyclists might have started to feel a certain
anti-bike sentiment from the District. Perhaps it was unrelated;
perhaps it was to attempt to dispel this notion, but soon after the
inception of the District's radar program, came the instigation
of the bike patrol program. This was up and running by the
time I came on board, but it was still sort of a novelty. The
official District's rationale for starting the bike patrol program
had to do with getting the trails patrolled in a quick and efficient
manner. I'm sure those anti-District cyclists would be more than
envious if they realized that rangers are free to ride any trail in
any preserve, including those closed to bikes.

As soon as I was eligible, after I finally finished my extended
probationary period, (Ya!) I took the bike patrol training class,
with gear-head Ranger Lars as the instructor. It was a one-day
class, and, to my mind, a lot more fun than your average training.
Lars went over some basics of bicycle maintenance and repair,
and we practiced trying to make tight circles inside one of the
parking spaces in the county parking lot and trying to ride up
and down the curbs. I didn't do too well at either of those two,
I but did come in near the front of the pack on the "race" up
the PG&E trail to the water tank. After getting outfitted with
uniform shorts, shirt, gloves, helmet, shoes, and a biking jacket
with RANGER written across the back in huge letters, I spent
three or four years happily patrolling the District on a bike.

It turns out that mountain biking is a lot harder than it looks. Yes, there are 18 or 24 or however many gears, but however low the lowest gear is, it isn't low enough for me. While hiking, if I find myself huffing and puffing while ascending a steep hill, I can just slow down. Still running out of air? I can slow down even more, to the point where, when climbing a peak at high altitude, I am actually doing the rest step—one breath every step. This doesn't work on a bike. If you stop peddling, you and the bike keel over. Watching the speedometer while trying to make it up the killer hills at the top of the Kennedy Trail, I discovered my keel-over speed is right at about 2.3 mph. At that point, not just my lungs are maxed out; my thighs are also burning and my body temperature has soared to the beet red face point. Isn't this fun? Actually, I loved it. Don't tell anyone.

With this newly acquired respect for the difficulty of the sport, I couldn't help feeling confused when checking out the average mountain biker at, say, St. Joseph's Hill. Some of these guys are fat, not huge, not obese, but quite often sporting a substantial beer belly, and with a derriere sagging over the saddle and straining the spandex. Yet there they go, rolling up the same hills that I know are just barely within my ability. What's the trick? I don't know. I never did figure it out, nor did I ever make it up those last two killer hills on the Kennedy Trail before my bike patrol days came to an end. Bummer. Here is a log from those days:

9/15/08: I went on bike patrol at Fremont Older today despite air quality issues. Haven't been out on the bike in months due to one reason (excuse?) or another. My neck has been bothering me, and biking definitely bothers my neck, and my knees have been swollen and painful ever since returning from backpacking this summer. So, I just had to get out and do it. Pretty un-eventful. Not a lot of folks out. I actually haven't ridden outside

Rancho since sometime early this spring, whenever the fire pumpers went back on the trucks and my bike hitch thingy in the truck bed went missing. I have been reluctant to try the rear-mounted bike carriers. With my luck backing up, just what I need is a big old something sticking out back there that I can't see. Seeing that accident about to happen is all too easy. And it is a hassle to take the stupid thing on and off. Most rangers who ride a lot just leave them on.

Yes, I did enjoy the biking, although I retain my reservations about the true compatibility of mountain bikes and nature preserves. Riding uphill, I couldn't pay the least attention to my surroundings. A dozen rare and illusive wild creatures could have been sitting on the trailside and I would have passed them by without noticing. My mind and body were given over wholly to my goal of ascending the entire trail, to the top, without once stopping. It was an absorbing aerobic challenge. Downhill was definitely not aerobic, but, as long as the hill was not too steep for me, it was really fun. Gliding down Rogue Valley at Rancho San Antonio, so smooth and straight, with about a 2% grade, I felt as free and happy as a child. I might even have exceeded 15 mph. Combine the athletic, aerobic uphill component with the free-as-a-bird downhill component, and it was altogether a very satisfying experience, but not a nature experience. The natural environment surrounding me was just a backdrop-- trees whizzing past, the distant view out across the valley--while my senses were intensely concentrated on the narrow strip of rocky and rutted roadbed in front of me. Biking has its place, but to really see, hear, smell and feel the land, you need to go on foot.

As alluded to above, my bike patrol days ended several years ago. The severe neck pain experienced while rattling down the trail in "turtle position" (hunched forward leaning on the handle bars with one's head held up) also started bothering me when driving over rutted, wash-boarded roads, and when playing water polo (same "turtle position"). It was no big surprise to be diagnosed with degenerative disc disease in my cervical spine. Unlike the chronic lower back pain, the neck pain does not respond to physical therapy exercises, and short of surgery (after which I would never be able to turn or lift my head again) the only "therapy" is drugs. I voted for the drugs, and, of course, avoiding those things that only make the problem worse, like water polo and mountain biking. But I sorely miss them. I bought myself a recumbent bike for toodeling around town, and that helps some, but I still miss the bike patrol. Maybe I just miss having that patrol alternative, another way of getting out of the truck that was not only sanctioned, but actually encouraged.

As I mentioned earlier, without bikes and dogs, rangers would have nothing to do, and, while bikes don't poop, they do leave behind their own variety of environmental degradation. Perhaps more so than any other user group, the rogue faction of the mountain bike community refuses to stay on the designated trails. These bad boy bikers love to go fast and furious and, if they had their druthers, would see us building trails that more nearly resembled black diamond ski runs, replete with ramps and jumps and obstacles. The District's pathetic 7% maximum grade trails apparently don't provide enough thrill factor, and obviously just aren't fun enough. These downhill maniac speed demons (mostly still in the "immortal" under-25-year-old age group) cut switch-backs, tear through grasslands, build jumps and ramps in the trail bed, create "whoop-de-woos," or "eyebrows" on the uphill embankments, and even surreptitiously build their own trails.

2/13/06: Just sunset now and still warmish. Beautiful pink and orange fading from the bottom of the clouds. We're having summer weather here in February. Quiet day. Didn't do much. Broke up the uphill ends of two "whoop-de-woos" where the downhill bikes go swooping ten or 20 feet up the upper embankments, making denuded, unsightly worn areas. It seems like there are ever more of these stupid things, giving the preserve the look of an outdoor gymnasium. The whoop-de-woos annoy me, but I also wonder if I'm not overreacting. Aside from looking ugly, how much real harm are they doing? Some erosion and habitat destruction, to be sure, but pretty minimal. Meanwhile, I'm sure the cyclists have no idea that they are in fact in violation of the rule that requires them to remain on the trail. So, I had just finished pulaskiing these two bits and here came three boys on bikes. Terry and I saw them using three "whoop-de-woos" higher up, so stopped and talked to them. Couldn't really cite them, as they are ignorant of their error. I don't think I was tough enough on them given they are the problem.

I would guess that a stereotypical bad boy biker would have a very hard time empathizing with my objection to the riding of "eyebrows." What's the big deal? So the path swoops up onto the upper bank a ways. So what. Unsightly? Good Grief. That's so petty, it's ridiculous. To him, (or her) the point is all about the absorbing-aerobic-uphill plus the free-as-a-bird-downhill. The vegetation and wildlife in one's immediate vicinity are a blur anyway. But to me, and many other visitors, rangers, supervisors, and even managers, they are ugly, wrongheaded, a plague and a nuisance, and they've got to go. The problem is that there no good way of getting rid of them. If you drag logs and brush across them, the bikers are equally capable of dragging the stuff right back off. They are just as committed as we are, and there are more of them. It becomes a battle of wills. We pile it on; they drag it off. This is not a solution. Stakes or spikes or rebar cannot be used because of the fear of endangering the trail crew when they are brushing the road. Should the giant flails of the mechanical brushing arm hit the stake/spike/rebar and send a chunk flying, it could kill someone. Should a cyclist should get hurt somehow on one of these staked-down anti-eyebrow devices, the District would be liable. The only safe and lasting solution is to fence off all the eyebrows. This has been done on a couple of them in St. Joseph's Hill, and the endemic flowers are slowly returning to the now protected serpentine soil, but brand new whoop-de-woos are developing just beyond where the fences end. Do we have to fence both sides of every trail?

1/1/07: A bright sunny morning although decidedly cool. I feel guilty sitting with the heater going in the truck. Yesterday I spent two-plus hours at El Sereno repairing the fence some visitor (read bicyclist) had cut in about two minutes. I had to remove bent-over t-posts with the high-jack lift, pound in new t-posts, string new wire and post new signs, just so the guy can come back and easily cut it all over again. I had found the fences cut the day before, and later that day at the Sheldon gate had had a sometimes heated discussion with a cyclist headed in. (I had stopped him to warn him we'd be closing in half an hour.) He said that those fences had really made him mad, that the little side trail we fenced off wasn't doing any harm, wasn't an erosion problem and had been there a long time. He said his Christmas cards this year feature a snow scene taken out there during last year's storm. He wants the fences down and asked how to make that happen. I tried to explain to him my reasons for putting them up. First of all, I said that side trail doesn't go anywhere. It is just a second trail paralleling the designated trail for some 50 yards and part of the objective of having trails is to concentrate the human use to a single corridor, leaving the rest of the land for the wildlife and native plants. Secondly, the trail has not "always been there." True, it may have been there as long as you or I can remember, but we really haven't been around all that long, and at some point in the not too distant past, this secondary route was not there. (Nor was the main trail, presumably!) If you had never had it, you wouldn't miss it and wouldn't be feeling deprived.

This plague of off-trail bikes, eyebrow riders, meadow rapers, and illegal trail builders goes on and on. Here is another courtroom drama featuring an illegal biker trail down a firebreak in Sierra Azul. This triple-wide, super-steep two mile long firebreak between Weaver Road and Alma Bridge Road was re-opened by CDF bulldozers in 1998 with the thought of halting the Loma Prieta Summit Fire. The fire never made it that far, but the black diamond bike run down the now broom-infested firebreak has proved unstoppable. It is awfully hard to catch these bad guys, though; you just have to luck out, to be in the right place at the right time. Short of the telltale vehicle pulled off on the roadside, we would never catch any of them.

1/11/10 I had court this morning, San Jose Traffic. I think with any other judge I might have lost, but I got Stonewall, who is known to be officer-friendly. I had to sit through six or seven cases ahead of mine (getting more and more nervous) and she found every defendant guilty, so I think that gave me confidence. My defendant had some good points I thought, and I felt bad that there was no opportunity to tell him that. I presumed he and his buddy had entered the so-called "Soda Trail" off Weaver, so my testimony was based on the fact that the top of the trail off Weaver is signed "Closed Area," and all my pictures were taken up there. But, in fact, he said they had entered off of Soda Springs Road at Gate SA20, which is completely unsigned. (That is now remedied!) When it was my turn to ask him questions, the only thing I could think to ask was why, then, was his vehicle parked near Gate SA19 at the bottom of the trail, and given that it was, why hadn't he checked the signs down there, if he knew that was where they were planning on exiting? I thought that was pretty clever of me, but Stonewall outdid me, bless her heart. She asked to see the public map of Sierra Azul, which I had brought in just to show the general area, and she pointed out that the "Soda Trail," doesn't even appear on the map. It is obviously not a designated trail. Guilty. Pay up.

I have found illegally constructed trails in nearly every preserve, and all but one of them can be attributed to bicyclists. Some of these are pretty elaborate affairs, not just earthen ramps and re-enforced embankments, but aerial boardwalks built of lumber and extending out from the hillside ten or 20 feet. I walk out to the end and can't imagine riding on this flimsy structure, much less flying off the end into thin air and hoping to land unhurt 30 or 40 feet away! These guys are nuts, and, of course, they have no training in trail building and no idea how much environmental damage they are doing, and they don't care. Trying to catch them in the act, with tools in hand is like trying to catch the dumper unloading his pickup off the side of the road, or the litterbug tossing the beer can, or the firewood poacher running the chainsaw, or the arsonist lighting the wildfire. Mostly we just clean up the mess. It is a red-letter day when you actually catch them red-handed, like this:

On Dec. 20, 2008 at about four in the afternoon, I saw a gray Volvo parked on the side of Umunhum Road near the PG&E power tower about a quarter mile above the Jacques Ridge parking lot. Why not just park in the lot? I pulled over and saw two teenagers hanging around outside the car. They said they were waiting for one of their dads to return; he was a painter and out in the area somewhere working on a painting. Weird, but not too weird, and there is nothing saying you can't park there if you want. I dismissed it; I'm gullible. About 15 minutes later I saw a teenager ride into the Jacques Ridge lot and park a small, but street-legal motorcycle. I stopped to warn him that there was only about an hour left until closing time. He said he was just going for a short walk. I did not connect the dots here and realize these two incidents were related.

After about another half an hour I happened upon Sheriff's Deputy Raymond, and we started chatting. I told him about the teens associated with the Volvo, which was still parked in the same spot, but now sans teens, and about the contact with the young motorcyclist. Raymond immediately smelled a rat. We went back to where the Volvo was parked, and I headed up toward the power tower where I knew there was an illegal trail heading down the ridge, but Raymond called me back and suggested that we first check the meadow behind the trees across the street. Okay, if you say so.

From the other side of the trees, looking down across the gray-brown of the early winter meadow, we sighted our boys at the bottom of 100 yards of freshly dug trail, tools in hand. Bingo! Raymond yelled something to our suspects like, "Stop! Police!" and all three boys sprinted for the trees. Now what? I figured Raymond and I would both go wait at the Volvo. They had to return sooner or later unless they were going to walk home, and it was getting darker and colder by the minute this being the eve of the winter solstice. Actually, just I went to the Volvo while clever Raymond charged down to the motorcycle, and, using a bike lock he apparently carries for just such purposes, quickly chained the bike to the fence, just in time to prevent the escape of our youngest suspect. The motorcyclist proved to be an unlicensed 14-year-old. Raymond called the kid's parents to have them come pick up their son and their motorcycle, then brought him up to the Volvo to wait. I meanwhile had detained the other two and was laboring with frozen fingers to fill in the JCR (Juvenile Contact Report, used instead of a citation forms in the cold and dark. The hood of my truck serves well as a desk because I can spread stuff out on it in the light of the cab-mounted spotlight. It also gives me a standard place to stand--beside the left front tire--and a standard place to put suspects—right in front of the grill. These three sat sullenly on the bumper enjoying Dumbo's engine heat while they fully fessed up to their crime.

It was kind of sad, actually. The youngest one, the motorcyclist, seemed to be the most messed up and the most unhappy. He said he was already in a lot of trouble at school and the only thing he really liked to do was ride bikes, but complained that there weren't any good trails to do the kind of biking he enjoyed. The tools, which we collected after Lars got on scene, were their parents', taken from their garages; they had been working on the trail for only a couple of days; they didn't know to whom the land belonged.

There was a certain part of me that sympathized with these boys. They were not rude or belligerent and readily answered questions and provided information. Could they really be this innocent, this naive? They knew that what they were doing was probably a violation of some law, but didn't at all understand why it was so wrong. They asked where they might be allowed to build their trail. Could they get permission to build it on District or County Park land? Could they help design a real biker trail and work with the trail crew to build it? They seemed so young and clueless. How could they know about the seemingly endless paperwork process that precedes any actual shovel work: the soil studies, the vegetation studies, the route planning and selection, and the permits from the various state, county and regional agencies? Even when you own the land, you can't just go out and start digging. All the same, these boys were doing exactly what bored and restless teens have been doing down through the ages, plunging in and taking action without worrying too much about the details, or the consequences. They had a fun and adventurous idea and they took the initiative and went out and actually tried to make it happen, and were severely punished for it. I respected their energy and enthusiasm and their desire to be outdoors actively and cooperatively building their dream, rather than glued to computer and video games like so many of their contemporaries.

I didn't feel nearly so sympathetic the next day when I came back to the crime scene to take pictures for the report. Stupid kids! How could they have done this? Their trail snaked right through the middle of a gorgeous little serpentine meadow. The picturesque rocky outcropping with its succulent Dudlea, a rare serpentine soil endemic, had been transformed into a springboard for a jump. The trail rampaged through the sunny, south-facing slope over the homes of suncups and shooting stars and jewel flowers; it cut through the boggy area at the bottom where monkey flower and the very rare Mt. Hamilton thistle live! How could they? I was outraged by the damage and saddened by the knowledge that this hillside would probably never recover. Non-native weeds love exposed soil and would quickly move in to this broken ground. There would always be a line of broom, star thistle, fillaree, and stinkwort swerving through the meadow. The line would gradually widen and spread and another small piece of paradise would be lost.

What would happen to those boys? Would they actually learn anything from this experience? If so, I doubt it would be the lesson I would have had them learn. Unfortunately, environmental education and youth guidance do not fit well into a detention and citation situation. Their emotions were running too high for them to actually learn anything. As usual, by catching and citing these guys, even though it may feel righteous and good, we won't change their behavior or solve the District's problem with illegal trail builders.

Given all the trouble the bikers cause, is it any wonder that I continue to basically dislike having them in the preserves? I have to work hard to remind myself that the majority of bicyclists are law-abiding. They mostly obey the speed limit; they don't ride eyebrows or fire breaks; they don't build illegal trails. What? They don't have the same way of experiencing and appreciating nature as I do? They don't know the names of the flowers and trees and don't intend to learn? Well, haven't I known and respected many a mountaineer for whom the same might be said? Maybe the best I can say for bikes in the preserves is that I understand that young people (mainly guys?) have always been drawn to the woods in pursuit of challenge and adventure, traditionally hunting and fishing. If bicycling gets them away from their computer screens and out onto the trails, maybe one day while grinding slowly up a hill they will accidentally see something—a snake or a paw print--that will intrigue them and lure them down off their high-tech machine to actually touch the earth.

13. Defensive Tactics

About every four months all District rangers and supervising rangers attend defensive tactics (DT) training. The area superintendents and the operations manager can attend too if they want. The training is very well done and worthwhile, and can even be a lot of fun, and yet I often dread it. I always feel so incompetent at defensive tactics, maybe because, with this particular skill set, there is always so much room for improvement. Maybe because, compared to my classmates—males 20 years my junior—I feel weak, pathetic and inept. We are actually extremely lucky to receive this quarterly DT time; many agencies offer no such on-going refresher training at all. Some agencies train only once or twice a year. Given that we seldom or never use any of these skills, the opportunity to practice them is a luxury—and a necessity.

We contract out for DT instructors, most recently with the Palo Alto Police, and have had some excellent instructors. They are keen to understand the policy restrictions we work under and they devise realistic scenarios, situations that we might actually come upon. There are usually only three to six rangers in DTs at a time, so there is lots of individual attention, repetition and practice. There isn't a test, so I can't actually fail, so why does my heart rate increase when I see DTs on the schedule?

According to District policy, rangers may not use physical force to gain compliance with an unruly suspect. Unlike a police officer, who is permitted, and expected, to physically capture and restrain suspects, District rangers may not so much as touch someone whom we are detaining for a violation. If a person I am citing starts to run away, I cannot grab them. If a cyclist I am citing starts to ride off, I cannot even touch their bike. I cannot "chase" people down, whether on foot, bicycle, motorcycle or truck, but I am allowed to "follow" them. Of course, even if I were to catch up with them, I am only permitted to, once again, command them to stop. This policy might sound awfully restrictive, but it is intended for officer safety. Touching suspects, whether to prevent their fleeing, or to affect a physical arrest, often provokes a fight. This is not a good idea, especially when you remember that, unlike cops, who are armed and whose backup is seconds away, we rangers are unarmed and operate alone. Our backup could be as much as an hour away.

Rangers are, however, permitted to defend themselves. I can, and am expected to, step deliberately out in front of the approaching motorcyclist, bicyclist or runner and command that they stop, and, should they continue to advance to a point where my safety is compromised, I can defend myself. The presumption is that a normal, reasonable, and compliant person is not going to run me over or attack me, especially as they are likely to get hurt themselves in the fray. Defensive tactics is about how to walk away from an attack unhurt, or at least alive.

So we practice interview stance and defensive stance, lunge step and side step, blocking and parrying. We practice giving commands, yelling at our DT partners to, "Stop!" and to, "Get down on the ground!" We practice kicking knees and raking shins with our boots and punching noses with our palms and elbows. We practice control holds and pain compliance techniques. We practice handcuffing people standing, kneeling, and lying on the floor. And, of course, we practice with the pepper spray and with the expandable batons that we all carry, drawing them and replacing them on our belts all the while keeping our eyes on our attackers. DT training sessions often end with some anxiety-laden scenarios, in which the instructors play the bad guys.

10-4-08: We have DTs today with an emphasis on the pepper spray, followed by handcuffing. I am suffering more than my usual performance anxiety. Not sure why. I am pretty bad at cuffing. I can never seem to remember "the moves," and the last time we did pepper spray I accidentally shot Bart in the face—and not with the fake stuff!

10-4-11: So we had DT again today, this time focusing on "personal weapons:" hitting, kicking, control holds, pain compliance techniques, and finally the "carotid restraint." This was the first time I ever remember being taught "pressure points" for pain compliance, like grabbing someone under the angles of their jaw and lifting up to get someone to stand up or pinching the skin above their triceps while helping them to their feet. The carotid thing was really interesting. I had heard about it, perhaps at the Academy, but never seen it done or had it taught. I've always heard it was a big no-no, a technique widely forbidden to law enforcement. Anyway, I volunteered to go first and both instructors tried, one after the other, to "carotid" me, but it didn't work. Basically you hook your arm around the neck of the person with your elbow pressed into their sternum, then lift and squeeze. It is supposed to cut off the supply of blood to their brain so they pass out, but its not supposed to injure the person. In our training, anyway, it wasn't always effective. Of course we only held it for a second, until the victim started to feel woozy.

I have never yet handcuffed a suspect, and the closest I've come to thinking of cuffing someone is when dealing with mentally ill people. They often seem passive and compliant enough that I could accomplish the cuffing easily, and strange and unpredictable enough that I just might like to have them in cuffs while we wait for the sheriff. I have never yet pepper-sprayed anyone either, or hit a living thing with my baton. I have drawn it a couple times when faced with bristling, snarling dogs, but have, on both occasions, been rescued by the dogs' owners. I have never in my life, (well, okay, in my adult life) even intentionally hit or kicked anybody.

I've never done any of these things because, as yet, I've never had too, and it would be fine by me if this status should prevail for the rest of my career, and indeed for the remainder of my life. I don't spend much time worrying about being attacked, probably because I've led an attack-free existence thus far. Maybe I'm too trusting and not suspicious enough, having never really been threatened with violence. So, what do I imagine would happen if some angry young man were to attack me? Well, unless I were extraordinarily lucky, I imagine I'd lose, despite all those hours spent learning to sidestep and back up. I hope I would survive the fight, maybe with some minor injury. I know there are some crazy and violent people out there, but there is really nothing more I can do to prepare for the chance that I might run into one of them.

This brings us to the gun question. District rangers are not armed. We have never been armed and I doubt we ever will be, but many District rangers would like to be. Many rangers are hunters or gun enthusiasts or target shooters. They are familiar and comfortable with guns. I am not. When I envision the unlikely scene of being attacked by an angry young man, the one where I come out with the minor injury, and I then add into the mix the presence of a gun on my hip, I see the statistical chances of my surviving the encounter going down, rather than up. And certainly the angry young man's chances of survival plummet. Either I get the jump on him and either kill or gravely wound him, or he gets the gun away from me and shoots me. The gun is a major liability and I don't want it.

I have all sorts of other arguments against arming the rangers, chief among them being that we would then truly become wholly, and solely, cops. The entire character of the job would change. We would become park police rather than park rangers. With all the money the District would have to commit to equipping and training and maintaining armed law enforcement rangers, they would not be interested in having those rangers doing resource management or maintenance projects. I enjoy those parts of my job. I want to remain a generalist ranger.

One of the only questions I remember asking the interview panel before I was hired was, "Has any District ranger had ever had a loaded gun pointed at them by a suspect." I was trying to gauge just how potentially dangerous this job could be. When the answer was no, I felt reassured that the job would not be unrealistically dangerous. Yes, I could always meet the one-in-a-million crazy guy and wish I had that loaded gun, but that could hold true anywhere, anytime, outside my job as a ranger. For your run-of-the-mill angry young man, my likelihood of getting shot or beat up is very much reduced by the District's "no touch, no chase" policy. When the guy threatens me, I aim to just let him go. Most people's anger subsides when they realize they are going to get away; they are not going to be caught; they are not going to be ticketed or go to jail. A trail speed ticket is not worth getting beat up over. When the violator starts seeing red and raising his voice in anger, I can just say, "I've changed my mind. You can go. I'll catch you later." Such person's next law enforcement contact is probably not too far away.

14. Bluebird Boxes

Every first of the month Terry totes up the previous month's resource management (RM) hours. Each field office is supposed to achieve some minimum number of hours as the rangers' contribution to the District's resource management efforts. I think Rose, the resource management boss, was envisioning us out there pulling broom and thistle and stinkwort, but other activities also count as RM, and appear much more frequently in Terry's tallies. Writing wildlife observation reports of mountain lion sightings counts as resource management, as does counting deer on the annual deer surveys, and waiting for the sheriff to show up to dispatch injured deer. There is some broom pulling, mostly when a ranger is assigned to a weekend volunteer project featuring broom pulling. There are always interesting incidentals like the Western Red Bat I found flopping around on the ground surrounded by excited and curious visitors. I moved it to the far side of the creek to quietly expire. Catching and moving rattlesnakes, as described earlier, also counts. For me, however, the biggest source of RM hours is undoubtedly the bluebird box program.

Across the United States every spring thousands of volunteer birders start checking their bluebird box "trails," a series of numbered birdhouses with easy-open sides, usually spaced out along a little used trail, disc line or fence line. It is not a District program, but is run by the Audubon Society. It was started many years ago on the East Coast in the hope of stemming the decline in the numbers of cavity-nesting birds by providing alternative "cavities."

These volunteer birders are a hardy and knowledgeable lot, appearing rain or shine at their self-appointed "trail," and able to distinguish a bluebird nest from a swallow nest by the appearance of a few feathers. They come prepared with a butt-pack full of specialized and often homemade tools and supplies—pliers, screwdrivers and screws for fixing the boxes, a tube of "Tanglefoot" to keep ants out, a little dental mirror for spying on babies hiding over the lip of the nest, small binoculars for checking the box from afar for the presence of parent birds, and, most important of all, their pocket-sized notebook usually with grid-ruled paper and filled with their tiny, precise script for keeping detailed notes and records for each box. Bird box monitors start each spring earlier than the earliest early bird because, at the end of the season, the on-line data spreadsheet calls for the date on which a nest first appeared in each box, and they wouldn't want to miss the first nest and have to leave a blank spot on the form. During the height of the nesting season, these volunteers check their boxes every week, usually on the same day, and even at the same time. They record the construction of a new nest, the laying of eggs, the number of hatchlings, and how many are believed to have successfully fledged.

All this commitment to the recording of tiny bits of data requires a personality completely different from my own. Nest box monitors are detail-oriented, fastidious, perfectionists: two of the three I have been working with are retired engineers, and the third is an accountant. I did try for awhile setting up a "trail" of my own of all of five boxes on the District's Rancho de Guadalupe property, but it was way too much work and I gave it up. Not the right activity for me. My boxes filled with bees and mice rather than birds, and it was hard getting out to check them every week, even though I cheated by putting them right along a drivable route. No, my bluebird box (BBB) RM hours have come from tailing along behind Ulf and Don and Joan, and it's one of my favorite ways to spend a morning at work.

4-18-05: Did BBBs this afternoon with Ulf. I enjoy his company and feel so privileged to get to tag along while he checks his boxes. I still am bad at identifying the various birds (bluebirds, nuthatches, flycatchers, wrens, swallows and a couple others) by their nests (sticks, grass, feathers, coyote poop) and the size and color of the eggs. Bluebird eggs are blue; I got that one. The babies are cute and it is fun to see them. My box in the garden at home, a present from Ulf, still has no success. Probably should move it off the fence.

My identification skills for birds, nests, eggs, and nesting materials have improved slowly over the years, and so has my interest in bird natural history trivia. I never before thought about the time factor associated with the laying versus the hatching of a clutch of eggs. Once the nest itself is complete— usually a joint effort--Mommy bird lays one egg a day (true of domestic chickens too) until the nest is full to her satisfaction, and to her body's ability to sustain egg laying. But all the eggs hatch on the same day, more or less. How can that be when the first-laid egg might be six days older than the last-laid? It seems that all the earlier-laid eggs just sit in the nest, uncared for and (here is the important part) un-incubated until that magic number is reached, and then the round-the-clock incubation begins. Only when warmed to the right temperature does the embryo begin to develop. Daddy bird helps out with this task in most of these species, either taking turns on the nest or bringing home take-out for Mom. Once the eggs hatch, the hardest work begins: the non-stop feeding. Unlike single parent human families, which can fare pretty well, single-parent bird families usually all die. If either parent bird gets lost to predation during this critical period, the babies stand almost no chance. Maybe the largest, strongest, first-hatched chick, who is always first in line and grabs the majority of the chow, survives if Mom just ignores the others. Checking BBBs does often bring home the cruelty of "the survival of the fittest."

5/31/11: This has got to have been the coldest May on record, and rain and clouds are forecast for the next week as well. Interesting that the annual grass still dies and turns brown even though the rains continue. Wet, cold weather is not good for raising baby birds. I checked boxes today with Ulf, and we found quite a few dead babies, sometimes their bodies withering away under their still living siblings. One box, which had six ten-day-old bluebirds last week, had no live babies, just three dead babies and a bunch of blue feathers on the ground under the nest. Ulf thinks that when the weather is cold, wet, or windy, the insects on which the birds feed do not fly, so the babies starve. It was so sad to open a box which last week contained a throng of eager mouths stretched wide as miniature tulips, then to open it this week to find them all dead and crawling with ants, just their smiling beaks remaining.

At least it was a glorious day for tramping around through the more-than-head-high grass. The quality of the light seemed like something from the High Sierra, so clear and sharp, and the sky so very blue in contrast with the enormous black and white columnar clouds. I followed Ulf up a slope, watching him push through a "cornfield" of purple mustard stems, and it looked like a painting of some old-time agricultural scene.

6/20/11: Spent an hour and a half with Don in the Fremont Older Hayfields checking BBBs. I was dreading being out in the full sun in the late afternoon of a hot day, but now all the boxes are in the shade, thanks to Don, who moved many of them after having too many cooked babies. I figured, this being the end of the season, we would have nothing but a few swallows, but no. Wow! There was actually a nest of Ash-throated Flycatchers with four babies about ten days old, and two nests with five bluebird eggs each. Bluebird eggs are so lovely, such a smooth, soft powdery blue, and a clutch of eggs is so heart-rendingly homey. I get a thrill every time. Of course, the babies are even cuter when they all pop open their enormous mouths and beg.

I admire the nest box volunteers. With their patience and dedication, and their quiet and careful observations, they have amassed reams of data on America's cavity nesting birds. I also acknowledge and salute the enormous body of nature knowledge, and wilderness experience lodged in their heads and hearts, and thank them for sharing it. If the famous American writer and naturalist Aldo Leopold had lived today he would surely have been a nest boxer. He kept such exhaustive records of all the critters on his property. He would fit right in. Curious that I cannot summon up the same admiration for the professor gathering mountain lion data with his capture and collar program as I can for the nest boxers and their data gathering program. Why does tagging and counting birds and fish and insects seem so acceptable and innocuous while collaring lions seems so wrong, or at least so sad? I don't know, but I acknowledge my apparent hypocrisy.

15. Suspicious Vehicles

I said that without bikes and dogs, rangers would have nothing to do, but then again, maybe I was wrong. The motorcyclists also keep us busy, not that we actually manage to catch and cite many of them, but we expend a lot of effort trying. Motorized vehicles of any kind are not allowed on the trails, including those trails which are actually patrol roads, but physically preventing cars, trucks, motorcycles and ATVs from entering is not as easy as sticking up a fence or a gate. There have to be gaps for the visitors to get in, as well as their horses, bicycles and wheelchairs. How do you make a pedestrian stile that accommodates a horse or a wheelchair, but not a dirt bike? This was not made any easier when the Americans With Disabilities Act declared that the existing standard was too skinny and we had to actually widen the squeeze stiles. (Even then, I had a group of "stroller moms" complain to me that the squeeze stile at Deer Hollow Farm, through which one has to pass to reach the restrooms, was too narrow to accommodate their doublewide baby strollers!) Basically, if someone really wants to get in with their motorcycle (dirt bike, ATV, car, truck), they probably can. Chains, locks, fences, gates, stiles, and strategically placed boulders are only speed bumps on their way to a good time riding the forbidden ground. My first-ever Motor Vehicles Prohibited cite:

12-5-04 I wrote my first ever "802.1" citation yesterday. It was pretty odd, actually. I was coming in the Mora gate at Rancho and saw someone up at the water tank, so I went up to say hi, but, as I rounded the tank, here came this guy on a motorcycle. I rather cluelessly figured he must be a contractor working on one of the antennae up there. It took my asking, "Who are you?" "What are you doing here?" and "How did you get in?" before I began to realize that this was a law enforcement contact. He just fessed up to riding right through the pedestrian stile. Said he wanted to see what was up there. I felt kind of bad for the poor stupid guy.

One incident I do clearly remember from the week I spent riding around with the four supervising rangers before I went to the academy, was catching a dirt biker riding illegally in the Monte Bello Preserve. I was riding along with Supervising Ranger Owen and I remember his glee as he spotted the suspect and took off after him in the patrol truck at truly amazing speed over the rutted dirt road. The motorcyclist turned tail and sprinted for the exit when he saw us, but then spun out and fell. "Got him!" exalted Owen, who grabbed the P.A. microphone and started hollering, "Park Ranger! Peace Officer! Drop your bike! Get off your bike!" while continuing to steer with the other hand as we flew over the ruts and hurtled toward our prey. Our prize briefly attempted to upright his bike, but then stood quietly and awaited his fate. It was a kid, a juvenile, son of one of the neighbors. I half-remember the crest-fallen look on Owen's face as he realized he would have to fill out a Juvenile Contact Report (JCR), rather than a regular adult citation, which meant he first had to find a blank form somewhere in his truck, which I now realize was probably a jumble of tools and equipment liberally mixed with deli sandwich leavings and snack wrappers.

As Owen laboriously filled in boxes on the JCR, I sized up our suspect. He was dressed from head to toe in motocross armor—chest guard, elbow and knee guards, shin and forearm plates—and, of course, a full crash helmet, all held together with tightening cinches and straps. He was quite imposing, something like a medieval knight, or a space alien. He was a lot bigger than I was, and younger, and no doubt stronger and faster. Given that he was entirely cooperative, and meekly signed his papers and provided his parents' names and phone numbers, I wasn't entirely intimidated, but as we drove away and Owen apologized for "going a little overboard" during the contact, I had realized that I had a lot to learn.

While we sometimes find suspicious cars, trucks, or ATVs in the preserves, these nearly always turn out to be neighbors, or former neighbors. I once found three unauthorized cars and about 15 people out in the middle of nowhere on Loma Prieta Ridge. Even from a distance I could see that this was probably not going to be a citation-writing kind of stop; there were several elderly people and a bunch of kids. Turns out they used to own that spot of land, and one of their former neighbors had lent them a key to get back in there and show everyone around the old homestead, that is, trailer flat. At least that's what they said. Actually I bet they still had, and still have, their own key to get through.

The most commonly encountered suspicious vehicles in the Sierra Azul backcountry are "friends" and "renters" of the owners of the remaining in-holdings within the preserve. Most of these in-holdings are peppered with bulldozed trailer flats and steep dirt roads leading down to them and their ancient trailers. No electricity, no running water, no sanitation. Their inhabitants drive unregistered rusty old pick-ups filled with debris. After a while, you come to recognize the regulars, the long-time inhabitants, but, in fact, there is a pretty steady turnover of renters and friends-of-renters. When I ask what they are up to out here on the ridge, all of them simply claim that they "live at O'Conner's." They have no way to prove it—their address is always a P.O. Box in Los Gatos—and I have no way to disprove it.

I was once detailed to meet a US Census Bureau worker and help him find the residents of the in-holdings out on Loma Prieta Ridge. While I am not forbidden by District policy to go on private property, short of some kind of dire emergency, I have no business out there, so, after driving him up to the boundary and filling him in on the names, physical descriptions, and associated vehicles, of as many locals as I could think of, and after warning him of the type of reception a government worker was likely to receive in their halls, I said, "I'll wait here." Most such locals have no love for the District, which they see as an imminent threat to their way of life (We might buy out O'Conner, and then where would they be?) They are deeply suspicious of inspectors, regulators, and bean counters of all stripes, for good reason. The census guy was back in half an hour. "No one was home."

One day, driving down Cathermole Road, which drops off the west side of Loma Prieta Ridge into the headwaters of Los Gatos Creek and Lake Elsman Reservoir, I saw, to my great surprise, one of these suspicious vehicles coming up the road toward me in a cloud of summertime dust. To come up from the bottom, they would have had to come through the San Jose Water Company gate. To have come down from the top, they would have to have come through two District gates. But this wasn't a Water District truck, or PG&E, or CalFire, or Fish and Game or anybody else official-looking. Who the heck was I shortly going to be contacting? Catermole Road is really, really remote, at least an hour's drive for the closest Sheriff, if I were obliged to call one. When we were about 20 yards apart, nose-to-nose, and somebody was going to have to back up, I could see the license plate, and quickly ran it. I saw this huge, burly man step out of the car. "Clear for 10-36 information?" asks Mt. View. Oh shit. 10-36 means confidential information and usually means the suspect has a criminal record. "Stand by just a minute." I got on the loudspeaker and told the guy to go back and wait by his car, which he did. Now I felt better. He was compliant. Turned out that my illegal visitor lived in the only in-holding on Cathermole Road, the Moses house, except that my suspect wasn't supposed to be living there, because he was a registered sex offender and he was registered to live down in Watsonville. He also had no authorization to be up on District land. He claimed he had emergency escape route rights up Cathermole Road, which wasn't true, but I wasn't going to argue. I didn't cite him. It wasn't worth it. He backed down and turned around and I followed. Later I met with the Sheriff down at Lake Elsman and he went up to deal with the sex offender registration problem. A few years later the District bought that property. It was a really nice house, well maintained with beautiful woodworking. I never saw Moses again.

One of Ranger Sandy's real talents is remembering the local residents, their names, their vehicles, their criminal records, and where they are currently living and with whom. Partially it is because he has the gift of gab; he will sit and talk with these characters for hours, and they will eventually forget about his uniform and spill a few beans. He knows who's sick, who's broke, and who's using (drugs). I'm not much for chitchat, and pretending to socialize with this crowd always feels so fake, and I am sure they can sense my discomfort. There are certainly times when I wish I had his talent, or at least the knowledge it yields, about the local backcountry population. Last winter

I was bullshitted by two motorcyclists who bluffed their way past me at a roadblock where I was stationed down at Loma Prieta on a "snow day." They claimed they lived down off of Loma Chiquita and needed to get through to get home. I was suspicious of these two because I was pretty sure I had seen these same two bikes earlier that day buzzing up and down Bear Creek Road in excess of the speed limit. These two jokers were just out joy riding, but that didn't mean they didn't need to get home. I even tried to verify their addresses via dispatch, and was more suspicious than ever when one guy came back with a Cupertino P.O. Box. I let them through. Sandy told me later (he was off duty that day) that the one guy lived at Garrod Stables, near Fremont Older, where he worked, and had been busted last year for poaching deer.

9/15/06: Hungry. I went and left my lunch sitting on the table in the office this morning when Terry and I rushed off to go catch bad guys. I bought a sandwich but still hungry. Just as we were coming on duty at 1300, dispatch called with a report of motorcycles in Rattlesnake Gulch and off-road vehicles on Loma Chiquita. I started for the top gate of Loma Prieta Ranch (Rattlesnake Gulch) and Terry went for the bottom one. I met Supervisor Murray at the top gate where we found nothing, either there or farther up the road where the ORVs and dirt bike trailers often park. We were about to clear when Terry reported that he could hear motorcycles approaching his position at the bottom gate, and then we heard him go 10-95 on three motorcycles. He was only about a mile away as the bird flies, but the road through the preserve is the worst: super-steep and full of boulders. I hate driving it. So Murray headed down through the preserve, "hurrying" along at less than five mph, while I "hurried" around the outside surface streets, including steep, one lane Mt. Bache Road, at about 15 mph. It's very odd to be gunning your truck while in second gear! Terry wasn't running their I.D. s and wasn't going Code Four (safe, secure), so I had to assume that he had

his hands full just keeping his eyes on those three until one of us got there. I
was sure Murray would beat me, but we arrived about the same time. Three
big boys in total body armor, two pretty quiet and one mouthing off about
how he knew all the secret ways into this place. It turned out that one of
the quiet ones had a felony warrant, so Murray cuffed him and we sat and
sat, waiting for Santa Cruz County Sheriff officers to come from downtown
Santa Cruz. I was glad we caught them, but equally glad it was Terry, and
not me, who made the stop.

That was a great bust and highly unusual. Usually those guys
ride through there with impunity. It takes an hour just to get to
the gate from the Foothills Field Office and it can't take more
than ten minutes to zip through there on motorcycles, so who
knows what they were doing in there all that time. Whatever it
was, I'm sure they're regretting it now, especially the guy who
went to jail. We later reinforced both top and bottom gate areas
with more boulders, and with cables, rather than wire fences, but
they still get in. It must be those secret back entrances that guy
was talking about.

My ultimate, and perhaps best, motorcycle story comes from
July 2008. This time I was the one who made the stop.

Late one afternoon, Roy, the Rhus Ridge caretaker, called to
say that he could hear motorcycles up in the hinterlands of the
Rancho San Antonio Preserve. I started up through Rancho
making for the Windmill Pastures area where I met up with
Ranger Lars, who had come up from the Rhus Ridge lot after
meeting with Roy. Rangers were also deployed to block off
the top of the Black Mountain Trail in Monte Bello Preserve
and to Hidden Villa to prevent the suspects' escaping out those
adjoining trails. Lars and I parked at the junction of the Rhus
Ridge Road and the Black Mountain Trail and then positioned
ourselves a short walk up the trail at a spot where it would be

difficult for the motorcycles to get around us. It wasn't long
before we heard them coming.

*(From my supplemental IR.) The first time Ranger Lars and I heard
the motorcycles approaching, we heard Suspect M's voice saying, "Rangers.
Don't stop. Just blast through." Ranger Lars at this point deployed his
baton and pepper spray and I deployed mine. We did not actually see the
motorcycles at this point.*

*It was several minutes later when we again heard the motorcycles
approaching. When they came into view, Suspect M was in the lead with
Suspect S close behind him. Ranger Lars was about ten feet ahead of me on
the trail facing the motorcycles with his defensive equipment deployed. We
started yelling, "Park Ranger! Peace Officer! Stop your bike! Get down on
the ground!" Suspect M rode toward Lars, then paused and looked like he
was going to stop, then accelerated straight at Lars, who stepped back and
toward the downhill side of the trail. Suspect S cut high above the upper
embankment of the trail avoiding confronting me and Lars. I saw him turn
down the Rhus Ridge Road toward the parking lot.*

*By then Suspect M had gotten past Lars and was riding right at me as
Lars scrambled to his feet. I continued to shout at Suspect M to stop his
bike and I continued to try to block his way. When he came abreast of me,
I pushed the motorcycle away, downhill, but my right foot and leg got caught
under the rear wheel, my pant leg stuck in the chain, and I was dragged off
my feet and down off the trail. Suspect M had his hands on the grips of
the motorcycle during our entire confrontation, since he was trying to control
the motorcycle off trail in the loose dirt. Both Suspect M and I got to our feet
quickly. I still had my baton in hand and Ranger Lars and I continued to
shout at Suspect M to sit down on the ground. Suspect M was yelling at us
that he didn't know who we were, and that we had come out of nowhere and
that he was not going to sit down and was not going to comply. After about
30 seconds he did sit down on the edge of the trail where he remained seated
until the arrival of the sheriff deputy.*

We waited about 20 minutes. Ranger Lars uprighted the motorcycle to keep it from leaking fuel. I took photos of the scene. Neither Ranger Lars nor I ever struck either suspect with our batons or pepper sprayed either suspect. Suspect M refused medical attention for the severe scratches on his forearms and said that he had gotten the scratches earlier during the ride that day and not during contact with Ranger Lars and me. He also said that he didn't know Suspect S and that he just met him while out riding on the trail. When we said that this seemed unlikely, he said that he didn't want to rat on a friend. He said he had entered the preserve at the gate on Stonebrook Drive, easily driving his motorcycle over the log stiles meant to prevent motorcycle access. He said he had been riding in the Neery Quarry (now within the preserve) and Windmill Pastures area all of his life, long before it became a preserve. He said he was sorry for running into Ranger Lars and me and that he would never come riding at Rancho San Antonio ever again.

When Supervisor Tony finally got on scene bringing along the SO, there was some discussion because Tony wasn't happy about transporting a suspect who had just attacked a ranger in the passenger compartment of his patrol truck, but there really wasn't any choice. The SO's Crown Vic was not coming up that hill. When we finally all got down to the lot we found that Suspect S had been stopped there by Ranger Patty, along with caretaker Roy, who was a military veteran and usually walked around sporting a 12-inch knife on his belt.. The county paramedics were there too, although nobody was badly hurt and Suspect M refused to be seen. Tony sent Lars and me down to the hospital (It was so late by now that our usual clinic was closed) to document our rather minor injuries, just some scratches and bruises. We felt pretty silly about being seen by a doctor for such minor injuries, but she seemed used to doing such documentary exams on law enforcement officers. In addition to the PC 148

Delay and Obstruct a Peace Officer and MROSD 802.1 Vehicles Prohibited violations with which both suspects were charged, Suspect M was also charged with Assault and Battery on a Peace Officer. Suspect S was cited and released; Suspect M went to jail.

My bruised calf was spectacular enough to draw the attention of my fellow swimmers and water polo players, who then, of course, got to hear the whole story. The attention and the kudos and my brief fame as a tough guy were all great except that I didn't really feel like I had done anything to deserve my reputation. I had just done what anyone else would have done in the same spot. I also felt guilty that my moment of glory was riding on the back of the suspects' degradation, especially Suspect M. I know that the motorcyclists brought their problems on themselves by their own actions and choices, but I still felt bad about it.

On several occasions after this incident I talked to Roy about how I felt. He had known Suspect M since childhood and said he was actually a pretty nice kid, just with no impulse control and thus always in trouble. That day on the Black Mountain Trail he had been drunk, which I had suspected. Suspect M hadn't wanted to hurt Lars or me or to run us down; he was just trying to get past us, to get away. Everything had spun out of control as his bad decisions mounted up. By the time my part in this drama arrived, Suspect M's finale had already been ordained. I guess I'm not really cut out to be the tough guy.

10-30-07 Need to get out on foot today. I've been trapped in the truck due to being the only ranger on. Everyone else is up at motorcycle training on Skyline. Yes, you heard right, motorcycles! Skyline has had them for some time now, but only on a trial basis, for patrolling Corte Madera. The idea is that we could then "follow" the bicyclists who refuse to stop. I don't hear them being used much, but now suddenly we're to get them too. For what?

We have very little single-track trail down here, almost none. We already have ATVs, which I've forgotten how to operate since I never use them. I scarcely hear anyone else using them either. How do they remember? I figured there was no sense in my doing the motorcycle training since I have no intention of using them either. Why would I? When do the other rangers think they are going to need to use them? It really just strikes me as wrong for rangers to be buzzing around on desert rapers. Noisy, dusty, destructive, and, with the helmet on, one can't see anything or politely talk to anyone.

As you can see from the above diatribe, I was aghast when I heard about the motorcycle program. To have rangers mounted on these environmental nemeses, motoring around the foot trails, runs contrary to my core beliefs about low-impact, leave-no-trace visitation and law enforcement in the preserves. It bothers me that, once again, I find myself in the lonely minority of opinion on this issue. Most rangers thought it was totally cool that they would be able to ride motorcycles at work. It would be fun. There would be lots of fun new gear to go along with the bikes. Most rangers love vehicles and machinery, and specialized clothing and gear. Call me a killjoy; call me a stick-in-the-mud, but motorcycles are unnecessary, dangerous, and the antithesis of my image of a proper park ranger.

Off-road vehicles are the bane of land management agencies of the California deserts as they struggle to confine human use to the roadways. While I appreciate the restraint of those motorized recreationalists who do manage stay on the road, I truly do not understand the allure of spending the day driving around in circles in a cloud of dust at a "Vehicular Recreation Area." The County of Santa Clara has a motorcycle park, a very popular and dangerous place judging by the number of emergency medical calls. While I was at one of my Park Management Program Interns' presentation days at West Valley

College, I listened to the presentation of a young woman whose internship involved training children to ride motorcycles at this park. I was disgusted. Her whole class was about how to safely handle and operate a dirt bike. She apparently gave them no training at all about the park itself, its natural features, its human history, or its wildlife. No, as far as her training was concerned, she might as well have been preparing them to ride around a garbage dump. The land itself was of no interest aside from its value as a recreational venue.

Our motorcycle program might have been easier to stomach if it hadn't seemed so unnecessary, such a big waste of money. Money that could have gone to buy and restore land, instead went to buy four motorcycles, two specialized trailers for hauling them, two sheds for storing them, all the associated costs of maintaining them, and equipping and training the ranger staff. And they are scarcely ever used. About once or twice a month I hear a ranger going out on motorcycle patrol, driving the motorcycle slowly around the trails. They could patrol the same trails on foot or on bicycle, or, in many cases, in the patrol truck, but riding the motorcycles is, for them, more fun. The original justification for their purchase was the following of fleeing bicycle suspects, but I can't recall a single use of the motorcycles for this purpose. Occasionally the motorcycles have been used to quickly search single-track trails looking for missing persons or medical aid victims. I can't recall if we have ever actually located the victim this way, but I do acknowledge that potential. The lost or injured victim would still have to walk out, as the motorcycles are too small for more than one rider.

The premium tool for locating lost hikers, much faster than an ATV or motorcycle, is a helicopter. Amazing but true, Sheriff's and CHP and CalFire helicopters seem more than willing to come out and fly over trails with their searchlight looking for stray hikers. I've only been on a couple of these, but in both cases, the people were found in short order once the copter was on scene. Next thing you know, the equipment-loving division of the District's Operations Department will be demanding their own bird.

16. Pichetti Pond

Arriving with the flood of other Italian immigrants after the Civil War, the Pichetti brothers, Vincenzo and Segundo, bought some virgin land at the bottom of Monte Bello Ridge, west of the agricultural heartland of the Santa Clara Valley. They imported grape stock and started making wine. They prospered, bought more land and imported Italian wives. Their descendents survived Prohibition by ripping out vineyards (all but enough for their 200 gallons worth of Zinfandel for "personal" consumption) and planting apricots and pears. The little pond at Pichetti Ranch was probably their stock-watering pond for pigs and cows and was probably originally connected to the year-round spring, whose waters now flow past the old winery buildings and down into Stevens Creek Reservoir.

The Pichetti family heritage is now well preserved as Pichetti Ranch Open Space Preserve. One of the smallest preserves, it is wedged in between Stevens Creek County Park, the Sunnyvale Rod and Gun Club, and Stevens Creek Quarry. I loved a former intern's description of a "peaceful" hike at Pichetti: the motorcycles on Stevens Canyon Road (RRRrrrrRRRrrr), the shooting range (Bang! Bang! Bang!) and the heavy equipment working at the quarry with their reverse gear warning beepers

(Beep, Beep, Beep, Beep!) Closed to both bikes and dogs, Pichetti Ranch would sit largely unvisited if it weren't for the winery, and the infamous pond.

This quarter acre puddle is decidedly ephemeral, more like a vernal pool, emerging in the winter, drying up in the summer. Even when absolutely full and flooding over the patrol road, it isn't more than six feet deep. It's warm shallow waters and gently sloping margins make an inviting breeding ground for California newts, Pacific tree frogs, Western toads, and myriads of insects with aquatic larval forms, such as damselflies and dragonflies. A mallard duck couple raises ducklings there every spring. The pond used to have red-legged frogs, now highly endangered on the San Francisco Peninsula.

The old farmhouse, winery, and associated buildings are preserved as historically significant, and are leased to a vintner who lives there, makes wine, and makes a tidy living operating the complex as a tasting room and event center. It's a win-win situation for the most part.

Wine tasting in the Santa Cruz Mountain has become a huge industry. The up-scale, well-heeled urban elite arrive in droves, especially on fair-weather weekends, and they more than fill the large gravel parking lot. Their children roll down the winery's green lawns, balance along the old stone walls, and play in the little spring-fed creek under the redwood trees. For those families brave enough to leave behind the familiar comforts of lawns, picnic tables and flush toilets, the broad and level Zinfandel Trail starts just across the footbridge, and the pond is less than a quarter mile away. The easy access and tantalizing lure of water tempt some of these suburbanites to leave the pavement perhaps for the first time. Their children might actually get wet and dirty playing in a natural environment. Wading into the shallows in pursuit of pollywogs and larval newts, the kids have a chance for a memorable, hands-on, direct science experience. That is, until I arrived and put a stop to it.

4-23-05: I was at Pichetti Pond again late this afternoon and contacted four different groups of parents with wet, muddy, preschool children armed with bags and pails of tadpoles. I confiscated the tadpoles and returned them to the pond and spent quite some time educating the public, who basically didn't see the harm in stomping all over the shallows. "No collecting" seemed to go over better. I found this same situation when I was at the pond on Saturday. I presented one mom, who was standing out in the pond supervising, with a written warning. Tony seems to feel I was overreacting. Doesn't anyone agree with me that we are doing environmental damage to the pond, and we're allowing these kids and parents their negligent behavior? Wading is prohibited for good reason and should be enforced. I'm not happy and don't know what to do. I can't get no support.

4-30-05: Still kicking kids out of Pichetti pond, although half-heartedly. The ten-year-old girl there today had caught a newt baby, I think. I'd never seen one like it before. It was a tiny salamander about one inch long with four miniscule legs and two pairs of external gills! Do California newts have external gills when young? She also had some damselfly nymphs and a Dobson fly larva. I couldn't get myself to forbid her squishing around the muddy shoreline. Is she really doing more harm than good? Am I? Wednesday's patrol meeting last week was devoted to this discussion. I was a distinct minority of one, worrying about the environmental damage of the squishing. Everyone agreed the collecting (to take home) was bad, except some wanted schools to be able to get collecting permits. Nobody (myself included) wanted to deprive kids of this fun and educational experience.

If the pond wasn't so very close, or if it wasn't so shallow and warm, or if it didn't have such a gently sloping shoreline making it so easy to wade in, maybe this problem wouldn't have developed. If, indeed, there were only thousands of similar ponds dotted around the peninsula, maybe this problem wouldn't have developed. But no, there was only one tiny pond, and thousands of nature-starved youngsters eager to plunge in. In some sense, splashing around in a natural pool with duckweed and cattails and water lilies ought to be part of every childhood, like a birthright, and I wished with all my heart that there were enough ponds to go around, enough ponds to support the trampling and squishing of every child in the Silicone Valley, but there weren't. Our continuing to ignore the problem at Pichetti could be wholly attributed to our unwillingness to deprive kids of this rather special experience. But ponds in California are exceedingly rare and special environments. In the whole of the District's 60,000 acres, there aren't more than a couple dozen ponds, most of them still active cattle ponds. The creatures that need a still body of water to mate and lay eggs are totally dependant for their survival on the integrity of these ponds. Their claim to the pond was thus undeniably stronger that that of the hoards of children, especially given the District's mission.

There was an ordinance on the books against swimming, which by definition includes wading. We just weren't enforcing it. And I seemed to have run into a brick wall of resistance. What to do? I needed a new angle, a new strategy, and I finally hit upon it. Some of the most gross and blatant violators of the (un-enforced) No Wading ordinance were the private preschools. On warm spring mornings when the pond was full of life, I could count on finding at least one 16-passenger van in the parking lot and an equal number of three and four-year-olds marching out to the pond in their water shoes and bathing suits. While I'm sure a few kids enjoyed collecting critters, most seemed simply to be splashing, wallowing and belly flopping in the muddy shallows. It was a sure-fire weekly outing for several of these preschools. It drove me crazy since there wasn't much I could do except kick the kids out and then try to educate the unhappy kids about the harm they were doing. I can't very well cite a three-year-old. The adult caregivers, whom I might cite, weren't in the water. In fact, they seemed to be rather overwhelmed by their charges, whose demands for food, water, attention, and comfort kept them from properly playing lifeguard. Hence my idea.

A few minutes of on-line research was all it took. It turned out that drowning was the second major cause of death of preschoolers, right after automobile accidents, and, even better, it seemed that "farm ponds" are the leading site of such drownings. I had a winner, and I knew it. Visitor safety is the ultimate trump card.

New signs went up, first in laminated version, and then in metal, specifying that wading and collecting were specifically prohibited. Ironically enough, the signs indicated that the prohibition was for the protection of the habitat of sensitive pond creatures! That was the net result, of course, but that was not at all the real impetus behind their installation. The rangers' "turn a blind eye" practice, which for so long held sway, seemed also to be slowly changing, and we no longer saw the preschool vans in such numbers. It was just not as much fun if you couldn't go in the water. Initially, I think, some of the rangers, and even OSTs were upset with me for forcing this issue into the spotlight, but their annoyance has now devolved into good-natured teasing. "Hey Frances, I saw some families with kids out at the pond. You better go string 'em up." Thanks. I'm on my way.

17. Emergency Medical Responder

A ranger gets to wear many hats. It's one of the cool parts of the job. Primarily, District rangers are cops. We spend more of our time patrolling, poking around looking for trouble, than anything else. We are trained as firefighters and certainly have the hats, as well as a wealth of other fire gear, but we do little actual firefighting. We are also maintenance workers, which is where I probably spend my second-greatest amount of work time, especially if pulling weeds and picking up litter get to count as maintenance. Yes, my glamorous ranger job involves lots of weeds and trash. Cutting up huge fallen trees with the chain saws and building and repairing split rail fences is more fun, and less denigrated, and we do get to do those tasks too, especially on weekends when the crew is off. Ranger flat hat, yellow firefighter helmet with shroud and headlamp, orange construction helmet with spring-loaded earmuffs, and…well, actually there is no real hat for perhaps the most important aspect of the ranger job, the medical hat. (The lack of an actual hat is a dilemma when it comes to playing "dress-up" with school groups to help them understand the job of a ranger. There are lots more volunteers for the firefighters' nifty coat and helmet than for the stethoscope and disposable medical gloves.)

We spend a lot more time training for medical calls than actually attending them. While some rangers have EMT (Emergency Medical Technician) training, most of us are lowly EMRs (Emergency Medical Responders). The District will facilitate time off and schedule changes for rangers to maintain their EMT status (once they have it), and pay for the class, but there is no such assistance for getting the EMT in the first place. The EMT classes at the local community colleges are completely oversubscribed since every firefighter candidate has to take them. Part of me would like to get my EMT, but a bigger part of me says, what for? The first aid skills and techniques I am allowed to use on patients are prescribed by District policy, and all are at or below the EMR level. Any more advanced skill I might learn to do at EMT class I wouldn't be allowed to apply in the field anyway. One topic covered extensively in EMT class is extrication, that is, cutting people out of mangled cars. District rangers, by policy, don't do extrications; we just wait for the fire department to get there. That, in fact, defines our role in an awful lot of medicals: wait for fire to get there.

Our role in an emergency medical response is to locate the patients, size up the scene for safety, evaluate the patients, and keep them alive until fire gets there and takes over. Most of the time, all of this is very straightforward and, well, easy. I locate the patient by driving my patrol truck right up to their reported location on the flat, dry road. I size up the scene by seeing the calm, cooperative patient sitting on the ground surrounded by the helpful bystanders waving me down. The patient has some sort of non-life-threatening injury or illness, and, in many cases, just wants a ride out to the parking lot. Keeping them alive is not a problem. Fire is on scene in five minutes or less, barely giving me time to do any sort of patient assessment, much less care. I spend more time writing the report than dealing with the patient.

Attending a bunch of these "easy" medicals is good practice though: practice driving with the Code Three lights and sirens blaring and five other rangers talking over themselves on the radio trying to attach themselves to my incident and asking me what they should do to help; practice driving steep, narrow roads crowded with strollers and bicycles while trying to hurry; practice being calm and professional when I come on scene—putting on gloves, introducing myself, getting permission to treat, etc-- and practice dealing with all manner of patients, non-English speakers, small children, people with dementia, autism, mental illness, and, of course, people in pain.

Responding to a medical call is always somewhat stressful because I won't really know what I've got until I get there. Even when responding to something, which sounds completely benign, I am always second-guessing myself and imagining the worst. What caused the patient to fall? How badly is he hurt? How will we end up transporting him out? To which entrance shall I direct fire and ambulance? Will we need a helicopter? The stress is exacerbated by the need to hurry, or the imagined need to hurry. City fire departments have rigid expectations about how fast an engine should be on scene to a call in their district, and city dwellers, rangers included, have come to regard this near-instantaneous response as the norm. In the preserves, in the "urban interface," and in any semi-wilderness area, none of this hurry really makes any sense. I am not suggesting that responders should stop and take lunch on their way to the next emergency call, but, on the other hand, when the call is already 15 minutes old by the time it gets to dispatch (due often to lack of cell phone service) and I can see that it will be at least another 15 minutes before I get on scene, there is no point in actually hurrying. Anyone with severe arterial bleeding will already have bled to death. Anyone without a heartbeat is long since brain dead even if CPR is in progress. Anyone with some other serious medical condition—stroke, seizure, diabetic emergency—is not going to suffer a greatly different outcome if I get there in 20 minutes instead of 15. So why do we continue to hurry when we all know this? One of the OSTs once told me his mantra when responding to medicals was, "Respond slowly. Maybe it will be all over by the time you get there." This sounds horrible, but may not be such bad advice. Partially true, anyway. By the time we get there, the window of time for any true lifesaving will have long since closed. We are just the start of the evacuation effort. So why do we hurry? We hurry because we know there is someone suffering and we want to help, even though, in the event of a truly serious medical, there is next to nothing we can do to relieve the patient's suffering. For the blessed drugs, they are going to have to wait for Fire.

I should mention that in addition to our semi-annual EMR training, we also have annual CPR for Professional Rescuers Training, Hazardous Materials (HazMat) training, Vector Control training, Incident Command System (ICS) training, Confined Spaces training, and Helicopter Landing Zone (LZ) training, and maybe some other incidental medical and scene safety emergency related trainings.

11-12-05: Yesterday was helicopter training , actually the second Stanford LifeFlight training I've been to. I guess they occur annually. The pilot talked about how to help land the helicopter; he's from South Africa and has a cool accent so I can usually recognize his voice on the radio. He said to put our backs to the wind and point to the landing spot and to face the truck into the wind, headlights pointing at the spot so as not to blind him. He'll be landing facing into the wind. Those were new ideas to me. The two flight nurses said they actually work in the emergency room when not on a helicopter call. Pretty interesting. Would all have been good if it hadn't been drizzly, windy and freezing cold.

At an established LZ, the pilot really needs no help from anyone on the ground to land the helicopter, especially if he has landed there many times before. Even so, there are at least a few useful functions for a ranger at an LZ. In the summertime, when the dust can be a couple inches thick, we use those otherwise useless fire pumpers on our rigs to water down the entire area, the wetter, the better. Otherwise the backwash from the rotor blades sends up a tornado of dust, plastering everything in sight, including the patient and rescuers. We also do duty as crowd control, keeping curious visitors out of the zone of flying gravel. We also get to talk to the pilot as he is approaching, just to assure him that all is well and the patient is packaged and waiting. Fire often seems happy to hand off LZ duty to the rangers.

One reason why we need all this training is that we just don't attend enough serious medical calls--calls with critically ill and injured people, multiple patients, multiple rescuers and helicopter evacuations—to keep all the requisite skills current. Any given ranger may end up on just one or two a year, a few more for those rangers working on Skyline and assisting with all the motorcycle carnage on Highway 35. No matter how much we train and prepare, every serious medical will also be a novel situation, and thus, to some extent, a learning situation.

I have never done CPR on a real person, only on training mannequins. This is kind of ironic since I am one of the District's in-house CPR and EMR instructors. All field staff re-certify their CPR every year, even though the certification, from the American Red Cross, is now good for two years. The half-day class also covers Blood Borne Pathogen training and all the legal and ethical considerations of providing emergency medical services to the public. Sometimes CPR class participants groan about having to endlessly repeat the opening sequence of steps for properly assessing the patient and initiating CPR, but we all know that, in a real situation, those steps need to be automatic and need to be correct, not the 30-year-old version still secretly residing in one's muscle memory.

I think I first took CPR as a freshman in high school in a wilderness first aid course taught by my mother. When I got to college, I got a job teaching swimming and doing lifeguarding, which required a CPR card. I was driven to become an instructor out of frustration with the boring, pompous, long-winded instructor at the local Red Cross unit. I figured, if I had to waste a day every year doing this, I might as well be dishing it out rather than receiving it, and doing a better job than this self-aggrandizing windbag didn't seem too daunting a challenge. So, I became a CPR, Lifesaving, and Water Safety Instructor, which opened various doors to employment as a young adult, and was certainly an asset on my resume when being hired at the District. I moved right into the in-house instructor spot.

The instructor's role with American Red Cross has become more and more that of a mere facilitator, maintaining, hauling, and preparing the mannequins, arranging the tables, and show the DVD. All actual instruction is done by the DVD; the books are almost superfluous, as is the instructor. My biggest contribution is simply as a time keeper, keeping the class running smoothly, cutting off the war story tellers, keeping the short breaks short. The most difficult part of the job is filling out the on-line form to get the students' cards, a task I off-load onto others as much as possible.

Wanda, Bart, Cory, Tony and Matt have all done CPR on real people in the line of duty. Perhaps there are others that I am forgetting about. None of the patients survived. A quick synopsis of their stories, as I was not on scene for any of them: Wanda was first on scene at the horrific accident in La Honda OSP where a young contract worker was squished to death when a pickup truck rolled over. She said she saw gray stuff coming out the ears when she pushed on the chest. Bart was first on scene of an apparent heart attack way out on the Black Mountain Trail in Rancho. He found the victim's loved ones doing CPR when he arrived and took over. Of course then he was stuck doing CPR on a corpse for 15 minutes until Fire got there to pronounce the patient dead. (As EMRs, we cannot stop doing CPR until we are too exhausted to continue, or the scene becomes unsafe, or an equally trained person takes over, and, with all the victim's family standing around, deciding that you are now too exhausted does not seem to be an option.) Cory, who lived in District housing, did CPR on his neighbor, with the victim's wife watching, until Fire got there. Tony tells me that, years ago, he and another ranger did CPR on a heat stroke victim up on the PG&E Trail at Rancho. The victim was a young man, terribly overweight and developmentally disabled, whose brother had taken him hiking on the hottest day of the year to get him in shape. It took forever for Fire to get there and I think they really did stop from exhaustion and to prevent heat stroke in the rescuers.

The only CPR medical for which I have a journal entry is Matt's story, so still second-hand:

Yesterday a guy died at Fremont Older in the parking lot. I missed the whole thing as I was up at the top of Soda Spring Road when the call came in. Matt was first on scene, in his civvies having been alerted by a walk-up report to his house. It was a 50-something man who had ridden up Prospect Road with his son and son-in-law and then reportedly collapsed in the parking lot, just keeled over, face first. Matt got to do a couple of minutes of CPR (he did compressions) with bystanders before Fire got there. Terry, who got there next and wrote the report, said it was pretty gross and traumatic. The guy was very blue, bleeding from his smashed face and mouth and had vomited. Then his wife and daughter showed up and were hysterical. Glad I missed it.

Maybe I will make it through my entire career without ever having to use CPR on a real patient. That would be fine by me. Patients given CPR in remote locations only have one outcome: death. CPR does not re-start the heart; it just moves a little blood around in the hope of staving off brain death until the drugs and defibrillator can arrive. People with heart disease might want to stick close to malls and casinos, where the security guards are all CPR-trained, and where, statistically, patients have the best chance of survival and recovery. Those malls and casinos can also afford to put AEDs (Automated External Defibrillators) at the end of every aisle, and train the security guards to use them. The District finally got some AEDs a few years ago, but they live in the offices and are primarily intended for employees to use on one another. When I next happen to be sitting in the office when a call comes in for a "person down with unknown medical at Deer Hollow Farm," I will grab the AED on my way out the door. My opportunity to be a hero may yet come.

I am also a big proponent of switching to Wilderness Emergency Medical Responder training for field staff. Working in a semi-rural setting, where Fire's arrival time is nearly always "extended," the urban panacea of "call 911" is not usually the best answer. The American Red Cross has dumbed down all its first aid training tremendously, since, after all, the evacuation and long-term care issues of dealing with the sick and injured have all but disappeared from modern life. Bandaging and splinting skills have been minimized. Why bother training people how to make a snug, stable arm splint, when the patient isn't going to be walking out, but getting a ride in an ambulance or helicopter? Technology is also rapidly eroding the territory of wilderness first aid. GPS devices and satellite phones facilitate helicopter rescues which would have taken days and now can be accomplished in hours or minutes. All the same, there are a few wilderness protocols which would make sense adopting for our job. We should not be starting CPR on pulse-less, breathless patients who are more than 29 minutes from definitive care. We should be able to stop CPR after 20 minutes if no AED has arrived. The Santa Cruz Mountains are not arranged in aisles, with AED machines and helicopter landing zones every quarter mile. The hiker still gets to assume some of the risk, to take on the task of self-sufficiency, to embrace the illusion of wilderness, at least for a few hours.

My in-house EMR instructor job is a little more involved than my CPR instructor role since it is a three-day class with lots of scenarios and practice time using all the equipment—backboards and wheel litters, oxygen tanks and airway adjuncts, bag-valve masks (BVMs), AEDs, blood pressure cuffs and stethoscopes, traction splints, tourniquets, epi-pens, and bandaging materials, plus any props and extras needed for the scenarios. As with the CPR course, I am really just a facilitator. Since I now find myself in the instructor role, the first aid class power seat, I get to design the scenarios, and I admit that it is very hard to come up with scenarios that will keep everyone busy and engaged without unintentionally creating something that is too challenging. I don't want students approaching "the scene" already resigned to failure, or complacency. I try to be the best instructor I can be because I know how much I loathe a poor instructor.

The first serious medical of my career was a helicopter evacuation from Wildcat Knoll in Rancho. It may have even been within the first week of my driving solo, certainly within the first month. I was just exiting the field office, coming down the driveway, when Mt. View came on the radio, "Any unit in the Rancho San Antonio area, ID to Mt. View." Okay, that means me. There was a little surge of adrenalin as I reached for the mike. "9L15" "Report of a woman with palpitations, difficulty breathing, and a heart history. Reported to be at the Vista Point on the Wildcat Trail." There was now a longish pause as I recovered from the huge hit of adrenalin before responding. I was the one now having palpitations and difficulty breathing. "Uh, okay. 10-4. I will be responding." Thank goodness Matt was right behind me and quickly took on the role of coordinating the onslaught of assistance, directing incoming units to the best access and making sure someone was meeting Fire to guide them in as far as Deer Hollow Farm and to transport their medics up the hill from there. The tension was enhanced by the dusky low light conditions of early evening as we headed up Rogue Valley, and it was nearly dark 20 minutes later when Matt and I got on scene with our patient. Matt immediately handed off patient evaluation and care to me and took on directing the approaching helicopter.

Our patient was woman in her 20s with some chronic heart condition. In the five minutes or so before the helicopter got there, I mostly learned how very difficult it is to do any kind of proper assessment under such conditions. It's cold and dark. Patient and rescuer are both stressed. It's noisy and confusing with the truck engines and radio traffic and flashing lights and by-standers asking questions and trying to help. I found her pulse was thready and erratic and, had we had oxygen in those days, she would have been on it first thing. As it was, I tried to help by wrapping her in a blanket and looking like I knew what I was doing by asking her SAMPLE questions (Symptoms? Allergies? Medications? Past medical history? Last meal and water/Last urine and BM? Events leading up to incident?) and trying to get a blood pressure. I also learned how awfully hard it is to get an auscultated BP under noisy conditions. I tried again and again and probably stressed her out worse than ever with my show of incompetence. I now realize that, under such circumstances, it is hopeless and just go for the palpated BP, or forget it. A single BP reading doesn't tell you much that you can't tell just by looking at the patient. It was my first helicopter landing and I was surprised when Matt came running over and said, essentially, to duck and cover because we weren't moving the patient and the copter was coming down not far away. We were both in firefighter jackets and flung ourselves over the patient when the rocks and gravel started flying. The helicopter was probably on the ground less than a minute, just the time it took to get her on the gurney and in the back door. Then they were away and would be landing within a few more minutes at Stanford Emergency. The little hilltop became suddenly silent as the distinctive sound of the receding helicopter faded away.

It was a very odd experience indeed, and rather a let down. One minute I was straining my brain and working as fast as I could trying to figure out what was wrong with our patient, how to best help her, and also trying hard to avoid screwing up by forgetting some crucial step, like getting her name, address and phone number for the report. Then, as soon as the helicopter left, I was done, for better or for worse. I didn't get to hear the rest of the story. It's like she flew off into a vacuum.

I feel a similar sensation of disorientation and loss on most medicals when the ambulance pulls away. We seldom learn what happens to our patients, whose pain and fear and problems were so close to us just moments before. I often feel like my patient was snatched away before I had a fair chance to help her. Short of the stereotypical burning building or frozen lake rescue scenario, it's pretty hard to be a hero in five minutes or less. Tony, my supervisor, was full of praise for my performance on my first big medical when he and who knows how many more vehicles finally pulled on scene well after the departure of the patient. I was feeling inept and guilty about my blood pressure taking skills failure, and I was embarrassed to receive praise for my miniscule role. We now had to clean up, to put stuff away and to get everyone back down the hill. But first we had to have the little schmooze session with the fire medics, in this case very little, since they never made it on scene with the patient. There was a little chitchat, and hand shaking, and back slapping and saying of, "See you next time." At least it affords an opportunity to pass off any bloody clothing (hazmat) to Fire and to restock our first aid kits from their stores. Perhaps the unspoken message of this quickie "de-brief" is: we all know that we aren't perfect, and we all know that, most likely, we all did not perform our functions flawlessly today, but it is okay. You are okay. The patient is okay. And there is always next time. We'll see you then.

Medical incidents come in two basic sorts, illnesses and accidents. Although illnesses—such as the case above-- can be life threatening, and certainly scary and painful, they do lack some of the drama and horror of blood and mangled body parts of an accident. Although I am spared all the gore and guts of working the Skyline Boulevard motorcycle raceway, I do get on scene of an occasional high-speed bicycle crash. In some of these cases, the cyclists were probably not even moving that fast. They just managed to land in unfortunate ways, with ugly results.

There was the middle-aged man in the Hayfields at Fremont Older on a stiflingly hot and airless day who totally blew out his ankle when his foot failed to detach from the pedal clips. Matt was first on scene and, by the time I got there, he and some helpful visitors had managed to free our patient from the bicycle.

Two visitors had grabbed the blanket usually used for keeping freezing victims warm, and were holding it overhead to provide some shade. Our patient was on his back in the thick dust holding stock-still with his teeth clenched in pain. It took me a second to realize what I was looking at when surveying the injury. His shoe was still on his foot and, aside from some scrapes on un-related body parts, there was no blood, but extending forward from the ankle, and entirely covering the laces of the shoe was a grotesque, fleshy bulge, his tibia (the larger bone of the lower leg). I thought the guy was awfully stoic to not be absolutely screaming in pain. Matt and I were halfway through carefully sizing and padding a cardboard splint when Fire drove up. They too didn't even try to cut off the shoe, just threw the splint on him and stuffed him in the ambulance.

5-29-10: I missed my doctor's appointment last week Tuesday because I had to respond to a fallen bicyclist on the Jones Trail at St. Joseph's Hill. I was the closest. The guy had been riding a "whoopee-di-whoo" and wiped out. He must have done a face plant because he had ripped open his right cheek from the corner of his mouth clear to his ear, although teeth seemed to still be in place. His nose and ear were also partially avulsed. Very icky and painful-looking and lots of blood. He was conscious and responsive, but he kept asking where he was, a pretty obvious case of concussion. His CSMs (circulation, sensation and movement) were good in both hands and feet, so maybe no spinal injury, but, of course, we were holding C-Spine (keeping his head and neck in line with each other)when Fire got there. Got to help with backboarding. Biggest problem was trying to get a truck on scene without a damn pumper in the bed, my truck being useless for this reason. Fortunately crew happened to be in the preserve and they were able to quickly unload all their gear and come to the rescue. The worst part of the whole thing was that it was raining steadily the whole time, so our poor victim was soaked and freezing, as were we.

That was a real rescue which seemed more like something a sadistic Wilderness First Aid instructor would dream up for a challenging scenario: a badly injured bloody patient with possible head/neck/spine injury, a backboard that doesn't fit into any of the vehicles provided so the students have to scramble to improvise transport and, to consummate the instructor's sadistic pleasure, a convenient freezing rainstorm. After that medical I started carrying an umbrella in my truck. Just that tiny bit of shelter would make all the difference. Somehow it is just impossible to think clearly and act decisively while one is getting soaked. The umbrella really seems to work great as anti-accident-in-the-rain insurance. I've never gotten to use it.

One more weird, ugly and unlikely accident that comes to mind was a broken arm at Rancho. This occurred on a bright, sunny, warm spring day, as I recall. The patient was a young woman, maybe in her 30s, who fell off her bike while cruising along the broad, flat, paved service road through the front meadow. She somehow managed to fall just right and land with her forearm directly on the lip of the pavement, where it ends and there is a little two-inch drop down to the dirt. Both the radius and ulna looked to have snapped at the point of impact and the distal part of her arm was inwardly rotated maybe 20 degrees and off-set from the proximal section. Amazingly, the skin was entirely intact. She was another very stoic patient who managed to avoid screaming as we carefully manoeuvred her amazingly twisted arm onto a nicely padded splint. When Fire showed up, she very gratefully accepted an IV with morphine while I got to asist the fumbling fireman in applying a proper sling and swathe. I think they don't normally splint anyone since the doctors at the emergency department just cut it all off again; they just package them on the gurney, throw them in the ambulance and go. That may be the only splint I've actually had time to apply before fire got there, probably because I was just one minute away at the office when the call came in, and because there were no extraneous circumstances, like rain, to deal with.

In general, Fire gets to Rancho lickety-split; there must be a well-worn pathway in every engine driver's mind from Station Seven on Stevens Creek Boulevard to the turnaround at the back gate at Deer Hollow Farm, their usual staging spot, while the rangers play Find the Patient. Of course Engine Seven's most frequented locale is also on Cristo Rey Drive: The Forum, a retirement community. Half of their total call volume must be for scraping up fallen 90-year-olds. I can only imagine how humiliating it must be to slip and fall, naked in the shower or on the toilet, and be too weak and frail to get back up, and then have to have a bunch of big guys in fire gear come rescue you. What we all have to look forward to! Sometimes fire engines drive back to Deer Hollow Farm just to practice and to train new drivers. So I was really disgusted one day when we had a serious accident at the farm and Fire got lost, went to the wrong gate, and took half an hour to get there. I don't know if they got reprimanded, but they wouldn't be the only ones to get in trouble for their response that day...

Sandy and I happened to both be on modified duty that day at Rancho. I was in casual office attire recovering from arthroscopic knee surgery; he was still out with his shoulder. When a call came in over the radio for "any ranger near Rancho San Antonio," there was no answer followed by a long pause. Finally Cory answered up: he was deep in Sierra Azul somewhere. Dispatch then gave Cory the details: a medical call at Deer Hollow Farm for a 60-year-old woman fallen near the pig barn. Now what? It would take Cory 45 minutes to get here. Fire should be here in ten. I thought that Maintenance

Supervisor Riley was around Rancho somewhere and he had EMR, and the farm maintenance guy at least had First Aid and CPR. My mind was chugging along as I continued filing acquisition reports and making file labels. Then Sandy appeared in the doorway, "Come on. Let's go." "But, we can't." "Who else is there? We're the closest, and most highly qualified, and this is much more important than anything you are doing here." "But…" "Let's go!" I think we responded in my truck, with me driving, out of uniform, and a little voice inside my head saying, "This is not a good idea. We're going to get in trouble for this," even though I couldn't think of any one specific, particular rule I was breaking. When we got on scene, I handled patient care and Sandy took down the information and handled radio traffic. The woman was a docent at the farm, and she had tripped over a toddler who had run out front of her, and she had fallen on her side. She was conscious, breathing normally, and fully oriented, but in a world of hurt, with severe pain in her left arm and shoulder as well as her left hip and leg. She said she had osteoporosis. Not much to do but monitor vitals, make her as comfortable as possible and wait for transport. It was frustrating but familiar sitting with a suffering person, reassuring them and waiting for Fire….and wait we did, almost 30 minutes. Had we been on some back road of Sierra Azul, 30 minutes would have been lightening fast. It's all a matter of perspective. I'm glad that, in general, on my job, there is no one with a stopwatch timing my performance. All the same, I felt so frustrated and useless just sitting there waiting. Moving her onto the backboard was agony. Lots of screaming now. How about some morphine, guys? Altogether I felt like Sandy and I had made a good job of it, even though I had struggled some in dealing with a patient flat out on the ground when I had a knee that wouldn't bend more than about

90 degrees and on which I could neither squat nor kneel. Yet I just knew we were in trouble, bad trouble.

Superintendent Bernie called me in the very next day. He knew that I knew what it was about. "So, if you knew it was wrong, why did you do it?" was his only question. I didn't have a good answer. I hadn't been able to think of a really good reason not to go, other than the certain knowledge that Sandy and I were getting ourselves in trouble. My only real concern, and my only actual difficulty, had been my stiff knee, and certainly not any worry that I would somehow goof up patient care because I wasn't wearing the magical expert-in-all-things uniform. My only question of Bernie was about exactly which rule it was I had broken. I felt his answer wasn't very compelling either. He replied that, while on modified duty, I had no duty to act, and that I could have hindered my recuperation by bending or twisting my knee while responding to an emergency medical. Yes sir, point acknowledged. Won't happen again. So, would I do it again? Will I do it again? We shall see. To quote Sandy," If you never get in trouble at work, you're probably not doing your job."

18. Outfoxed

6-29-10: Most interesting incident recently was the two dead gray foxes I found dumped up behind the Powder River gate at Twin Creeks. They were still quite fresh when I found them, no ants, no smell. I couldn't see any bullet wounds, only some small lacerations. The female's left front leg was shattered in multiple places, although the skin was intact. It was ever so sad seeing them dead there together almost curled around each other, male and female, like a lovers' suicide. Their beautiful soft gray pelts and thick glossy brushes had been so recently alive. Damn whoever did this! My lead suspect is Rod, the local private property caretaker who recently got chickens.

Supervisor Bart later confirmed my suspicions about the caretaker. Rod had been bragging about his shooting of the foxes until Bart began pressing him for details, pointing out that it is a crime to kill foxes out of season without a depredation permit. Rod then began some serious backpedaling. Doesn't matter. The poor things are dead, and Rod is probably a hopeless case. I don't know that I could ever make him understand why the shooting of those foxes was wrong, not just illegal, but morally wrong. To him, foxes are sly and evil predators sneaking in to massacre his innocent, valuable, chickens. But gray foxes are a locally threatened species. They are being out-competed by invasive European red foxes, which were imported years ago by yet another ignoramus with the thought of chasing them around and shooting them in an English style foxhunt. Gray foxes thus need all the help they can get. Domestic chickens, meanwhile, are about as endangered as human beings. The value of a flock of chickens is as nothing compared to the value of a breeding pair of gray foxes.

In discussing this tragic incident with some of the other rangers, I was shocked and disgusted to learn that there is in fact a "season" for hunting gray foxes. Per California Department of Fish and Game, a licensed hunter can kill an unlimited number of gray foxes every year between November and February. How can that be? That too is wrong. Furthermore, while I am on my high horse, the whole system of issuing "depredation" permits is wrong. Currently, if a fox eats one of your chickens, or a mountain lion eats one of your sheep, or a bobcat eats one of your rabbits, you can get a depredation permit and go retaliate. The predator pays with its life. All you lost is a chicken. And the loss of that chicken was entirely your own fault. If you own livestock, or pets, it is your responsibility to house them so they are protected from predators. Shooting all the predators is not a sustainable option.

To continue the sorry saga of never actually arriving in time to nail the bad guy or save the victim, but rather just getting to document the event and clean up the mess, here is another mysterious death:

9-27-06: I was going to go out on a longer foot patrol on the Woodrat Trail, but a couple hundred yards up the trail I found a dead great horned owl. So very sad, but I thought maybe I should rush it in for West Nile virus testing, which has to be done when the birds are fresh. Ants had started in on its eyes, but it didn't stink. There was some matted blood near the "wrist" of the underside of the right wing and, I think, a very small wound there, which didn't look big enough to have caused even that much blood. How big is a BB hole? Tragically, I can hear another great horned owl calling over and over again right now as I write; I can hardly stand it. Maybe not true, but I guess it's the mate of the dead owl. I am so sorry. The dead owl is so beautiful, all intact, its amazing claws and the tough pads on the bottoms of its feet, which remind me of the skin on my cat's paws. I wish that owl would stop calling. It's making me cry. I hid the body on site since Murray said the West Nile testing place is only open Monday to Friday, 9 to 5. Sad, sad, sad.

I'm not sure why I wanted to try to get this owl West Nile virus tested, since it looks like it probably died of injuries, most likely from being shot, but possible from running into a power line or a plate glass window. I suppose I just wanted to feel like I was doing something, even though it was obviously too late to do anything. Maybe the staff at the testing place would at least share my grief and frustration. It felt so cold and cruel to just fling that beautiful body up into the poison oak thicket, which is what I did.

West Nile virus kills mostly birds of the corvid family—crows, ravens, jays, mocking birds, blackbirds, etc.—but birds of prey—hawks, eagles, falcons, owls, etc—are also susceptible, and Santa Clara County Vector Control had asked us, at our annual vector control training, to record and report dead corvids and birds of prey and to bring fresh birds in for testing. They were tracking the spread of the virus, which was thought to have entered California from China. Vector Control's real concern is not for native, wild birds, but for the commercial chicken supply. The virus is actually spread from bird to bird by a distinct breed of mosquito, so the chief weapon against West Nile virus is mosquito abatement. Of course, humans can also contract West Nile disease, although it doesn't kill us as readily as it does the birds. So, in this case, our efforts at stemming the tide of

West Nile's spread, although motivated by selfish self-interest (protecting our chickens and protecting our own species) may, in fact be more especially benefiting our endemic feathered friends.

Getting back to the owls, my other great horned owl story has a happier ending. I had always heard that there was a great horned owl nest in the enormous eucalyptus tree at the Mora Road junction at Rancho, but, although I could often hear them calling in the area, I could never find their nest, so I really rather doubted its existence. Then, early one spring day, a baby great horned owl appeared, sitting right at the base of this tree, right next to the main drag out to Deer Hollow Farm. By the time I got on scene, luckily enough for me with Ulf, my bluebird box monitoring buddy, there was a tidy crowd of visitors gathered around, happy to relate the story of how it had come crashing down. Baby owl was adorable. It looked like a stuffed animal, a tubby ball of fluffy gray downy feathers, with two enormous yellow leathery feet poking out the bottom, and two huge yellow eyes. If approached, it would raise its short, fat gray wings, just covered with feather stubble and hiss at us, but it couldn't fly and it couldn't run. It was altogether very defenceless. We had to rescue it. Yes, I know, our policy calls for letting nature take its course, but that's not what would have happened if we had left Owl where it was. Someone else would have rescued it, I hope, or someone would have taken it home as a pet, I fear. Had it not fallen right next to the busiest trail in the entire District, and had we therefore not been forced to rescue it, we would have had to leave it where it was and it would, no doubt, have become coyote food. The parents may have found it, and may have continued to feed it, even on the ground, but they couldn't have defended it for long. So Ulf and I got to be the heroes. It was fun and satisfying. We just scooped Owl up and stuck it in the dog carrier and drove it over to the Wildlife Rescue of Silicon Valley. They were the true heroes of this story, as they got to raise Owl along with another baby great horned owl of about the same age, who was turned in a few days later. Both birds were eventually released to the wild. Happy Ending. Happy, happy, happy.

19. Neighbors

Wouldn't it be nice to own one of those houses that backs onto a preserve? Imagine looking out the back window or walking around the back yard and seeing wild nature spread out all around, and vistas of forests and meadows instead of fences and houses! Of course, in this imaginary back yard, no boundary fence mars the marvelous view and the bright spring days and clear starry nights invite strolls out into that land, mindless of any silly, man-made limitations on individual freedom. Over time, it might start to get a little foggy just exactly where that pesky boundary line was supposed to be and the flower beds, fruit tree orchards, picnic grounds, solar panels, bocce ball courts, and llama pastures (all of which are encroachments we have dealt with) just might start impinging onto a little corner of the public land out there. It is interesting that some people who wouldn't dream of invading the private property of their other neighbors, somehow view the public lands of the Open Space District as less sovereign. Discovering and investigating these encroachments is a part of my job which I find very interesting.

Our long-serving legal counsel once said, as part of some presentation, that when she was hired, she expected that a good part of the job would be liability lawsuits from people who had hurt themselves while on District lands, but no. She said almost her entire job was about land—land trusts, life estates, management agreements, conservation easements, access easements, and all the ins and outs of the rules of real estate and encroachments. Litigious land arbitration is hardly surprising in the San Francisco Bay Area, a region with some of the priciest real estate in the country. Because neighboring homeowners have laid down such extraordinary sums to escape the rat race and the riffraff of the metropolis, they are very protective of their rights to property and privacy. This leads to the formation of homeowner associations and private roadways, which end up blocking public access to preserves. In order to gain political support for local land purchases, the District has even made agreements with such homeowner associations specifically honoring their rights. How about the rights of the visitors who have paid for the preserve land with their taxes? Part of my job is enforcing the parking prohibitions along these stretches of private road, a task I find more discomforting and onerous than interesting.

Living next door to an Open Space District preserve might be nice in some respects, such as having a great and unspoiled view off the back deck, but, I admit, there are some clear downsides. In some places, such as Mora Road at Rancho, visitors park in front of neighbors' houses, bringing noise and litter. Deer and raccoons and mice and coyotes who live in the preserves find the rose bushes and garbage cans and compost piles of suburbia to be irresistible dinner invitations. And, of course, Open Space neighbors are always worried about wildfires. Neighbors or near-neighbors living within walking distance of a preserve do have the very enviable privilege of being able to go for their daily hike, walk or run on a trail through woods and meadows without ever having to get in their cars, but they still have to follow all the preserve rules once they are there, just like all the other visitors, which can come to seem rather onerous. If you live right next to Bear Creek Redwoods, which is open to the public only by permit, you too have to get a permit to enter. If you live just down the street from El Sereno, you have to put your dog in the car and drive 20 minutes over to St. Joseph's Hill to take the dog for a walk in the woods; dogs are prohibited in El Sereno. If you live at the end of Mora Drive near Rancho and want to take your out-of-town guests up to the vista point after dark to show them the lights, you still have to be out be a half hour after sunset, even though you live right there.

Of course that permit that you have to get as a neighbor wishing to enter your neighboring preserve isn't just the usual run-of-the-mill, good-for-one-day entry permit issued upon request to the general public. Neighbors can get special neighbor permits, which are good for the entire year. So who counts as a neighbor? Do our properties have to touch? How about a block away? How about a mile? Special privileges can be a slippery slope. One neighbor privilege situation that I find unfair is off Allen Road at the back entrance to La Honda Creek OSP, in the Skyline patrol area. There is a small parking lot there that requires a permit, but only to park, not to enter the preserve. La Honda Creek OSP is open to the public, but, in effect, the only people who can actually use it, without the delay and forethought of getting a parking permit, are the neighbors. Allen Road is a private roadway and is lined with "No Parking" signs and there is no other way to get there, short of a long hike along the highway.

Another example of neighbor clout and privilege is the Blackberry Hill piece of Sierra Azul. Blackberry Hill Road, like ever so many roads bordering District lands, is a private road, and the section that passes by the trail entrance gate with its small parking turnout, is actually District property. The trail leads up to an old house flat with some still-living fruit trees and a fantastic view of the valley floor. We had occasional problems with teens going up there and partying. So the locals convinced the District to post our whole stretch of road with "No Parking" signs, thus precluding access to anyone but the neighbors. Nice for them: how about the rest of the general public whose land this is? The locals, of course, claimed they were concerned about someone going up there and starting a fire that would threaten their multi-million dollar homes. Interestingly, the Mercedes and BMWs that usually parked in the turnout were the sons and daughters of the very people who wanted it shut down. It was their own kids up there smoking and drinking. Now these busybodies call to complain every time there is a car parked in the turnout. We respond slowly. They can call the Sheriff if they are that worried.

I can appreciate trying to cultivate good relations with our neighbors, giving them the benefit of the doubt, and asking nicely to get transgressions to cease rather than immediately slapping them with a misdemeanor citation or a major lawsuit. Being accommodating might often be the cheaper and faster solution, especially when dealing with extremely wealthy neighbors, such as our Bear Creek Redwood neighbor, Wendy. Somehow, when the District bought this piece of property from the timber company (after it was logged because we couldn't afford it before the logging) we missed the fact that her makeshift llama pasture was almost entirely on our new land, and it took several years for us to discover this and take her to court. I was thoroughly disgusted that she actually won, claiming she had squatters' rights to the land. This part all happened before I was hired, but I did get to witness the part where our crew built, entirely at taxpayer expense, a nice, new, high-quality fence around her llama pasture. I didn't help to build it, but I could sympathize with the crew guys working in the hot sun while Wendy thumbed her nose at us.

We got her back though, a little bit. Sandy happened to be out patrolling up near her boundary when he heard the sound of a chain saw working. He parked his truck and crept up on foot while waiting for Cory to come fill for him. They watched as Wendy felled and bucked up several small trees on our property about 25 yards inside a Powder River gate from her house. They could have busted her for that alone, but Sandy held off and waited and, sure enough, here came her boyfriend in a pickup truck. He dismantled part of the gate so the chain could be slipped over the top of the post, and drove on in and they started loading the firewood into the pickup. Then Sandy and Cory busted them. Cutting our trees, vandalizing our gate and illegally driving a vehicle onto our property: All misdemeanors, and no benefit of the doubt. This time Wendy did not win in court. I'm afraid all District staff took some vindictive pleasure in that bust.

9/6/06: Interesting foot patrol today. Went out yesterday on Dyer Creek in BCR and found a built trail and probable residential water system, but didn't follow it all the way out because of the paranoia about marijuana growers. I didn't want to be accused of not following the rules. So went back today with Murray and investigated further. The trail does lead to a residence and the spring box and plumbing look old enough to predate the District's ownership, which Murray says gives them a prescriptive easement to the water. Hmmm. Seems screwy to me. There is also an associated trail up the ridge leading to a little built table and stools in a redwood fairy circle. Probably an encroachment, but probably not worth pursuing. It seems the neighbor here is some big donor to the District.

I was told that the northern half of the BCR purchase was allegedly bought with funds this wealthy old neighbor lady provided, so we would be turning a blind eye to her little trail and such. Patience and time would solve this problem. Our benefactress will pass away; the property will change hands and the little trail will melt away. But some such little trails have real staying power and getting rid of them proves harder than we imagined.

There used to be a District regulation sign halfway up the Rhus Ridge Trail in Rancho San Antonio, incongruously marking an old deer trail. I finally remembered to ask about it at a patrol meeting and Sandy told me that he had installed the sign some years before because there had been a lot of use on that trail coming up from a neighborhood in Los Altos Hills. "But," I argued, "It's not an official trail. It doesn't show on any maps, and putting the reg sign there makes it look official and invites even more use." "Well," he argued, "people coming in the unofficial way still need to know the rules." "But it is superfluous. We don't need two trails going from Los Alto Hills to Windmill Pastures." I was amazed that the supervisors and even Bernie, the Superintendent, didn't back me up. Humans are very reluctant to change features of local geography once they have become established in their minds as the norm. This little use trail had the additional merit, in some minds, of having been established by Liz Duveneck Dana, daughter of the founders of Hidden Villa, who were big proponents of the District. "The trail is really overgrown and hardly used. We should just pull the reg sign," I pleaded, but it was no use.

Then, when the South Area Outpost office opened a couple years ago, the preserve assignments were changed. I lost El Sereno, but gained the Windmill Pastures part of Rancho. The annoying, illegal Rhus Ridge Trail alternate was now in my area. I decided to try the old adage, "It is easier to get forgiveness than permission," and rather quietly pulled the reg sign and, in its place, plunked in a "Closed, Not a Trail" sign. No one seemed to care. Lars even volunteered to help me figure out how to drive to the private water tank in Los Altos Hills where the trail started. Perversely, now that it was illegal, someone had used saw, loppers, shovel and polaski to thoroughly open it up again! Aarrgh! I planted a "Closed, Not a Trail" sign at the lower end, where our property started just past the private property of the water tank. I pulled a lot of brush, including a lot of poison oak (to which I seem to be partially immune) over the neatly constructed earthen steps. I traced these earthen steps around to the back gate of a fancy house near the water tank, but couldn't get any interest from Bernie in going after this neighbor for illegal trail building and encroaching onto District land. "That trail has been there a long time," Bernie said. "You can try to close it if you want, but good luck, and I don't think we need to be citing people out there."

I have been engaged in a running battle with the trail builder ever since. I destroy her steps and pile brush on her trail and she rebuilds the steps and cuts through my brush piles. Then, in a stroke of luck, I found where our friend had built a second trail, with the same little earthen steps, descending from the other side of her house into the canyon and ending at a shady flat she had constructed under a grove of buckeye trees down by Hale Creek. Nearly the entire trail is on our property. Suddenly Bernie became interested. I had to write a report, take more pictures and meet with the District's real property guy in charge of encroachments. I haven't gotten a response yet, but, while I am at it, I certainly intend to include all of our neighbor's misdeeds in my report. The ball is finally in my court and I intend to get a slam-dunk.

We the field staff do love to gossip about our neighbors. Our nouveau-riche neighbors in their stone castles, surrounded by high walls and fences with electronic gates and security cameras, provide much less grist for the gossip mill than do some of the old hill folk living in the nooks and crannies of the southland. These aging hippies, fanatical libertarians, survivalists, recluses and, in a few cases, petty criminals, are much more colorful and interesting characters then the lords and ladies of the stone. Both sorts of neighbors often seem to resent us, the rich folks because they have to pay property taxes, which pay the salaries of us "useless public employees," and because they dislike the whole idea of "the commons," public spaces where their status is not acknowledged and where they are reduced to rubbing elbows with the great unwashed public, and are obliged to follow the same rules. Poor folks have more obvious reasons to resent us, as we seem to sit more comfortably in the wealthy camp. We drive around in shiny new trucks, and we wear clean, expensive uniforms. Part of their dislike is akin to that of the wealthy: they both hate "the government." Castle dwellers and trailer dwellers alike have moved to the fringe of the megalopolis because they value freedom, liberty, and independence, but both groups fail to acknowledge that without the District—a.k.a. the government— protecting this buffer of open space, they wouldn't have their surrounding open, undeveloped land. They too would be in the thick of it. Maybe deep down inside they realize this and resent us all the more for it!

Some of these apparently poor people are anything but. One woman I know, in her early seventies, lives in a horse trailer, an old, single-stall-sized horse trailer, covered with blue plastic tarps to keep it from leaking, and she single-handedly cares for about 40 horses. Her property is an hour's drive south of Los Gatos in one of the most remote corners of the District. She has no electricity or running water and spends most of her time hauling in water and feed for her herd of semi-wild horses, which keep escaping onto District land. She loves it out there. She loves the wild land that surrounds her. She loves her unconventional life.

She told me she figured she had enough money, if she didn't eat very much, to finish her days out there. Meanwhile she is sitting on many thousands of dollars worth of land. She is living as she is entirely by choice. Now there's a character.

Or take Larry: like something out of Appalachia, he is unemployed and lives up on the slopes of Mt. Umunhum with his toothless father, a developmentally disabled son, and a daughter, who works at a convenience store. They too own that chunk of land, (although, unfortunately, it turns out, not the exact chunk where their trailer sits!) Larry is always very friendly and amiable and always stops to say hello. He has a little snow plow that he attaches to the front of his pickup, and he plows Umunhum Road on snowy days. The first time I met him, I saw this bearded bear of a man, with a huge beer belly, get out of an old pickup and come strolling toward me. He had long, unkempt hair and a graying beard, and he was wearing an enormous pair of none-too-clean overalls and no shirt. I'd be willing to wager he had no other clothing of any kind underneath either. Yet his broad smile was infectious and welcoming and I was immediately disarmed and liked him right away. Another character.

The other guy who lives off Umunhum Road is legendary. In his prime, Dick used to patrol the boundaries of his land dressed in camouflage and carrying a loaded shotgun. The story goes that he would shoot over the heads of the teenagers headed up to check out the old Air Force Station, scaring the heck out of them. He was a very effective deterrent. Thank goodness he never hit anyone. He probably misses those good old days before the District put a stop to his fun. He still wears cameo, but he's too old and sick to patrol.

Sierra Azul, at 18,000 acres, is the largest District preserve, and its long outline surrounds all these long fingers of private property, like Twin Creeks, and its interior is pockmarked with numerous small in-holdings, like Larry's place. Many of our Sierra Azul characters aren't actually the landowners, or even renters, but paid caretakers for absentee landowners. Where the owners find these guys and what kind of value they think they are getting, I cannot imagine. Actually Rod, Bilbo's most recent caretaker on his Twin Creeks property, is not that bad. He has cleaned up the place a bit and he seems more industrious than his predecessor, but I am suspicious that he is poaching game, and I am still angry with him for blithely shooting the mated pair of gray foxes. But, of course, he doesn't see it that way.

Mr. Reggie's caretaker, Ollie, is another story.

10-9-05: I'm staffing the lot here at Jacques Ridge for a shift, having relieved Matt, and Murray will relieve me at 1700. It's a crazy thing and not easy to explain. One of our neighbors, Reggie, claims that his property extends down and crosses the Woods Trail. We say it doesn't. So last night Owen and I dealt with a call from Santa Clara County Parks and SO saying that Reggie was threatening to cut his way into the lock chain at SA06 to access his property that way. He was advised not to do so and to talk to the administrative office on Monday. So he didn't cut into the gate, but he does have the Woods Trail blocked off about a half mile in from here. His minion Ollie and some buddies are here at the lot telling visitors that the trail is closed. So, we are here telling folks that it is not closed, but to please avoid trouble and just go somewhere else for today. Supposedly, legally Reggie has to enforce his claim to the property or lose it to "eminent domain," and today is the day. The sad thing is that this same charade went on last year and nothing has been done since to fix the problem. Actually, for me, it's rather fun and interesting sitting here intercepting all the vehicles coming through. Amazing to me how many folks are out just driving around.

10-2-11: Henry has gone to close Ravenswood. Bart, Terry and Cory are south, and, like yesterday, it's deader than a doornail. I did the weekly update earlier today and got it done really quickly as nothing happened all week of any consequence. Okay, I thought of something, but it isn't anything new. In fact, this situation has been going on since before I joined the District. It was last week, Tuesday I think, and I was down south because I had to meet the Port-a-Potty guy and take him up to the base. Just as I was cruising up Hicks heading north again, Riley radioed saying a visitor had called to complain that there was a group of people on the Woods Trail with a white van who had closed the trail and turned her around. So, I headed out there and Terry, Mr. Leadfoot, managed to catch up with me and arrived at almost the same time. We found Ollie and his housemate Leach and a woman—a really trashy looking woman—named Didi with the white van, the "No Trespassing" signs, the lawn chairs, coolers of beer, and two off-leash dogs. Empty cans and cigarette butts littered the ground. They were doing Reggie's annual closure of the Woods Trail, to "keep the District from claiming a prescriptive easement over the trail." They won't say how they got in. They must have a key to one of the existing locks on the gate, probably ours. They pull this stunt every year, but never before, that I know of, including driving a vehicle in. They also close Mt. Umunhum Road every Fourth of July, also claiming that Reggie's property extends over Umunhum Road. Anyway, same old thing. If not for the larger issues involved, I could have cited Ollie and company for a slew of misdemeanor and infraction violations.

Who knows where Ollie would go if Reggie ever sold out to the enemy, the District, that is. Speculation is that he'd probably just move in with some of his drinking buddies down in Twin Creeks. Ollie has no source of income, unless Reggie is paying him. With his intimate knowledge of ranger and sheriff comings and goings, probable possession of a District key, and safe perch halfway up the mountain, he is a prime suspect in some of the on-going metal scrapping at the old Air Base and along the Hicks corridor. Now if we could only catch him in the act.

Some of our other "problem" neighbors, the sources of good chin-wagging ranger stories, probably wouldn't have made the list at all except with the help of their dogs. Like this guy:

3-14-07: Crew Supervisor Riley showed up to fill for me to go give Mr. M another Dogs Prohibited and Dogs Off Leash ticket. This was his fifth such ticket. He had threatened to bring his attorney and I was worried about another big confrontation like the other night when Cory and I cited him, but today all went smoothly. This time Mr. M's dogs had been out again harassing crew, who were scouting the broom field, and I had been called over to deal with the situation. I was thinking the damn dogs would probably already be back in their yard by the time I got there. They were, but they came charging out barking and growling onto the service road when I drove past in the truck. I wanted to call Animal Control and have them taken away to doggy jail, but Mr. M's neighbor came out and leashed them and helped get them into the garage. Mr. M actually came home from work to receive his ticket.

It took seven tickets (two more from Cory for launching golf balls off their back deck) but the M's finally got the message that the large meadow behind their house was not their property, as much as they and their dogs might have come to think so, and, in a plea bargain agreement—i.e. they didn't pay a cent on any of those tickets—they agreed to build a dog-proof fence around their yard. So the problem was solved, but it didn't feel very satisfying. I guess I wanted some kind of apology for the trouble they had caused, some kind of acknowledgement that they were at fault. Compromise doesn't feel like victory.

And finally, my favorite encroachment story of all: In the spring of 2006, Sandy was looking north from St. Joseph's Hill, across Lexington Reservoir and Highway 17, and saw a bulldozer at work near a grove of eucalyptus trees halfway up the arid southern flank of the ridge near El Sereno OSP. That bulldozer could well be within El Sereno, he thought, pulling out his patrol map book and Thomas Brothers Guide. Comparing contour lines and the landmarks provided by a line of P&E towers, he figured he had spotted an encroachment, and reported it to his supervisor, Murray. Now someone needed to get out there on the ground and do some further investigation. The problem was, that although it was easy to see how the bulldozer had made its way in—straight up from the private property off the side of Highway 17—we needed to access from our own property. The closest point looked to be from the PG&E tower out at the end of the Serenity Trail, which, as the bird flies, couldn't be more than a half-mile from the eucalyptus grove. Murray decided to give it a go. He reported making several hundred yards across a steep slope through thick chaparral before quitting and dragging himself back the way he had come. Murray reported this to Sandy, who responded, "Well, you know, there is an old roadbed that goes right out there off the end of that first big switchback on the Aquinas Trail." "What? Why didn't you tell me?" "You didn't ask."

Before anyone else could beat me to it, I headed out there the next day, having gotten Sandy to show me his proposed route on the patrol map. It is about a mile and a half of old roadbed and it took me over four hours on foot—as well as hands and knees-- one-way the first time I did it. The first quarter mile or so was the worst, because the roadbed had "slipped out"—that is to say, slid down the mountainside, leaving a steep escarpment behind--in a couple of places, and these short steep sections were covered in impenetrable chaparral. Covering 25 yards of manzanita, buckbrush, chaparral pea, mountain mahogany, chamise, and lots and lots of poison oak, armed only with a pair of loppers, was very slow going. Of course, I was wondering the whole time what had happened to my old roadbed and if I would ever find it again. Even with the aid of the old roadbed, which, to my huge relief reappeared on the same contour line, progress cross-country through this vegetation was miserably slow. Crawling, climbing and slithering on my belly through the wormhole I created, I followed the roadbed across two small drainages. At the second drainage there was an old water tank, and the amount of undergrowth lessened, as though whoever had placed the tank had, during some years in the past, cleared the road a couple times.

Abruptly I reached a junction where a second road down a side ridge took off to my left while the main road continued straight. Both roads were completely clear of vegetation and covered with bulldozer tracks. I went to the left, walking upright for the first time in several hours, and shortly found myself out on top of a little vista point I now call Spooky Knoll, in honor of Spooky, "the best dog who ever lived," whose wooden headboard and epitaph still grace this hillock. From here I could look south back across Highway 17 to St. Joseph's Hill, not so very far away as the bird flies. A zip line from here to the top of the Flume Trail across the way would make a mint. As well as the bulldozer tracks, there were now Jeep tracks galore coming up the nose of the ridge, and then descending by yet another road. Several clusters of bay laurel trees had been hacked to the ground and bulldozed into heaps, presumably to improve the view. I took pictures.

Following the dozer and Jeep tracks for another half-mile, I reached the euc grove. What a mess! Mature oaks, madrones, and laurels had been sawed off at waist height, with the stumps left standing, like a person cut off at the knees. The smaller stumps had been ripped out and dragged into big ungainly piles along with the felled treetops and all the smaller bushes and undergrowth. Several acres had been thus denuded and were now a maze of crude flats with steep connecting roads between the enormous heaps of dead. Who would do something like this, and why? None of the flats seemed large enough for a house, being rather long, skinny, and not especially flat. There were no survey stakes or flagging tape, and the flats and connecters seemed to run willy-nilly across the mutilated hillside. Later, when describing this devastation to my co-workers, I would call it the work of "recreational bulldozing."

Off to one side and just above two enormous eucalyptus trees, which had been left standing, was a very small pond. It was contained by an earthen retaining wall below and seemed to be spring fed, as there was no stream running in. It was full of reeds and cattails and pollywogs—a little bit of heaven in the middle of a massacre.

I took a lot more pictures, then wearily made my way back through the wormhole to my truck, enlarging it as I went. Back at my truck, I found, not to my surprise, that I was crawling with ticks, and even after brushing them off my clothes and combing them out of my hair, I was still picking them off my hairline as I drove away. Back at the office the next day I wrote my report, which took nearly as long as the trip out there, fighting with the computer to get the pictures off the camera and into the evidence section of the report, all correctly sized (which the program does not do for you!) and neatly labeled. I expected that everyone would want to come see this bulldozing disaster, which did seem to be on our property, but my description of the route seemed to put people off. It was several months later when I finally got out there with one of the planners with a handheld GPS unit. A couple of planners had tried to get out there with the backpack sized unit the week before and hadn't made more than a couple hundred yards before getting lost and bogged down in one of the slip-outs. We dragged along three or four District boundary plaques attached to U-channel posts and a sledgehammer for pounding them in. The GPS accuracy was not great, so we stuck the boundary posts well uphill from where we suspected the boundary truly lay, about 20 yards above the little pond.

About six months after my initial visit and several more trips through the tick and poison oak hole, now more caterpillar sized, I finally got to meet the culprit himself, Oscar. The District land protection specialist and I got to ride up in Oscar's Jeep, me in the back where there was neither seatbelt nor seat, straight up the rocky road off the side of Highway 17. Oscar was tall and very thin and tanned, and had an aging hippie look to him with his thin gray hair pulled back in a ponytail. He said he still did a lot of surfing and he seemed somehow pretty laid back and easy-going, despite never once cracking a smile the entire visit. He said his father, or perhaps his grandfather, had showed him about where the property ended up there near the euc grove. He totally admitted to the bulldozing and tree cutting, but gave the impression that he didn't understand what we were so upset about. He was improving the place to his mind, clearing out all that underbrush and extra trees. But, he claimed, he was all done up there now. We showed him where we had placed the t-post boundary markers, explaining that the GPS was not real accurate and we had tried to be conservative and neighbor-friendly. We parted with a hand-shake agreement that we would both treat the area as a "no-man's land." No more cutting, earth moving or driving. I think we did actually shake hands, although he still didn't smile.

Maybe six month after that, I made a trip out there with Matt. He had seen, looking across from St. Joseph's Hill with the binoculars, what looked like a travel trailer parked in the no-man's land. Unbelievable, but in fact merely a slight escalation of Oscar's on-going disregard of our un-written agreement. The bulldozing and tree felling had stopped, for the most part, but the familiar Jeep tracks were everywhere. The trailer was parked on one of the flats, just barely below and right next to one of the boundary markers. It was like he was taunting us! "Nah, nah! What are you going to do about it?" More pictures and another report to send down to the encroachment specialist, who then got to write another useless missive of polite and pathetic pleas to Oscar.

The better part of Matt and my visit was our cross-country hike from Oscar's up to join the Serenity Trail, thus completing the route that Murray had tried to do the year before. Matt and I however ended up much higher on the ridge, not at the lowest tower where Murray had started. If our route could someday be made into a real trail, there would finally be a loop trail possibility at El Sereno, rather than just the existing out-and-back.

What finally got the ball rolling for the boundary survey was a trip with the head of the Real Property Department. I had made up some more boundary markers and he asked to come along to see the area of conflict and help me drag and pound. When we got out there and I showed him around, he was furious, the first of the co-workers I had seen, besides myself, to look outraged by Oscar's mess. He had me stash the new markers in the bushes (I showed him where I knew for sure that Oscar had moved some of the previously emplaced markers. They had done no good.) and said, "We are getting a survey." Yeah!

I got to meet several times with the surveyor and his assistant. They were originally from Czechoslovakia, from Prague, and had great stories of lives under Communism and their roundabout escapes across the Iron Curtain. Meanwhile, they enjoyed asking me about the District and about the natural history of the area. They said they mostly worked in downtown San Jose on giant construction sites, so it was fun for them to be out in the woods. It reminded them of the forests of their homeland. I had spent most of the day prior to their first visit further clearing the route to the point that one could now largely walk upright with only occasional climbing over and ducking under. No more crawling. On a later visit the surveyor showed me how he had found the brass corner section marker from 1968 buried in the leaf litter near Spooky Knoll. He had some old maps of the area that showed a "triple tree," a tree with three trunks, which, fortunately was still standing just north of the Jeep track road. With a compass bearing and a distance from the tree they had found the marker. Then came the hard part. To find the exact on-the-ground location of the boundary, the surveyors had to "chain" the entire route from the corner marker at Spooky Knoll all the way to euc grove. I missed out on seeing this process, which would have been interesting, although very gruelling, carefully measuring the angles between each successive chain length distance across a half-mile of rough terrain. I did get to help on the day we marked the actual boundary. I held a striped pole still and carefully moved it right or left, while the surveyor sighted through a scope from the last known point along the line, and then we marked and planted a wooden survey stake. These stakes marked the line where a fence would ultimately be built. I took a lot of pictures of the wooden stakes, presuming that Oscar would move them before we could get the fence up. As the survey results came in, I whooped with joy of vindication, I almost hugged those guys around the neck: it was all ours—the euc grove, the devastated area and, best of all, the little pond. We were in the right; Oscar was in the wrong. So there.

I didn't get to help build the fence, though I wish I had. There is a nice photo of the trail crew posing by the finished product out at Spooky Knoll with the great view in the background. The grass in the foreground is green and everyone is smiling broadly, looking like they are having a really good time. Building a fence out in a remote area does sound like a lot more fun than mowing and weed-whipping the trails at Rancho for the nth time. Of course, to get all the fencing materials and equipment out there, they first had to re-build the old road. As an existing road, the restoration of the old roadbed counted simply as "clearing." We didn't need to get any special permits from the state or county. Crew had to put in new culverts at the two washed-out creek crossings and fix the slides and slip-outs. Fixing and clearing the road probably took more time and effort than actually building the fence.

While they were at it, crew also brushed out the route Matt and I had used to connect from the Oscar-route up to the Serenity Trail under the PG&E towers. Part of this connector is also an overgrown old road, but, unfortunately, not all. The mountain of permits needed to build the half-mile or so of actual new trail, and the expense of that mountain, brought my hopes of a quick and easy completion of the "Serenity Loop Trail" crashing down. I think that others, most notably Superintendent Bernie, also had also harbored similar hopes because the entrance to the Oscar Trail, although still signed "Closed, Not a Trail," actually got a gate, not just a fence.

And thus matters have stood for the last several years as the chaparral in the connector route has re-sprouted and regained much of its former height. We have had to make several additions and fortifications to the boundary fence, both at Spooky Knoll and at the euc grove where I found Jeep tracks going around or through our fence, and the need to maintain the boundary fence has meant the need to maintain the service road. Someday there will be a loop trail. The slow steamroller of bureaucratic decision-making just needs a little cog quietly steering it in the right direction. Me, perhaps.

20. Coyote in a Jar

5/3/11: We got a call from dispatch that someone at the Bear Creek Redwoods stables was reporting a coyote with a glass jar stuck on its head. She gave Terry, who was closest, the RP's phone number, but there was no more real information other than that it had fled downstream into the bushes from the reported area, the creek confluence below the stables. I was en route to Fremont Older so told Owen I planned to divert south to help Terry look. He said nothing at first but a few minutes later was back on the radio indicating that we shouldn't waste too much time on this detail today since the preserves were full and staffing was low. Of course, I had been thinking the same thing, but, with this supervisor's chiding to rebuff, I started to think of reasons this call had merit. The primary one, of course, was that the poor coyote was suffering from fear, initially, and then also from thirst and hunger. It was going to die a slow agonizing death. Wasn't that enough to at least justify the effort? Then there was the question of how the jar came to be on its head. Was someone baiting coyotes, or was this a case of curiosity killed the cat (dog)? We looked around for an hour while I tried to imagine how we would remove the jar should we actually find the coyote. We had catchpoles, and with the jar on its head, it couldn't bite us. Ultimately we were UTL, of course. Rats. Now I won't be able to sleep for thinking about it.

We never did find the coyote, or its remains, but this story says a lot about what a limited role District rangers have in actually protecting wildlife, especially when it comes to preserving the life of an individual animal, or even preventing its suffering. In general I understand, and agree, that the focus needs to be on preserving species, not individuals. Half-dead animals are left un-molested to quietly expire unless they are clearly within sight of visitors, where they might pose a hazard, if only a psychological one. We call the sheriff to come dispatch deer with broken bodies trying to drag themselves off the highway. We collect birds with broken wings and beaks which have crashed into windshields and power lines. Usually they die in the cardboard box long before we get them to Wildlife Rescue of Silicon Valley, and we know that this is the most likely outcome, so there is no hurry. At least we have spared the public the sight of their dying. Are we actually doing anyone a favor here by thus sanitizing the park-visiting experience? Should the Open Space be as sterilized, as un-natural, as Disneyland? No, it's just easier to move the poor thing than to respond to a good many more calls as the daily parade of visitors all discover the same suffering critter.

Part of me understands and agrees with the sanitizing strategy because I find dealing with sick and injured wildlife to be one of the most stressful parts of the job. Like our animal-loving visitors, I too want to rescue every suffering individual, man or beast, and the great importance placed upon responding to sick and injured humans contrasts so poignantly with the near total disregard given to individuals of other species. I understand, but I don't understand. Here is another recent incident along the same lines:

11-15-11: I happened to be in the office when the call came in for a skunk acting erratically in the county park, so headed out here and found it, no problem, tottering around along the path between the equestrian lot and the restroom lot beside the creek. It actually doesn't look too bad. Its coat is fine, and, although it is small, it doesn't look emaciated. It looks like it is hunting for worms or grubs right now. But it is staggering somewhat and why is this nocturnal hunter out in the middle of the day? Worst of all, it allows people to walk right up to it. Could it be rabid? Is it merely blind, or deaf? Conan and Zack also came out and took a look, and we decided to at least close off the trail while we figure out what to do. So I am guarding the now-closed trail because our habit-bound visitors will just go around the caution tape if I don't. Zack has gone back to the office to try to call Animal Control to see if they will come out.

(Later) So Animal Control said to call Vector Control, and Vector Control said to call Animal Control. Finally, a supervisor at Vector Control said that if the skunk were on private property they would trap it, but they would still have to call Animal Control to come and euthanize it. But he did make the useful suggestion of pre-covering the live animal trap, bated with cat food, with a disposable blanket, as a precaution against being sprayed. Zack and Tony arrived with the cage and the cat food and a yellow plastic blanket. I didn't actually think we would succeed in trapping the skunk, but I was wrong. We put the cage down about five feet away and, after first trying to get in the wrong end, Pepe le Pew walked right on in. Amazing! But then the door failed to fall shut. What to do? I was so totally surprised when Zack strode over, extended his baton, and gave the cage a sharp rap, which did the trick. Zack is positively averse to all things smelly, dirty, or, worst of all, diseased!

I missed the grand finale, as it seemed really silly for all three of us to stand around and wait for Animal Control. Part of me was maybe secretly hoping that they would refuse to come, and another part maybe didn't actually want to witness the end. Zack told me later that the officer had a five-foot long pole with a remotely triggered hypodermic needle on the end, which he used to first tranquilize the skunk. The coup-de-grace could then be delivered at close range. Truth be told, Pepe probably had a much easier death than he would have had we not intervened, but we didn't rescue him, didn't save him. There were no heroic rangers in this story.

21. Down and Out

5-22-05: Last night Joe and I didn't get back to the office until almost midnight. I had come upon a visitor at SA08 at about 2100 who said he had run out of gas and could I give him a ride to the gas station and back. One look at this guy told me I didn't want him anywhere near me. He said he had been there since the night before, and had been trying all day to get someone to give him a ride. He was talking a mile a minute, was grimy and unwashed and had open sores on his face. I didn't know quite what to do. He said he had no friends or family willing to come and get him. Then he went and locked his keys in the car! I asked Mt. View to see if the Sheriff would respond and Ranger Joe, with the Ops Manager as a ride along, started my way as well. I gave him a wool blanket as he had no coat and ran his car plates and his identifying information, all of which came back clear. Nonetheless Joe and the OM (who reportedly was opposed to coming down to fill for me at all as it was clear that it would lead to getting off late) seemed equally suspicious about him when they got there. Finally the SO arrived, frisked him, sobriety checked him and opened and searched the car. One of them finally ended up giving him the ride he needed. A total meth addict. Poor guy.

There are some sad parts to my job. Dealing with the drug addicts, the mentally ill, and the homeless can be very trying, and kind of scary. These guys are crazy, and seeing their erratic, abnormal behavior can be unnerving. They talk to themselves and to inanimate objects; their eyes wander around and never seem to entirely focus; they repeat themselves, and their answers wander off into nonsequeters. They are filthy, often have obvious untreated physical illnesses or ailments such as rotten teeth or open wounds, and they stink. Homeless people are not necessarily paranoid schizophrenic tweekers, but even the most sane and rational homeless person has reason to fear me. Any contact with law enforcement means trouble for these down and outs, and they know it. They stand to lose what little they have, be it their possessions or their freedom. They are right to be apprehensive, as am I to be cautious.

A big part of my job is supposed to be helping the preserve visitors and, of all visitors, these guys are perhaps most obviously in need of help. But my help? I'm afraid not. Like most police agencies and many municipalities, the District is not set up to deal with these, the neediest of people. They are not our problem, and our only interest is in getting rid of them, getting them off our land and as expediently as possible. While my dealings with the homeless and almost-homeless populations of the Silicon Valley are quite limited, especially when compared with the experiences of a city police officer, I find that the homeless always leave me with the bitter taste of futility in my mouth. I don't actually help anyone or solve anything. I just help to get the problem out of the way, out of the view of the normal park visitors, back under the rug where difficult problems end up.

12/26/08: Home alone again for Christmas last night, but not really. Family Christmas in Colorado this year, and I have to work. I went to my friend Stacy's for a late dinner while they had dessert. I didn't stay long. The quiet house is kind of nice after a long day. It was nice to get to talk to them about my day, which was kind of lousy. Zack found a vehicle crashed over the side of the road near SA08. It came back as a rental, but looked more like someone had been living in it. In heading up Umunhum Road to fill for him, I found the associated driver wandering down Hicks Road, soaking wet, cold, hungry, confused, probably mentally ill and homeless. I ended up transporting him back up to SA08, where I found Zack and Santa Clara County Sheriff gathering information for reports. The tow truck driver finally agreed—after the Sheriff refused-- to take him along back to the rental agency at the airport. I felt sorry for him so abandoned and alone on Christmas day.

I guess the true Good Samaritan would have given the guy the shirt off his back, or at least all the money in his wallet. I don't know what the most helpful action would have been. What was going to happen when they got to the rental agency? They probably threw all his worldly possessions in the dumpster and took away the car, the only "home" he had left. Maybe we should take these guys down to the nearest homeless shelter. If they refuse to go inside out of the rain, at least I don't have it on my conscience that I left them outside in the cold and wet. Here is a very similar story from the same area a few months later:

2/29/09: Earlier today I responded down to Reynolds Road to act as a translator at Cory's stop with an undocumented Mexican driving an unregistered piece of junk van which he said belonged to a man where he lived. Of course, by the time I got there from Rancho there were already three other ranger units and four other sheriffs on scene, and they had managed to communicate enough to decide what to do: tow the vehicle. The sheriffs, who were making shamefully derogatory, racist remarks amongst themselves, did agree to give the guy a ride back down to Camden Avenue where maybe he could get a bus. I gave him $5 for bus fare. He seemed like a decent guy and I felt bad for him. He was all wet and muddy from *scrambling around in the wet bushes collecting aluminum cans and other recyclables. He told me he had been working at Hicks Creek Ranch (the horse stables the District bought out last year) but was now unemployed. He said his brother had been killed at Hicks Creek Ranch a year ago in a tractor accident. Cory said he remembered a memorial up on the property. The guy pulled his tarp of recycling out of the van onto the roadside. Maybe he can come back for it.*

Sitting here warm and dry in my comfortable suburban home, it is easy to forget that a huge percentage of the world's population lives more or less as that Mexican man was living— scrambling for a living, scratching out a meager income from the discards of the wealthy. That man wasn't a beggar or a tweeker or any other sort of hopeless drain on society. He was industrious and hard working and deserved much better than he got, it seemed to me. His encounter with District rangers resulted in the loss of what I would guess was a week's worth of collecting work, all of which was stored in that unregistered van. I agree that we can't have unlicensed drivers driving unregistered vehicles around, but it does seem like that man got an awfully raw deal. Couldn't we have done something more to help? Couldn't I?

6/23/12: Chantal and I had an interesting 5150 last week on Wednesday. We had been running radar at St. Joseph's Hill together and she was giving me a ride back out to my truck at SJ03, Lexington Reservoir, when we passed this strangely dressed young man. No shirt, super-baggy nylon athletic shorts hanging off his hips exposing his boxers, and huge blue plastic glasses frames without lenses. He was skinny and had a cleanly shaven head. He avoided making eye contact and barely muttered a "hello," in answer to Chantal's friendly greeting. Down at the gate, a woman flagged me down to describe the strange young man she had talked to about 15 minutes earlier. He had told her he was headed east into the wilderness and asked for directions, said he needed to get out of civilization, maybe go to Nevada. Same guy, of course. So I headed back in Gate SJ03, and Chantal, who had taken off, came back in SJ01. I found him near the summit, and by the time Chantal got there five minutes later, I told her to call the Sheriff because this guy was nuts. He talked about selling his soul to the devil and the devil telling him to cut his wrists. He said he was a bad person, a racist and an alcoholic. He said over and over that he couldn't go back to civilization because he always got fucked and he was scared of being attacked by the gray aliens. He was also very passive and meekly submitted to my patting him down. Turned out Mt. View police had had several recent contacts with him. What to do? He was unwilling to sit down. That suggestion seemed to upset him. I said we should give him a ride out to where the cops could pick him up, but Chantal was totally opposed to putting him in my truck, even handcuffed. We just asked him to walk out with us following in the trucks. It took about 45 minutes and there was confusion on the radio about whether we were meeting the Los Gatos police at gate SJ01 or the Santa Clara County Sheriffs at Gate SJ03. Could one agency or the other go ahead and clear? And someone was giving bad directions to the Sheriff for how to get to the gate. The problem was that I didn't know for sure if he would turn left or right at the critical junction. Anyway, we met Tony and Henry and Los Gatos PD, and they checked him out and took him in for a 72-hour psych hold. By then it was 11 pm and I still had to drive back to the office and write the report. Tony seemed pretty unhappy about the entire incident, saying that things could have been done better and that he was going to get the run tapes from dispatch and discuss them with Chantal and me. Since I was in charge of the incident I was getting worried.

What will become of this young man? Will he spend his life in a world of delusion, getting "fucked" at the psych hospital? Or, if they decide he is not actually a danger to himself or others, will they release him? Will his family, at the address on his driver's license (identification card, actually), take him back in? Someone had been taking care of him; he was very clean and he had $500 in his wallet—State Disability, according to the police. When his family tire of him, or grow too old to care for him, will he end up on the street? Does he have any hope of security, happiness, or freedom? Something about his pathetic quest for "the wilderness" rang home in me. "Civilization" had "fucked" him with cops and handcuffs and psychoactive drugs and locked wards. As he said over and over, he didn't want to go back there; he couldn't go back there. But where else was there for him to go?

This next story, one of my favorites, features a drunk and has an amusing finale, but anyone who has ever had to live with an alcoholic will know that alcoholism is not actually funny, despite its being so portrayed in all sorts of stories and dramas. Alcoholics are addicts, just like stoners or tweekers, who are not normally played as harmless buffoons. Unlike the down-and-out-drunks with multiple other problems, this guy must have had some money, and he still had at least one friend.

I think I must have been at the office when the call came in that there was an older man, possibly disabled, stumbling and tripping and meandering his way in toward Deer Hollow Farm. I drove out to the Farm rather hurriedly and didn't notice anyone, but then doubled back when I realized that I must have passed him. I spotted him near the permit parking lot, basically just walking along, alone, but staggering and weaving slightly. Using the P.A., I told him to stop, but he didn't. I parked and went to stop him in person, but he pushed me away. About then the ambulance showed up (Fire Engine 7, with their medics had also driven right past him. They were still down trying to get turned around at Deer Hollow Farm) and two big, young medics went over to talk to our patient. He pushed them away too, but they tackled him, wrestled him to the ground and then onto the gurney, and tied him to it. One of the medics lost his glasses, which got broken in the fray. Meanwhile, quite a crowd had developed to watch the action, including a middle-aged woman who kept trying to get my attention. When the medics finally got him tied down and were checking him out, this woman told me that the man was her long-time friend, and an alcoholic. He had been drunk when she arrived at his house to pick him up, but she decided to bring him along anyway, hoping to help him. Within a few minutes the medics had reached the same conclusion: the guy was just drunk. They drove him out to the parking lot and off-loaded him into the woman's car. It made a pretty good story, what with the wrestling to the ground and the broken glasses and all, but then several years later, the story got better.

As a low-level peace officer, I am not automatically exempted from jury duty. I still have to show up and sit in the cold steel folding chairs in the waiting room with everybody else. This time, much to my surprise, I made it all the way up to being one of the 12 potential jurors being questioned by the defense attorney. I told them right off that I was a ranger and that I did law enforcement, even if it mostly consisted of dog off leash tickets. The defendant was accused of drunk driving, and the defense attorney, a slimy-looking character, bald with a gray ponytail, was excusing all sorts of people, most of whom seemed much more innocuous than a peace officer, for one reason or another. Sometime during the second day of jury selection, as I sat idly staring at the defendant while half-listening to the prattle of his lawyer, I realized that I knew him. I had finally placed him as the drunk of several years before at Rancho. Two days earlier, at the point when the judge had asked the pool of potential jurors if we recognized any of the parties involved—the defendant, the cop, the attorneys, etc.— we had been standing as a blob in the back of the courtroom and I hadn't really been able to see, which hadn't worried me at the time. Then, when we potential jurors were in the audience seats, the defendant was facing the other direction. When I got called into the jury box and had time to sit and look at this guy I had thought that he looked familiar, but not until sometime on the second day did it strike me who he was. Now, what was I supposed to do? Should I just raise my hand and say that I recognized the defendant as the drunk guy who beat up the paramedics at Rancho a few years ago? There wasn't really an opportunity provided for doing so. It would be really embarrassing and just might prejudice the whole trial. Should I ask to see the judge outside of court? That seemed silly and was probably prohibited. So I sat through the rest of the day in a quandary. Finally on the morning of day three, Mr. Slimy threw me off without cause. Thank goodness. I found out later that the guy got convicted (surprise, surprise), and have enjoyed telling the story of my dilemma ever since.

Finally, bottoming out the list of down-and-outs in the preserves are the suicides. Suicidal people sometimes come to parks to kill themselves. Perhaps these are places that were special to them, places where they could temporarily forget themselves, forget their sorrows, their loneliness and their mortality.

My first suicide started with a vehicle left in the Rancho parking lot overnight. The late shift rangers from the night before had left the usual note on the whiteboard in the office alerting the earlies the next morning of a vehicle locked in. It was a small sedan parked in one of the upper lots. Lars found it still there and, in checking it out, saw a hand-drawn map on a piece of notebook paper on the dashboard. After the sheriffs got there and broke into the car, we examined the map and tried to figure out what it was a map of. It was quite neat and tidy with clear, bold lines and landmarks clearly drawn and labeled, "gate," "sign," "road," "path," "tree," and an X, but no indication of which gate, path, or sign we were talking about. I thought it might be the St. Joseph's Avenue area, but Lars was arguing for the Mora Road gate, and I realized he was right, so we all trooped over there, three or four sheriffs and as many rangers. Using the map, we headed down the Mora-Ravensbury Trail, then turned left on what our victim showed as a dotted line out onto an un-trailed ridge.

Somehow it hadn't really dawned on me what we were looking for. Nobody had said a single word about suicide. Maybe no one wanted to bring it up, as though that would precipitate its being true. I was walking around with one of the deputies rather enjoying myself, like it was a treasure hunt. Where was the X? Who would be getting the kudos for finding it? The deputy actually spotted him first, then pointed him out to me before calling for the others. I was sort of shocked at our grisly discovery before I realized, in observing the deputy's demeanor, that, of course, this is exactly what he had been looking for the whole time. Not a hidden treasure, not a pot garden, not a geo-cache, but a "hanger."

He was suspended from the strong limb of an oak that stuck out over a short steep gully eroded into the face of a grassy oak-studded hillside. We made our way down across the gully and over to the trunk of the oak, and we congregated where he must have stood while preparing for his own death. It is a nice spot, with a broad view south across the grass and trees, with no roads or houses in sight. The rope was tied to the tree trunk, and then slung over the big limb. He must have used a stick to grab the loop and drag it back to where he could get his head through it.

His hands were tied to his belt with shoelaces, "So he couldn't change his mind," said the deputy. He was casually dressed in new, clean clothes and was wearing brand new sneakers, bought just for this occasion, it seemed. There was a bag over his head. Oddly enough, I can't recall what kind of a bag it was, but I was strangely grateful for it. Somehow the idea of seeing his face was too much. I do wonder if my imagination of the face wasn't worse than the reality would have been. Why did he cover his face?

Then we had to wait several hours for the coroner, while "guarding the crime scene." I sat on the grassy hillside and yakked with the deputy while others closed and "guarded" the Mora entrance and the Mora-Ravensbury Trail. I liked the coroner, a rather jovial and loquacious black woman, not at all the pale supercilious worm of my stereotype. Under her direction, we got him cut down and hauled over to where she could get a look at him. With us all watching, she gave him a cursory once-over, matter-of-factly displaying the dependant lividity of the lower limbs and the receding of the cuticles of the fingernails. I guess she was gauging a rough time of death. She found his wallet in his pants pocket and one of the deputies ran the number. Name. Date of birth, and now, date of death. He was 40 years old. I stared at the face in the driver's license photo. The real face remained covered the whole time. Even the coroner didn't remove the bag, for which I was, again, peculiarly grateful. Then we zipped him into the body bag, put him in the wheel litter, and rolled him out to the hearse.

As with other crimes, if suicide must be thought of as a crime, I felt the familiar frustration of our failure to arrive in time to help this guy. Maybe we could have saved him, talked him out of it, rescued him from himself. I suppose it's just wishful thinking. Had we saved him yesterday, he would have returned next week. Like the homeless and the nut jobs, the suicidals are not our problem.

Here is the Incident Report from the other suicide victim I found, once again, a "hanger:"

Synopsis: On January 17, 2010, at 1055 hours, a dead body was found hanging from the rafters inside the pool house at Hicks Creek Ranch. Santa Clara County Sheriffs Office and Coroners Office responded, investigated and removed the body.

Statements: None

Investigation:

Initial Observation: While on patrol checking the abandoned buildings at Hicks Creek Ranch, I saw what I thought was someone standing in the pool house.

Crime Scene: Hicks Creek Ranch is off Reynolds Road, about one tenth mile from the intersection with Hicks Road. The area is gated and marked "Area Closed." It was operating as a horse stables but has been deserted for several years, and many of the buildings, including the pool house, are dilapidated and infested with rodents. The pool house consists of a single room, part of the floor of which is missing. In this area there were the remains of a recent small campfire, a metal bowl and an empty soup can. On the floor next to the missing section was an unzipped, ripped sleeping bag, a butter knife, a wadded-up shirt used as a pillow and two small pieces of the gray cotton sweatshirt, the rest of which had been used as a hanging rope. There was an empty packet of Marlboros on the floor and a second packet with some more garbage just outside the entrance doorway. Midway between the sleeping bag and the body was a pair of crutches.

The body was hanging from a ceiling beam, which was about eight feet off the floor. It was hanging from several sections of torn gray sweatshirt tied together. The body's white tennis shoes were hanging just a few inches off the floor and between his legs was a block of wood about 15 inches tall. There was an extra shoe with no laces near his right foot. His hands, which were hanging roughly at his sides, were tied together with a black cord, like a sleeping bag binding, which ran behind his back. He was wearing two long-sleeved collared shirts under a red polo shirt and two pairs of pants, blue jeans underneath and kaki denims on top. On his lift wrist was a disposable plastic medical bracelet, which read, "Fall Risk."

The body looked to be that of an Asian male. He had straight black hair with just a few strands of gray.

Evidence Taken: The body and associated clothing were taken by the Santa Clara County Coroner.

Action Taken: Believing I was observing a Closed Area violation, and seeing that the person did not seem to be behaving normally, as he did not try to hide having apparently seen my vehicle, I called for Santa Clara County Sheriff to respond at 1055 hours and I staged at the junction of Hicks and Reynolds to wait for them. Sheriffs Officers met me at about 1115 hours and I returned to the scene with them. They attempted to call the person out of the building, and then entered and found the body as described above. I waited at the vehicle until the scene was found to be safe, and then entered with Supervising Ranger Tony, who came on scene shortly after the Deputies. They examined the body for signs and life, found him cold and pulse-less with dependant lividity and pronounced him dead at the scene. Supervising Ranger Tony took some photos, and then we waited for the Sergeant, who arrived on scene at about 1200. He also examined the body and the scene and then called for the coroner. Ranger Zack, who came on scene at 1125, staged at Hicks and Reynolds to escort the coroner, and then cleared. The coroner arrived on scene at about 1430 followed about a half hour later by the body removal team. The coroner examined the body and associated clothing. She said that the man had not been dead for more than a couple of days. She mentioned finding some kind of chronic condition with his left leg. She found a large scar on the right wrist. In his pockets she found about three dollars in change, a phone card, a lighter and, in the left breast pocket of his innermost shirt, a note. The note was on an 8.5x11-inch piece of unlined paper carefully folded inside a similarly sized piece of what looked like gift-

wrap. It was written on both sides, in large, smooth handwriting, in what the coroner said was Vietnamese. It did not look to be signed. The body removal team bagged the body, cut it down and carried it away. I cleared at about 1500.

It would be fine by me if I never find another "hanger." I found this guy even more depressing than the first one, maybe because it looked like he was impoverished and disabled. He was cold; he was probably wearing every stitch he owned, and I can't help but think that he was hungry. He died with a mere three dollars to his name. The pitiful remains of his last painful days were there on display. Who was he? There was no I.D. Possibly an illegal immigrant? Maybe he didn't speak English, if we assume he wrote the note, supposedly in Vietnamese. What did it say? Did the coroner even have it translated? It was heartbreakingly sad. One real mystery was how he even got there. Hicks Creek Ranch is miles from the closest bus stop or grocery store. Had he made it that whole way alone, on crutches? Was he actually heading for Hicks Creek Ranch, or had he just ended up there? What was his story? I feel guilty to this day that I never pursued any answers, and that his death is still, at least figuratively, hanging over my head. I like to believe that this man had at least one friend left on Earth, because starting several weeks after his death and continuing sporadically for many months, bouquets of flowers would appear, left on the ground near the gate to Hicks Creek Ranch.

I know of a few more suicides that I was not involved with in any way. I think it was Ranger Dwain who found a guy who had blown his brains out in a car parked along Skyline Boulevard. Another ranger found someone dead in a car with the tailpipe exhaust re-routed to the interior. Then there was the body that turned up in the creek in Corte Madera weeks after we stopped looking for the missing person; the head was missing and was never found. Finally, I know of three other hangings, one at Bear Creek Redwoods, one at Purisima Creek Redwoods and on in Sierra Azul on the Woods Trail. In all three of these cases, cars were known to have been parked overnight and the associated bodies were then found nearby. I didn't hear too much about any of them. I guess there wasn't too much to say.

10-22-11 Another quiet day, at least down here. I guess there was another suicide up at Purisima found this morning, hanging. The vehicle had been overnight in the lot two nights and there had been some unsuccessful ATCs (Attempts to Contact) but, according to Henry, who filled me in when I came in at noon, this morning some visitors found a backpack beside the trail and looking off into the woods, a body swinging from a tree. Every time there is another suicide, I am reminded of the two I have been on. I thought maybe one would get used to it after a while, but I'm kind of upset right now. Horrible memories and pictures I can't get out of my head. Why would anyone choose hanging? So painful and gruesome.

Not my first choice for my own death, not that I will most likely get to choose. Getting hit by a train would be quick, but that causes a lot of fuss and bother cleaning up the mess. How about freezing to death? Supposedly elderly Eskimo women, recognizing their uselessness, would intentionally wander off into a freezing snowstorm and quietly expire. Of course I hate being cold, which just might nix that. But once one starts to be ALOC I understand freezing is not bad, rather like falling asleep. Just fade away, and with any luck, the body will be consumed by scavengers rather than found. Being killed and eaten by a mountain lion actually might be okay if I were killed by a nice, swift bite to the neck. Of course, then that wouldn't be suicide, would it? Drowning is out. I know all too well the panic of not being able to breathe under water. More than anything, falling is out. No Golden Gate Bridge for me: acrophobia rules. Poisoning and pills and guns all leave a mess. There should be no body. Just walk out into the void, alone. All gone.

22. This Little Piggy

The District has a pig problem, and not with escapees from Deer Hollow Farm. These are feral pigs, the descendants of European wild boar, which were intentionally introduced to many parts of North America with the happy prospect of then hunting them for sport. I guess it seemed like a good idea at the time, at least to the pea brains who introduced them. These monsters now rampage across California's remaining wildlands, rototilling meadows and turning wetlands into muddy pig wallows. They eat mast fruits like fallen acorns, bayberries, walnuts and hazelnuts, and they dig for tasty mushrooms and for the bulbs of rare native flowers such as Zygodene lilies, brodeas and blue-eyed grass, which they sniff out with their long snouts, and grub out with their protruding tusks. They are huge beasts. An adult boar can weigh up to 400 pounds, the size of a small bear. A sow can give birth every year to ten or 12 piglets, which, when little, resemble their domesticated counterparts and are absolutely adorable. That doesn't last long. Agencies that allow hunting, such as the National Forest Service and the Bureau of Land Management, may be able to combat these piggies' prodigious reproduction rate somewhat by allowing an unlimited number to be taken, but the District doesn't allow any hunting at all. Even the pig eradication guy is not allowed to just go out and shoot them. He has to find them and trap them, and then he can shoot them, but only very quietly.

5-31-05: Interesting morning. I got to go to Bear Creek Redwoods this morning and meet Dick, the pig trapper, and learn how to use the radio antenna thing to see if a pig could be in one of the three traps. Each trap has its own frequency. They are on little transmitters actually attached to dog collars left over from Dick's hunting dogs. When the door slams shut, trapping the pig, its weight pulls a little magnet off the transmitter. Two of the traps we visited today had pigs trapped in them. He shot the pigs using very small bullets (22 caliber) and then used a winch attached to the back of the cab of his pickup to pull the pigs into the bed. It was sort of sad seeing these animals, scared but curious, come snuffling over to the bars, getting shot three or four times, squealing and squirting blood before falling down and twitching for 20 minutes. I guess you get used to it. Anyway, I'm supposed to go out tomorrow morning and check the traps and yet be on time for the 800 "customer service" training. I therefore asked to come in at 600. Goodie, goodie.

Dick told me that he would be happy to use a much larger caliber gun and just put the animals out of their misery, but the District didn't want the sound of gunfire echoing out of the preserve. The suffering of that beast in the above account (which I nonetheless believe deserved to die along with all his kith and kin!) still haunts my memory. Another odd thing about the trap-and-then-shoot program is that the dead pigs are just hauled to the dump, the landfill. Dick said sometimes he took them to a tallow factory, but usually it wasn't worth the gas to truck them over there. I asked if he couldn't donate all that pork to a homeless shelter or a food bank. No, because they are not USDA inspected, and besides, he said, "You must have noticed how awful they smell." I had indeed. "That's about how they taste too."

I can't remember if Dick got paid by the hour or paid by the pig, but either way, at some point a few years after that journal entry, we severed our contract with him, and now no active pig control is in force on District land. I think State and County Parks have also had to cut their funding of pig control. I know some animal lovers would find this to be great news, given the horror of their deaths, as just described, but doing nothing is not a sustainable option. They are not native animals. They don't belong here and are presumably displacing native species as they expand their number and range, tearing up fragile habitat along the way.

I suppose mountain lions might tackle a juvenile pig, but why eat pork when so much fresh venison is easily available? And why should a lion risk its life going after a stinky quarter-ton animal with the thick hide and vicious tusks? Visitors, in fact, might better worry about being crushed by a herd of stampeding pigs than being throttled by a hungry mountain lion. Pigs have poor eyesight, are easily startled, and pack quite a wallop when they impact with the front of your patrol truck, as Cory found out. His patrol truck was declared totalled after he collided with an enormous pig on Hicks Road one night. He hit it dead on; the airbags deployed and the pig was dragged along under the truck for some 25 yards. Probably that was a quicker and kinder pig extermination method than death-by-trapper, but not one the District is likely to adopt. Very efficient extermination as well: it was a sow, so we lost a patrol truck, but prevented the birth of thousands of future piggy-pests.

23. More Medicals, Anyone?

The San Andreas Fault runs more or less north-to-south through the Santa Cruz Mountains, which themselves run more or less north to south, down the spine of the San Francisco peninsula. Streams, which should flow east or west toward San Francisco Bay or the Pacific Ocean, instead sometimes get trapped in the fault zone and make long detours north or south on their way downhill. Stevens Creek is a prime example. It flows south for some ten miles before escaping the fault zone and turning east to flow into the Bay. Stevens Canyon effectively separates the main ridgeline, Skyline Ridge, from the more easterly bulk of Monte Bello Ridge. While Steven's Creek's lower reaches have been dammed and concreted and canalized to the point where it is hard to find, much less access, the upper ten miles, above Stevens Creek Reservoir, have largely been saved as County Park and Open Space District lands. The Canyon Trail, a long, straight, ten-mile downhill, from the Monte Bello parking lot on Page Mill Road to Stevens Creek Reservoir--in combination with a climb back up the broad back of Monte Bello Ridge on Monte Bello Road--makes a fine and very popular, biking loop.

In the winter, Stevens Canyon is enticingly dank and dark. Soft, thick green moss carpets the stones and tree trunks. The brief hours of sunlight seem not to penetrate the cold blanket of air in the canyon bottom, and there are very few visitors. It feels very wild and wooly, like real wilderness. But on a hot summer's day, the deep canyon can be attractively cool and shady, that cold air now a welcome relief to sweaty visitors, most of them mountain bikers who either loop back up Monte Bello Ridge or up the Grizzly Flat or Table Mountain Trails. Neither of these loops is short enough to be attractive to the casual day hiker, so the bikers have The Canyon pretty much to themselves. And they ride like maniacs.

Near the bottom, maybe a quarter mile above the ford across Stevens Creek itself, there was an eroded and abrupt crossing of a small side creek. The trail, a narrow but smooth and predicable single track, at this point suddenly dropped about six feet sharply down to cross this small tributary and, just as abruptly, climbed straight back up the far bank. If you knew it was coming, and knew that you weren't up to it, you could avoid this treacherous crossing by quickly veering left and taking an alternate trail 25 yards or so up the side creek to an easy, level crossing. But if the novice or uninitiated rider didn't know it was coming, or if they didn't realize what a difficult and advanced skill it was to so very suddenly switch from steep downhill to steep uphill, they would ride right into this trap, perhaps at high speed. The front tire would hit that sudden, steep uphill like a stone wall and the cyclist would go flying straight over the handle bars. At least one young rider was badly injured here.

I wasn't first on scene; I think maybe county parks rangers got there first, but I walked in from "the bottom" with the firefighters, pushing the wheel litter with the backboard and medical supplies. (An enormous landslide blocks the old road a couple miles above the reservoir, and the road abruptly becomes a single-track trail. Firefighters and rangers have to stage their vehicles at the slide and walk. Thanks to this century-old slide, there is no public highway up Stevens Canyon.) At least in this direction the large and heavy bags of supplies can ride in the litter. When we came on scene, the initial rescuers were with the patient, a young woman, down in the mini-ravine, with one of them holding C-spine "in the position found," just as they should. The patient was crumpled up sort of on her belly with her head bent forward toward her chest...post face plant position. She was wearing a helmet, which probably saved her life. It was nice to come on scene with Fire because I got to just watch and help as needed, but had little actual responsibility. I held up the IV bag, and fetched the backboard straps and helped to roll and lift and carry, but I didn't have to make any decisions.

Our patient was conscious, breathing and "alert and oriented times four," which means she managed to answer the four standard questions: What's your name? Where are you? What day is today? What happened? (Person, Place, Time and Event) but had pain upon palpation in her neck. Well, what were we going to do? We couldn't leave her there. We couldn't carry her out in a crumpled, face down position. We had to straighten her out enough to get her on the backboard and safely strapped down and, before we could do that, we had to roll her over. Unfortunately, all that straightening and rolling, no matter how slowly, gently and carefully done, would require moving her from the only position in which the Red Cross, and District policy, says we are allowed to stabilize, treat or transport patients: the position found. Good thing Fire was on scene. If the ambulance were sitting right there next to the patient, we could just slide her face down, curled-up form onto the backboard and lift her onto the gurney. I know that has been done with crumpled patients on the roadway, but this gal had a half-mile ride in a wheel litter coming up. Exigent circumstances forced our hand. For once all the "extra" District, County Park and Fire personnel were actually useful. We were all needed for manipulating backboard, patient, IV lines, oxygen tank, tubes, blankets, straps and wheel litter. Unfortunately, of course, her CSMs (Circulation, Sensation and Movement in the extremities) deteriorated during this rather lengthy process. Where she had reported no difficulty feeling or moving her feet and toes before the move, she now reported numbness and tingling in her legs. Did the move cause this? Could we have done anything differently, and better? I don't think so.

She was pretty quiet, I would say silent, during the long and probably painful half-mile ride out to the ambulance. It is actually slightly uphill most of the way out, since the trail goes up around the giant slide, and, even with the wheel taking most of the weight and the patient being a rather small person, it seemed to me a strenuous ordeal keeping the litter steady and level and quiet as we tried to rush her out.

I had not realized that our patient's boyfriend had been on scene and taking photographs non-stop during the entire rescue. Most people, myself included, do not have the presence of mind to take pictures during medicals. That's why most of those photos in wilderness medical textbooks are staged or taken during training exercises. Nobody, I believe, thinks to drag out the camera when they witness their girlfriend take a face-plant into the embankment. I guess now that phones and cameras are an all-in-one electronic gizmo, the boyfriend could defend himself saying that he took the pictures while on the phone with the 911 dispatcher.

I don't actually remember when his photo journal started, but quite a few were taken at the scene of the accident. Then there are photos at the emergency room and of the x-rays of her neck showing shattered vertebrae. Then she is in the hospital bed all hooked up with tubes and wires, and finally, in the final slides, our patient several months later, is at physical therapy learning to walk again. The boyfriend sent copies of his documentary to the various agencies involved in the rescue as a thank you for helping. This seems like a second rather amazing feat: to have had the presence of mind to record which agencies those were! I guess he could just read it off the shoulder patches in all the pictures. It was great to see that our patient was walking again despite having broken her neck and damaged her spinal cord, and great to see her enthusiastically tackling the parallel bars in those final frames, but it was also sad to realize that she would probably never fully recover. Her athletic prowess took a severe hit that day in the canyon, and while her drive and spirit may be intact, her body will never be quite the same.

That strange and difficult creek crossing, the site of the accident, was eventually fixed, several years later, after another serious accident. The county had to install lengthy stretches of chain link fence on both sides of the gully to keep the daredevils from continuing to ride it. The safe and wimpy route is now the only possibility.

The worst accident I've attended in my career to date, even worse than the young woman in Stevens Canyon, was, again, a bicycle crash, this time a 14-year-old boy in Fremont Older Open Space Preserve.

Fremont Older is perhaps my least favorite preserve. It is named for Fremont Older, a wealthy San Francisco newspaperman of the early 20th century. His old house, which belongs to the District but is leased out, still stands on the property and District docents lead tours through it in the spring. Like Rancho, this preserve is easily accessed and heavily used, being nestled up against Cupertino and Saratoga, and, like Rancho, it has seen hundreds of years of intensive human use—road building, brush clearing, cattle grazing, and mowing and terracing for vineyards and orchards. The Hayfields area, through which one strolls for a view of the city from Hunters Point, is a grassland of weeds. Wild oats, foxtails, soft chess, rip-gut brome, Italian rye, wild mustard, star thistle, burr chervil, filaree, and a few other grasses and forbs are all introduced European natives which have out-competed and completely eliminated whatever the original grasses may have been on this gentle, sunny hillside. The woodland and chaparral areas retain more California natives, but there are huge groves of introduced blue gum eucalyptus trees whose toxic leaves and bark poison the ground for other species and effectively create a monoculture. As a plant enthusiast, I find Fremont Older depressing, but a typical plant-oblivious recreation-minded visitor probably would find my objections to the preserve rather ridicules. Most visitors love the open grasslands around Hunters Point, especially in the winter when they are green. Perhaps the only desirable remnants of this agricultural past, to my mind, are the many still living and producing 100-year-old apricot trees hiding down off the trails.

Not only is Fremont Older quick and easy to get to, but it also allows use by both dogs and bikes--which Rancho does not--and it gets lots of both. The tiny dirt parking lot holds only about 15 cars and is overflowing every sunny weekend. Because of all the people with their animals and machines, Fremont Older is both a law enforcement and a medical incident hot spot. Many of the cyclists here are beginners or intermediates. Experienced riders might ride through it merely as part of a bigger loop. Despite its popularity amongst novice riders, most of the trails are anything but level, and some are quite steep and rutted as well as crowded with large groups of runners and dog walkers. When I see paunchy parents riding in with their elementary school-aged and adolescent children on their shiny new bikes, I know I can expect to see them all a short way up the trail on foot pushing their bikes up the hill. They would have a better time riding the levees down along San Francisco Bay, where it is flat. The trails at Fremont Older are just too challenging for beginners, especially children. The Ranch Road, the site of the awful accident with the 14-year-old, was too steep for me to ascend back in my bike patrol days, and, for the same reason, I would never attempt to go down it either; it was too steep.

The day of the accident was clear and sunny and the preserve was busy with visitors. I was up on Coyote Ridge running radar in the euc grove with Joe when the call came in for a bicyclist down on the Ranch Road. Joe and I hopped in my truck and sped over there. That is, I remember doing my best to be speedy, and remember Joe fuming and suggesting that we stop and switch drivers because I wasn't going fast enough. Obviously we were getting a big jump on the response time simply by being in the preserve to begin with. As we approached the Ranch Road junction in the Hayfields, we could see panic-stricken people yelling and waving us down. Our patient was about 100 yards down the Ranch Road right at the bottom of the big steep hill, over on the side in a shallow gully, lying on his back. He was in a state of constant motion, with his arms and legs making clawing, climbing motions, his jaw opening and closing and his eyes circling around without seeming to see anything. He was in a strange state of altered consciousness, not oriented to name, place, time or event, in fact, not responsive at all, except that he would very briefly stop moving when I called his name. There was nothing we could do for him except get him out of there and to the hospital ASAP. We tried to hold C-spine, but just holding his head produced more motion to his neck because his whole body was in motion. The jackets that bystanders had attempted to cover him with wouldn't stay on because of this constant motion, nor would our blankets. We ended up sort of half-heartedly trying to hold him still. Any actual effort to forcibly hold him down produced squeals and shaking and seemed to make matters worse. I remember, with shame, working to put a cervical collar on him and getting completely befuddled by the mechanism for turning the flat (for storage) plastic, foam and Velcro slab into a cervical collar, even though I had done it before under less stressful conditions, and many times in training. The tunnel vision of adrenalin was in full force. The one thing we could have done that might have actually helped was getting him started on oxygen, to get some more oxygen to his brain, but we didn't carry it in those days.

The boy's uncle was on scene and completely distraught, though trying hard to maintain self-control. He said this was their second visit to the preserve and he had been following his nephew on the trails that day. He said he saw his nephew hit something in the trail, a rut or a rock or perhaps a water bar, and then go flying over the handlebars and land on his head. The poor man felt terrible. There was no way to dismiss the seriousness of the injury, and he felt entirely responsible.

Fire was on scene in about ten minutes, although it felt like forever and we helped to get him properly collared and backboarded, although this produced lots of squealing. A helicopter must have been on order from the get-go, because by the time we had him on the board, it was waiting for us on the flat up near the Ranch Road junction. I was completely oblivious of the helicopter's arrival. I think we just lugged him up the 100 yards of road on the backboard. It was too steep for the gurney and there wasn't time to turn my truck around.

The final drama of this horrible day was the arrival of the boy's mother. I saw her, and some other relatives, coming slowly up the Cora Older Trail just after the helicopter had cleared. She headed straight for me, (or maybe I headed for her?) and asked about her son. Was he alive? How was he? Nobody told me this would be part of my job. I told her the best news I could: that he was alive and on his way to Stanford University Hospital. I didn't tell her about the weird squeals or the disturbing limb movements or the vacant vacillating eyes.

I phoned a week later and reached the uncle, who said the boy was still in a coma, but a medically induced coma. I wish to this day I had called again, but I felt like too much of a nosey intruder in this family's grief. It is hard to imagine a truly happy ending to this story. Could he have fully recovered? How much brain damage did he sustain? Certainly this accident would have a major impact on this young person's whole life. I am still grieving for that boy and his family. My own son was, at the time, also 14 years old.

And a couple more medical rescues also featuring juveniles, one being my youngest patient ever:

The last stretch of the service road from the Rancho San Antonio parking lot back to Deer Hollow Farm runs alongside a small creek. On some maps it bears the amusing and cool name of Green Dragon Creek. This dragon has dug itself down deep into its bed as the years have passed, and its meanders have become wider and wider trying to turn themselves into oxbows. This is the nature of creeks and rivers when left to their own devices; the stream keeps eroding the bank away. But what about when there is a road built right next to the stream, right at the top of that eroding stream bank? Just short of the Farm there was a spot where the road was under imminent threat of falling into Green Dragon Creek, so our crew undertook a project to shore up and reinforce the creek bank in this spot, to keep the creek from meandering any farther toward the Farm.

They built a pair of short retaining walls out of old railroad ties, each wall about five feet tall, offset from one another by a couple feet, so that, in the 10 to 12 feet between the road and the creek there were two short walls and a skinny, sloping terrace. At the very top, right along the very edge of the road, they built a wooden fence about four feet tall with wooden posts and a handrail on the top and two other wooden rails below it. It looked great, very tidy and harmonious with the setting, but not entirely childproof, as it turns out.

Lars and I were at the office when the call came in for a 4-year-old child fallen into the creek near Deer Hollow Farm. We both hopped into my truck, flipped on the lights and sirens and headed out there. Trying to drive Code Three through thick crowds of pedestrians is both hazardous and frustrating. Most of the time, the large groups actually try to get out of the way, but they are leaderless, disorganized and oblivious of the needs of the driver. Seeing a large blaring, blinking behemoth bearing down on them, each individual heads for the closest side of the path. In other words, the crowd divides equally in half and each demi-crowd shuffles over and blocks the edge and shoulder on their half the road, leaving insufficient room in the middle for me to pass. Then they stand there waving and extorting me to pass through even as I watch half dozen wiggly toddlers and squirmy preschoolers already breaking free of mom or dad, itching to run back into the middle of the road. This is when it is nice to have two rangers in the truck. I can drive and answer the inevitable requests for updates on the radio while Lars mans the loudspeaker, encouraging people to all move to one side—the driver's side-- and to pick up their little kids. The longest half-mile in the District is between the Foothills Field Office and Deer Hollow Farm.

Arriving on scene, we found only a few people waving us down rather than the crowd I would have expected. Everyone was just strolling past, oblivious of the drama below, because from the road the patient was not visible. "Where is the injured child?" I asked one of the women who had waved us down. "Down there," she said pointing down into the creek, "He went through the railing." Peering over the edge I couldn't see much of anything. The intervening terrace blocked my view of the creek bank. "Where is he now?" I asked, "I can't see him." "He's still down there, and also his mother." Okay, now I can hear Mom calling out for help. She must have just realized we were on scene. Donning my medical gloves I clambered down to where I could see Mom, a heavy-set woman, cradling the head and shoulders of a small child who was lying on his back holding perfectly still. They were hauled up on a tiny sandbar on the other end of the retaining wall. When she saw me she started calling out, "Hurry! Hurry! He hit his head. We need get him up now. We need get to hospital. Fast! Fast! I am nurse. I know." I called up to Lars to hand me down a child-sized C-collar from my first aid kit while I was still within arm's reach of the road, then splashed on over to my patient.

He was alert and responsive and watched me with big, scared eyes. He was absolutely soaking wet and shivering, although Mom had wrapped him in her jacket, as big as a blanket on him. I got permission to treat, which was a bit redundant since Mom was already yelling at me what she wanted me to do. I got the kid's name and tried to question him to test his level of consciousness, but just got blank stares. "He does no speak English. Just Russian. But I know he is bad. I am his mother. His eyes are not normal. Look at his eyes. Something is wrong. Do something. Help him! Help him!" Her rambling pleas went on and on, mixed with crying and moaning in anguish and frustration. A quick once-over revealed nothing but cuts and scrapes, aside from a nasty goose egg on his forehead. I showed the little guy how the C-collar would go on, sliding it up my own chest and pretending to wrap it around my neck, Mom insisting the whole time that he didn't need it and she could just hold his head as I had showed her, and which she claimed to already know. Lars and Bart came struggling down the embankment and through the creek with the backboard just about then, and suddenly I realized that I had never tried to strap a tiny four-year-old onto an adult backboard. The strapping system required by County Fire protocols at that time still called for "box straps," which very few of the rangers had totally mastered because "box straps" are complex and confusing. I only knew the system as well as I did because I was the first aid instructor, and I was eager to go ahead and give it a go on a child. Supervisor Bart said no; fire was on scene up top and would be down in a minute and we would let them do it. Okay. (Rats!)

Mom meanwhile was becoming more and more hysterical, moaning, pulling her hair, crying and yelling at us to hurry up. I had taken over holding C-spine after getting the collar on and now, with nothing to do, she seemed to really lose all self-control. I could understand her frustration with the delay and certainly sympathized with her intense worry about her child, but didn't understand why she didn't spend at least a little more time and effort comforting the patient, sitting quietly with him, telling him it would be all right, since none of us could speak Russian to communicate with him directly.

When fire got to us, they tried to get Mom out of the way, telling her she needed to calm down and to leave the scene so they could work. One of them even started dragging her away, at which point the patient, who, this whole time had been very quiet, only whimpering occasionally, started crying and stretching out his arms and calling to her. She broke free of the fireman and now, of course, was more in the way than ever. Plus now the patient was crying and struggling against the firemen trying to apply backboard straps. What a mess. Don't you know not to separate a mother from her injured kid? Someone up top had cleverly thought to send the winch cable down off one of the trucks, so we could just hook it onto the backboard and basically pull the patient straight up into the waiting hands of the crew up on the road.

Once mother and child were safely in the ambulance and underway, I found the same women who had waved us down who, it seems, were also Russians and relatives of the child. They now explained that the little boy had been leaning forward through the railings throwing rocks into the creek while the adults were chatting, and he had apparently lost his balance and fallen. I crawled back down and took pictures for the report of the wall of reinforcement. I found crushed grass on the little terrace between the railroad tie walls. The terrace probably saved the kid from greater injury—two five-foot falls versus one ten-foot fall. In the end, our patient turned out not to have been badly hurt at all. One of the rangers saw him and Mom walking out to the farm a few days later. He said Mom flagged him down and thanked him for our response and even apologized for her behavior. A third railing joined the existing two lower railings very shortly after this accident.

Part of the hiring process for the ranger job are some practical tests such as a pretend vehicle inspection (yikes!), a tool identification test, and at least one scenario, which the candidate then has to write up as an incident report. The scenario starts out as an enforcement contact—in my case, Superintendent Bernie illegally fishing, accompanied by his prohibited and off leash dog—and then the scenario switches suddenly to a medical when Lee came running in yelling that he had been bitten by a rattlesnake. The test is to see whether the candidate will let the compliant and clueless fisherman go with just a warning in order to focus on the medical problem. Medical trumps law enforcement, although, I'm sure, there will always be exceptions. Incidents involving both these components, like the following, are usually rather interesting, although they often turn into multi-agency clusters with too many chiefs and not enough Indians, or vice-versa.

The automated entrance gate at Rancho closes a half hour before the posted closing time. The thinking is that no one would want to come for just half an hour, and that anyone arriving that late would probably end up being late getting out of the park. The exit gate is also automated, but only to open in the morning; it is not set to close at any particular time. The rangers close it with a key once all the cars have left. Newbie visitors often ask me if they will get locked in if they aren't out by the posted closing time. I assure them that we probably won't lock them in, but we probably will give them a parking ticket for after-hours parking. They don't find my answer very reassuring! In fact the likelihood of receiving such a ticket is quite high as there is nearly always a ranger prowling the lots at closing time. We are there to write parking tickets, sure, but that last half hour of the park day, the last half hour after sunset, is also the witching hour when problems come out of the woodwork. All those all-day hikers and last-minute runners now return to their cars, and at least one of them will discover that they have lost their keys somewhere on the trail, or locked the keys in the car, or that they have left their lights on and now have a dead battery, or that their spouse (child, parent, friend, etc.) who took a different route and was supposed to meet them back at the car, is nowhere to be found.

On a warm summer's evening a ranger can just about count on working late. Even if all the cars' owners return only slightly later than on time—and try to flag me down to complain about their parking tickets—there could still be more visitors out there in the preserve who didn't park in the parking lot at all. That is why we are scheduled to work for an hour or so beyond closing time. We do try to locate all the "lost" and "missing" visitors, but we are also hoping to catch at least a few of the naughty people intentionally using the park after hours, those people who know they are going to be late and so park out in the neighborhood somewhere. So, once the lots are clear, the ranger stuck on Rancho closing shift (often me) needs to go check all the usual spots: De Anza Knoll, the Mora Road water tank, and Hunters Point down at Fremont Older. Sometimes we never do find the visitors associated with those last lonely cars in the parking lot, and we do just lock them in. There is a pay phone at the restroom and a sign on the gate telling locked-in folks to call the Sheriff to let them out.

Heading up to check one of the usual after-hours hangout spots, I usually turn out my headlights and approach using only the running lights, or no lights at all on moonlit nights. I can often get very close indeed before the people notice me. They are all looking out the other way, at the lights. (Doesn't anyone else find it sad, seeing the huge extent of the city? During the day, the urban forest kind of hides it, but in the darkness the orange glow of a million streetlights tells all.) All the lights of Silicon Valley are spread out below. Most people seem to really enjoy looking at them. They are drawn to these vista points and will sit there mesmerized, like moths around a flame. It's amazing. If there is a late car down in the Prospect Lot at Fremont Older, 90 percent of the time I will find the offenders up on Hunters Point. If the lights-gazers aren't doing anything but gazing, and it isn't terribly late, I seldom break out the ticket book. The offenders are often neighbors who ought to know better, and are thus more culpable, but who might also be forgiven for wanting to take a stroll out their back door and in the moonlight. If, however, these night owls are smoking, drinking, riding bikes, or starting campfires, I am much more inclined to cite them.

The Mora water tank vista point at Ranch is easily accessed by parking on Mora Drive and coming in the back gate. Although near the preserve entrance Mora Drive is signed "No Parking," our late night visitors probably figure they can get away with it while they run up to the hilltop to enjoy the view of the lights, along with a beer and some weed. According to some of the old timers around the office, there used to be a lot more action up there, with tens of teenagers, kegs of beer, and young couples romping in the grass. They regale us with tales of chasing kids around the hill, stopping a few while the rest got away, escaping out the gate to their cars. Ah, the good old days.

So, one balmy evening after a hot day, and with the lots clear, I headed up to the water tank. I had my headlights off and was trying to be stealthy and quiet, as usual, and, what do you know? I got some action. Not like the old days, but something. Three seated figures were silhouetted against the orange glow of the city. I called in my 10-95 and Zack headed up to fill. I could see my suspects hurriedly tucking and stuffing, but still there remained a litter of fast food wrappers on the ground when they stood up and approached the truck, as directed. They looked like high school guys and, sure enough, they were all 17-year olds. Rats! I don't like citing juveniles, even when the offense is only an infraction and I can use the regular adult form and don't have to fill in a JCR (Juvenile Contact Report). But, even if I decide not to cite them, it was late enough I should at least issue written warnings and not just wimp out and give scold-and-release verbal warnings. And cutting paperwork of any kind means that I am supposed to contact their parents and advise them of the contact. Well, let's see. What should we do? Any weapons? No. Any smell of marijuana, tobacco, or alcohol? No. Anyone look drunk or stoned? No. Well then, what are you guys doing up here?

They said they were in the marching band at the local high school and had been at band practice all afternoon and were just up there chilling and relaxing. Okay, let's see some ID. Of the three, only one even had a license, which is not unusual nowadays given the price of insuring a car for a young male driver. Of course, our driver had had his license less than a year and was thus not allowed to be driving other juveniles around at all, much less late at night. Well that solved that part of it. We had to call parents to come collect their kids, (except the driver) so I might as well cut paperwork while we wait.

About then Zack arrived and started going through some of the same routine questions I had just covered. He was the "cover" officer now, while I was gathering addresses and phone numbers and calling parents and filling in the written warnings. Zack can be a little more by-the-book and security-minded than I am, which is not a bad thing in a peace officer. With parents en route and forms filled out, I called the boys over one at a time to my "desk," the hood of my truck, to sign their written warnings. The last kid was standing there, pen in hand, ready to sign, when...Wham! He hit the ground like a stone. From fully conscious and alert to completely unconscious and unresponsive with no warning at all. Time for a paradigm shift to medical mode. Shake and shout, "Are you okay? Are you okay?" "Zack, call for Fire." Actually he was already doing just that. Our perpetrator-patient was only out for 5 or 10 seconds, just long enough to scare the heck out of me, and then he slowly started coming around. He seemed rather groggy answering the first set of who-where-when-why questions, and he seemed to be in no hurry to get up off the ground, even to sit up. No, this had never happened to him before. No allergies or medical conditions. He said he wasn't taking any prescription medications, or using recreational drugs. Pulse and blood pressure both okay. No difficulty breathing. No headache or pain anywhere. What happened? What was going on?

When Fire got there they assumed patient care, re-doing everything I had just done, freeing me and Zack to deal with the other two kids. Zack was now becoming ever more suspicious of the driver-kid who kept asking if he could leave, since he had a valid license and a car and had signed his written warning. He was the only one of the three carrying a backpack, a fairly full and fairly heavy-looking backpack, and when Zack had asked, almost as his first question upon arrival at the scene, if he could have a look inside, driver-kid had said no. Asked what was inside, he had said it was personal. Zack now asked again, and was again denied, only increasing Zack's suspicions. Were there drugs in there which might explain his friend's sudden loss of consciousness? Pulling me aside, Zack suggested that, given that our enforcement stop had turned into a medical, we might have PC (probable cause) to search the backpack against the kid's will. I was opposed, saying that there were other, more likely explanations for the fainting spell, like being extremely dehydrated from having been at marching band practice all afternoon in the hot sun, and, with three 17-year-old boys, the "personal" stuff in the pack was just as likely pornography as drugs. So, we didn't search it, and we will never know. It might have made a better story if we had. As it was, Fire eventually cleared the patient, and gave him a clean bill of health. When the parents arrived, they too said they were unaware of any previous fainting spells. Interestingly, they seemed more willing to see a connection between marching band practice and recreational drug use, and seemed skeptical of my dehydration theory. Like most parents coming to collect their kid on a hilltop late at night, they seemed genuinely worried about their kid, his welfare and his future. They thanked us for calling them and for doing our bit to watch out for their children. I think we made the right decision in this case, but I don't think Zack thinks so.

I never got on scene for this next perpetrator-patient, but I did have to write the report with my second-hand information:

3/1/11: Interesting incident early yesterday morning just as we were logging on. County Fire was already on scene at the Sheldon Road entrance to El Sereno. Someone had called from the Los Gatos Coffee Roasting Company reporting having seen a naked man lying in the trail somewhere in the preserve. When fire got to the gate, the man was only about 50 yards inside the preserve walking toward them. He was completely naked except for a ragged polo shirt. He spoke only Spanish and thus was only able to communicate with the ambulance driver, whom he told that he "had gone to see why the water had stopped." The firefighters speculated that he had been out in the sub-freezing cold for several nights and was also probably dehydrated. The most likely scenario was a marijuana grower who got "voted off the island." Bernie attributed his lack of clothing to impaired judgment resulting from hypothermia. He may be right, as others then brought up the case of the family stuck in the snow in their car. When they eventually found the Dad, who had gone off to look for help, he was not only dead, but also naked, having gradually pulled off all his clothes. Weird.

Speeding, in my own fashion, south from the office, I was hoping to get a chance to speak to the patient, but arrived just in time to see the ambulance pull away. Darn! My Spanish is pretty good, and I might have been a better interrogator than the ambulance driver. All the cops, sheriffs, paramedics and firefighters were still milling around exchanging facts and fictions at the roadhead, but since the victim had walked right out to them and didn't speak English, there hadn't really been anything for them to do, and there wasn't much to tell.

As I wrote earlier, wilderness first aid instructors love to dream up sadistic scenarios for their students. A certain West Valley College instructor seems to enjoy torturing his students by taking them on a camping trip where they will be forced out of their beds in the middle of the night to go search for a reported "missing person," who, naturally, will have multiple serious injuries when they do find him. Of course, the instructor has an entire class of 40 or 50 students to keep occupied, so all these scenarios feature wildly improbably accidents, such as the ten "victims" found unconscious, or semi-conscious, in the avalanche slope with concussions and broken femurs and flail chests, all of whom are also secretly suffering from hypoglycemia. It's the Diabetic Dayhikers' weekly outing gone awry.

Like everyone else I know, I hate being on the receiving end of a sadistic scenario. It seems to be the instructor's intent to make sure that no one escapes with their ego unscathed, to make sure that everyone "fails" at least some part of it. Is failure supposed to prepare us for dealing with real emergencies and real patients? How about setting students up for success and self-confidence instead? Why not save the fractured femurs and avulsed limbs for skills practice sessions and use the after-dark-and-raining scenarios to practice more mundane and practical problems such as evacuating the wet and freezing person with a badly sprained ankle.

The mass-causality scenarios of these wilderness first aid classes do not crop up very often in real-life wilderness first aid. There is almost never more than one patient. I say almost never because, in fact, I had one: I was first on scene at a bike accident with two badly injured cyclists. After the event was over, during the de-brief and back-slapping session that stretched out over several days, I had a chance to ask the rest of the ranger staff about multiple patient incidents. They recalled for me the time when the brushing tractor hit a hornets' nest and a bunch of the crew got multiple stings, and there was, of course, the horrible accident when a contractor's pickup rolled over out in La Honda Creek OSP killing one of the workers riding in the back and injuring a couple others, but I was off duty both those days and only got the stories second-hand. All in all, very few incidents involving multiple victims when compared to the emphasis given to triaging patients in first aid class, and never can I remember a class scenario having two patients and a single rescuer, as happened to me.

I was driving south along Coyote Ridge at Fremont Older when dispatch called for "any ranger near Fremont Older." Good Samaritans on scene were reporting two bicyclists down on the Fern Trail. 10-4. I'm en route, and wondering what's up with the two patient thing. How could that be? Chantal and Cory attached themselves as well, heading for the Prospect lot to meet Fire, while Dumbo and I turned off on the Fern Trail to look for the patients. Fern Trail is drivable but not driven any more because we are trying to turn it back into a single-track trail, rather than a patrol road. But, this being an emergency situation, I figured I would set back the restoration process a bit in the interests of finding the patients sooner. The fallen cyclists were actually at the far southern end of the trail, just a couple hundred yards down from the much more drivable Vista Trail at the bottom of a long steep hill with ruts and water bars.

There was a small crowd of six or seven people there helping them, and two dusty, bloody men lying side by side reclining against the trail embankment, not moving. I let dispatch know I was on scene, confirmed that there were two patients, directed everyone else to use the Vista Trail, put on my gloves and grabbed the first aid kit. My patients turned out to be brothers, with similar Hispanic names, at least to my gringo ears. They were both big, beefy guys, who both spoke tolerable, if accented, English. Moving back and forth (and changing gloves each time!), getting permission to treat, asking about chief complaint, checking for severe bleeding, checking LOC and checking vitals, one of my biggest problems turned out to be remembering who was who. These two looked so much alike they could have been twins, not just brothers! It was awfully embarrassing to keep needing to ask them their names!

One of my better moves early on was appointing volunteers to assist me. I handed one guy my pocket notebook and pen and told him to just write down everything he heard. Two others, with gloves, became C-spine holders. Neither brother was reporting head or neck pain or loss of consciousness but C-spine precautions were certainly called for, given the mechanism of injury (MOI), and the extent of their other injuries, and the damage to their helmets. The MOI was, indeed, an interesting question. The bystanders reported that they had not witnessed the accident but seemed to have come upon it shortly thereafter. They said the brothers were in the middle of the trail and had asked for assistance to get moved to the side. It was nice that they were now out of the way of any further cyclists and could now lean on the embankment, but really, one should never move an injured person unnecessarily. Neither brother could accurately report exactly how they had both come to fall in the same place. Had one fallen and the second guy run into him? Had they both hit the same water bar or rut? No answers were forthcoming. One thing for sure: they were undoubtedly going way too fast.

Not only did they look alike and sound alike, but they also had very similar injuries. Both reported severe right side arm, shoulder and rib cage pain. One, additionally, had severe pain in the thoracic and lumber region of his entire back. I chopped off their shirts, jackets, and backpacks with my medical scissors, something I rarely get to do. Neither reported difficulty breathing, but I was just sticking my one oxygen bottle on the patient reporting back pain, who also looked sort of pale and sick and I suspected might have some internal bleeding, when Chantal came on scene with Fire.

I gave the captain the low-down on what I had done so far, and he immediately called for an "air ambulance." Cory headed on over to help land the helicopter at the LZ by Garrod Stables. Suddenly there seemed to be Fire guys everywhere, re-doing all the secondary survey stuff I had been doing, but probably not getting their patients mixed up since they didn't have to go back and forth. They started an IV on the more critical patient, I assumed so they could get him some morphine before moving him, but no, despite loud cries of pain, we rolled both of them onto backboards. The one guy was crying uncontrollably by the time we got him on the board.

When the dreaded box straps came out, Chantal and I enjoyed a small moment of glory. The two of us managed to get the first guy strapped in with only one minor foul-up, which we quickly rectified. So, seeing our competence, the firefighters, who had been helping us to wiggle and wedge the straps under the backboard on the uneven ground with the 250 pound guy on it, threw us a package of straps and directed us to go strap in the second, less critically injured brother. It felt good to be competent, and especially to be "caught" being competent. Scenarios should be like this.

We lugged one patient up the hill on the backboard to the ambulance waiting at the top, and the second patient rode up in the back of my pickup and was stuffed into the helicopter for his ride to the hospital. It was over. The sudden silence. I felt the sensation of exhaustion as all that adrenalin left my body. We cleaned up the debris at the scene and loaded their bikes—nice, new, expensive models, according to our bike experts—into the trucks for storage back at the office. I retrieved my notebook and thanked my assistants and took some photos for the report, still shaking my head over this bizarre double whammy of an accident.

24. Ravenswood

The District has two tiny preserves that are not in the Santa Cruz Mountains: Ravenswood Preserve and Stevens Creek Nature Study Area. (Why Nature Study Area rather than Preserve? Who knows.) Both sit on the waterfront of San Francisco Bay, one in East Palo Alto and one in Mountain View, and both are integral parts of the regional effort to create a pedestrian and bicycle path ringing the San Francisco Bay. I do wonder sometimes why we bought these lands in the first place and why we haven't long since traded or sold them away in exchange for property up in the mountains, in the heart of the "green belt" that is our mission. Perhaps having some District land actually down in the flats where most of the voters live, or perhaps our inclusion in the planning of the Bay Trail has something to do with it. Along with the National Wildlife Refuges and the many small cities the trail will pass through, we too will get to have a say in the building of this dream trail. The trail section from Palo Alto south to Alviso, which runs alongside the Nature Study Area, is, in fact, already complete and open to the public, and it is a big hit especially with recreational cyclists. Imagine a ten-mile stretch of graveled bike path running through marshes and tidal flats with flocks of waterfowl and wide vistas across the water. Better yet, there are no cars and no uphill; it's all flat! That's my kind of bike ride.

Cyclists coming north on this wonderful trail cross through the Palo Alto Baylands, enter the promising-looking Ravenswood Open Space Preserve where the "whole-access" trail appears to continue north, but shortly they find themselves curling to the east and then to the south where the trail ends at an observation platform. What? Looking at a map, the frustrated cyclist can see that there are further sections of the Bay Trail open to the north, in Redwood City around Bair Island, but the only way to get there is back on the city streets. You can't get there from here, and it will be this way for a long time, as long as it takes the construction crews to finish the Hetch Hetchy project. The trail north needs to go straight through the middle of what is now the western terminus of the new tunnel under San Francisco Bay for the Hetch Hetchy aqueduct. It could take years, decades even, to turn this dotted line on the map into a solid one.

Meanwhile, politics and a lot of money from POST (Peninsula Open Space Trust) have transformed several old, disused salt flats to the north of Ravenswood into an extension of the Don Edwards National Wildlife Refuge. Huge bulldozers tore through the levees, scraped the saltpans and built artificial little islands as hoped-for shorebird sanctuaries, safe at high tide from four-footed predators. For now, the area still looks pretty shell-shocked, barren and sterile, but the tide comes in twice a day bringing new life and new hope.

In Ravenswood proper, federal Recovery Act dollars, awarded to the city of East Palo Alto, have recently transformed the weedy wilderness of Cooley Landing into the embryo of waterfront park. A century or more ago Cooley Landing was an important port for the transfer of redwood timbers from the Santa Cruz mountains to gold-rush San Francisco. Most of the port infrastructure was now long gone, but there remained an historic boathouse, as well as a mothballed dredge supposedly constructed from timbers salvaged from San Francisco after the earthquake and fire. (Funny to think that those dredge-construction timbers may have made a round trip to San Francisco and back!) The plan was to turn the old boathouse into an interpretive center and to possibly even have a boat launch for non-motorized craft. The first step has been to tear out nearly all the existing vegetation, including mature oak trees, and to cover the entire point of land with a five-foot thick cap of dirt. This little peninsula, Cooley Landing, had obviously been capped once before--the trees all sat five feet down inside rounded bowls—and even so the PCB count at ground level, the legacy of an old dump site, was said to be quite hazardous. So the capping really did have to be done. All the same, I was very sad to lose this little junkyard wilderness of dumped concrete mounded with thistle, mustard, fennel, and wild radish. There was a native gray fox den somewhere out there, probably in the maze of broken concrete. Over the years I had seen mama fox with various litters of darling puppies. Their habitat is now gone, transformed into another human playground, and around the extensive new parking lot, the human vegetation of choice has been planted: lawn grass.

I found a dead gray fox off the end of the levee trail in the new Don Edwards Wildlife Refuge just a week or so after they had finished bulldozing Cooley Landing. Its body was too far gone to tell how it had died, and I don't know that it was the same animal, but it just rubbed salt in the wound of my feeling of loss. I know I should be happy that Ravenswood is being cleaned up, improved, and made accessible for the local under-served human community, but the pre-existing wildlife community does not seem to have been as well served.

One really great aspect of the redevelopment project has been the automatic gate. No more driving 30 to 45 minutes each direction from Rancho just to lock the old gate to the preserve every evening, and, of course, another giant waste-of-time drive back the next morning just to open it up again. Patrol (rangers) and crew (OSTs) have shared this task for years, with crew opening the gate on weekday mornings and patrol handling all the gate closings and the weekends. It was a hassle and a drag on both teams. For a while, during my first couple years at the District, a caretaker lived out there in a trailer. He opened and closed the gate every day, shooed out the bums, and called the cops on the kids drinking beer and doing doughnuts in the parking lot. He picked up litter, watered his potted plants and mowed the entire landing every spring. We didn't know how good we had it until he left. The next caretaker was a troublemaker and a bum and caused more trouble with his troublemaker-bum friends out there than his minimal help with the gate was worth. When we finally managed to get rid of him and his dilapidated trailer, we gave up on having a caretaker.

Suddenly, with no one guarding it, the vandals and graffiti artists took over. The historic wooden boathouse, a building the size of a gymnasium, which was completely boarded up on the ground floor, was now constantly being broken into. Furthermore, since it sits on the strip of land in the middle of Cooley Landing which belongs to the City rather than the District, we would have to call East Palo Alto police to come out every time and take a vandalism report. East Palo Alto's public works department would eventually come and re-board it up. E.P.A. police usually wouldn't come. It was just one more abandoned building in a city of abandoned buildings, but it was scary for us patrolling out there in the menacing shadow of this huge, derelict boathouse. The cops said it was too far from town to attract the homeless, but we regularly found encampments under trees in the preserve, and the boathouse was a lot nicer than that, and not much farther out.

We had to get past the boathouse to go check on the historic dredge, which was on District land. The dredge, of course, was also constantly being broken into and re-boarded up, but by us, and in a more timely manner. The attractive nuisance value of a couple derelict structures a half-mile out a deserted dirt road from an impoverished community with high youth unemployment shouldn't be too surprising. All the same, it was the dredge that burned first. Why the arsonists didn't manage to get the boathouse at the same time is a mystery. The dredge burned completely; just the various metal bits were left sticking out of a pool of stagnant charred black water, where it had formerly floated. Now, without the dredge to check, we rangers had even less cause to go beyond the parking lot, and the poor old boathouse's slow slide into ruin accelerated. Every possible surface was covered with gaudy graffiti. All the windows and doors were smashed and broken and even some of the exterior walls were ripped open. In the summer of 2013, the boathouse fulfilled its destiny and, like the dredge, burned to the ground in an arson fire. The future interpretive center will be cheaper to construct and probably a more suitable size and shape, but will lack the old boathouse's connection to the past.

Although getting there is certainly a pain, I have always enjoyed patrolling Ravenswood. Evidently, along with everybody else, I too have crawled through the torn and cut chain link fence and accessed the slowly rotting redwood boardwalk under the line of PG&E towers along the edge of the bay. It is a little unnerving because the boardwalk is only two boards wide and sometimes one of the boards is missing and the remaining board bends down toward the dark mud five feet below as I approach the midpoint between the support pilings. Of course, that is part of what makes it an adventure, plus the additional uncertainty about whether I am even supposed to be out there. I also like to walk from the far observation platform out into the pickleweed and cordgrass at low tide. I bring a plastic garbage bag and my litter stick and follow the ribbon of debris left by the last high tide. Despite the debris, it is nice out there. I like squishing along alone, obsessively picking out bottle caps, tennis balls, and old sneakers while lapsing into a meditative state induced by the wide monotonous view of mud and waterline, the bowl of sky and clouds. It is quiet and peaceful, except for the sounds of wind and birds. It stinks slightly of rot, as a marsh should. I have never met anyone else out wandering along the boardwalks or through the tidal flats, but I have seen their footprints, between those of the harvest mice and the raccoons, and feel a little kinship with those other souls, human and otherwise, out in this lonely place, this marvelous, lonely place.

There are no dogs allowed at Ravenswood, and while I sometimes feel like I have to strain to explain to visitors why certain preserves should be closed to dogs, down here by the Bay, it seems like a no-brainer. Dogs chase birds. Every time I have been to Bair Island, just north of here outside Redwood City and part of the National Wildlife Refuge, my explanation has been reinforced. Dogs are allowed there, on leash, but I see unleashed dogs running wild everywhere, chasing each other, chasing balls and chasing birds. The pitiful remnant of the marshes of San Francisco Bay provide a crucial resting and feeding ground for migrating birds heading north and south on the Pacific flyway. They often arrive stressed and starving, and they don't need to be harassed by our pampered pets. So I should have no qualms about handing out dog tickets at Ravenswood, right?

Unfortunately, most of the visitors to Ravenswood are from East Palo Alto, and many of the residents of East Palo Alto are poor immigrants from Mexico, and South and Central America. While they might see the "No Dogs" picture sign, they certainly have no experience in their home countries with law enforcement actually dealing with the sort of minutia that is my bread and butter. They fail to realize that we are serious. I also find it hard to give $150 tickets to people who obviously have no money to spare and for whom taking a day off work to go to court means no money for dinner. I give out a lot of warnings.

Repeat offenders are another story. They have been warned already; they have been cited before, and here they are again. In one case, the repeat offender was a tall, handsome, young black man with two large, unfriendly, unleashed pit bulls. When I entered Ravenswood, I saw them coming toward me down the path and immediately called for East Palo Alto (EPA) police to assist. This guy wanted trouble. On his previous contacts with my co-workers, he had been derisive, arrogant, dismissive, and rude. I figured I would need backup. He didn't try to run or evade me, and he did leash his growling dogs, all the while reminding me that I was a racist pig and that the only reason I was citing him was because he was black. I was profiling him. I was harassing him, etc. He didn't want to give his name, but I already knew his name. EPA police were quickly on the scene—it's a tiny city and well patrolled— and the young blond cop seemed to recognize my offender, for whom she was all smiles. She gave me a rueful look when I explained the problem, then stood talking and laughing with the suspect while I filled out the citation, both of them giving me disdainful glances. It couldn't have been more obvious that she sided with the violator and was surely even telling him as much. After he signed his citation and left, she chewed me out for citing him. "These people have no other place to go. This is the only real, natural park anywhere around here. Where else are they supposed to go?" I was upset, of course, that she couldn't at all see my point about dogs chasing birds, but even more upset that she would so blatantly disrespect another peace officer right in front of a suspect. Really bad.

As a counterpoint, one of my early experiences with EPA police at Ravenswood stands out because of the officers' humane and professional conduct. I came to lock the gate one evening and found a beat-up old pickup in the parking lot absolutely jammed full of junk. I ran the license plate and it came back stolen. I retreated back to the entrance gate, a couple hundred yards away, to wait for EPA police. Then I saw a bedraggled young black woman coming up Bay Road toward the preserve carrying a small red plastic gas can, apparently empty. I got out to see what was up with her, and while trying to question her, it eventually dawned on me that she was our suspect! She was a mess, dirty, and unkempt and she kept breaking down and crying and complaining about all her problems, but not very coherently. Fortunately EPA got there in a minute or two and took charge. They made the connection to the stolen vehicle in no time. It turned out that the truck belonged to her sometimes boyfriend, but she had "stolen" it so many times before, i.e. taken it without his permission, that he had told her that the next time he was going to call the cops, and so he had. One of the officers patted her down, then cuffed her and tried to get her in the back of the patrol car, but she was crying now worse than ever, saying that the handcuffs were hurting her. The two cops had been very gentle and calm and quiet handling her, and now I was sort of startled and definitely impressed to see the sympathy and concern as they actually loosened the already not at all tight handcuffs. After she was in the car and they were making ready to take her away, one of the officers said, "Boy, she needs a hit bad." I, of course, hadn't recognized her behavior as that of someone in withdrawals, but they had. Given that, I was even more impressed by their professionalism.

A final favorite Ravenswood story comes from a very typical, and ultimately, completely uneventful afternoon when I arrived out at Ravenswood to clear the parking lot and lock the gate. As I approached the parking lot I could see that there was still at least one car to get rid of, and, as I got closer, I could see two teenage Hispanic boys with bicycles lounging on the bench near the lot. No helmets, of course. I parked and went to talk to them about the helmet regulation. They were clueless about the helmets, and they seemed intimidated by my presence. They probably didn't even own helmets. As I was talking to the boys, I saw two huge Tongan guys coming across the bridge from the near observation platform. They were, presumably, the owners of the vehicle here in the lot. As they got closer I saw that each huge man had a tiny Chihuahua on a thin pink leash trotting alongside. The mismatch of man and beast gave my funny bone a jolt, and the two Hispanic kids, following my gaze, shared my appreciation of the contrast. I went to talk to the Tongans, who had arrived in the parking lot. They claimed cluelessness about the dog prohibition, and at least the dog-lets were on leash, so I started filling out written warning forms. While I was doing that, and keeping an eye on the two teenagers still occupying the bench, I heard another car approaching rather slowly up the badly pot-holed gravel drive from the entrance gate, and turned to see a low-slung older model American sedan with two young black men inside. I stopped writing and watched as they circled twice through the parking lot, giving me, and the Tongan men, and Hispanic boys unblinking stares, their loud rap music thumping out their open windows. "I wonder what they are up to," I said aloud, shaking my head. "No good," said one of the men, "No good," and we all laughed. Another day in the neighborhood.

25. Oh Deer

I was pulling into work one day in my personal vehicle and met Ranger Matt accelerating down the office driveway looking excited and concerned. He slowed to a rolling stop and filled me in through the rolled down windows. It was a unique and bizarre situation: Two bucks had reportedly been fighting just off the trail in Rogue Valley and were now stuck together, unable to pull free of each other. Could I get changed and logged on with dispatch and then meet Conan (District resource management guy), and drive him out to where Matt would be standing by, waiting for CA Fish and Game halfway up Rogue Valley? You bet I could! This promised to be a very interesting incident. F&G pulled in right behind me and Conan; two wardens and their vehicles, with all their weapons and equipment. The bucks, both probably at least four pointers, were not more than 20 feet off the trail. One was now dead and was lying on its side on the ground. The second buck, who was still on his feet but looked exhausted, had one of his antlers caught in the corpse of his former opponent, and was still feebly jerking and twisting his head. I thought the antler was stuck in between a couple ribs, but, as it turned out, it was only caught in the skin. Conan and the two F&G guys hemmed and hawed over their options for a good quarter hour, but, amazingly, decided to try the most straightforward, if not exactly cautious, approach. Matt got video of the whole thing. One warden just walked quietly over, squatted, and sliced open the tough deer hide, freeing the antler. The live buck, now unrestrained and less than a foot away from the warden, pulled his head free and seemed to freeze for a second, looking quite confused and almost as though he was considering charging the warden, then turned and bounded away. Pretty gutsy move, Warden.

Aside from birds and bugs, deer have got to be the most commonly seen wildlife of the preserves. They are ubiquitous, year-round residents, so common a sight that I scarcely give them a second thought. It is always strange, therefore, to see foreign tourists carefully creeping forward toward a grazing deer herd busily taking pictures, or to hear the excited exclamations of a group of school kids as they see their first large wild animal. About the only time I pay much attention to the deer, other than as a food stuff for mountain lions, is when we have to find and count them for the annual deer survey. The best thing about the deer surveys is that the assigned ranger also gets a volunteer helper, who actually does most of the work. At least in my truck, the volunteer properly fills in all the persnickety little boxes on the form for every deer we see: where and when (obviously), sex, approximate age, and, if male, the number of "points" on his rack of antlers. Strangely enough, to my mind, when counting "points," you only count the bigger side. So, for example, if a buck has three points on one antler and four on the other, he is called a "four point buck." Why not a "seven point buck?" That is just how it's done. Every fall we meet our volunteers in the late afternoon and, at the appointed hour, we start driving slowly along our prescribed routes. We keep the windows down unless it is raining, and our eyes and ears open. As it gets darker and darker, we use the truck's spotlight and giant flashlights to find our subjects. The deer's big brown eyes reflect the light beams and look like two glowing white coals on the dark shape of their bodies, giving them an oddly sinister aspect. (Deer poachers also take advantage of this trait. They drive rural roads "spotlighting" or "glassing" for an easy kill.) My assigned volunteer and I mostly amuse ourselves quietly chatting. Sometimes we see other crepuscular critters; barn owls, striped skunks, woodrats, western toads and tarantulas have made the list of incidentals, and helped spice up a long, slow and usually rather cold evening in the truck. That's deer surveys. Next fall we do it all over again.

10-3-11: Rain! The first rain of the year and it's only the beginning of October. This is good. All that horrible dust is going bye-bye. The smell is wonderful, the smell of wet dust. I'm happy.

I'm meeting my volunteer for deer surveys at 1730. I imagine this rain will put a real damper on the number of deer we see. Oh well. A month ago there were so many bachelor bucks hanging out in the front meadow, really big guys showing off their antlers, mostly, it seems, to each other. Since the antler-stuck-in-the-dead-deer incident a few weeks ago, the group seems to have disbanded. Maybe that fight marked the actual start of rutting season. Maybe we should be doing these surveys a month earlier. Last year my volunteer and I saw only a couple deer all evening, which was disappointing and dull. This year could be worse, given the weather. Hopefully the volunteer is a good conversationalist. I really don't know the point of these surveys, other than just bean-counting curiosity, and I doubt it is even that. Probably something to do with CA Fish and Game and their selling of deer tags. I don't think the District is behind this. While I don't mind doing it, I do wonder if all this data ever gets put to any use.

26. Let it Snow

1-24-08: I went down and checked out the snow at Loma Prieta this morning. There was just a little along Summit, then it suddenly started getting thicker and thicker as I drove up Mt. Bache Road and Loma Prieta Way. I passed one near collision with one car off the road. I ignored the young men sledding down the snowy hillock just inside Gate SA32, which is clearly posted closed. Now, driving through unbroken powder, I made it up to the Mt. Madonna junction, where I turned to face downhill, and parked. It was still snowing, though not very hard, adding to the foot of snow already on the ground. It was foggy and dead quiet. I put on my gaiters and gloves and wooly cap and shuffled off through all this incredibly soft, dry, white snow up to the Loma Chiquita junction, enjoying the quiet, the solitude, and the beauty of a rare snowy day.

Every couple of years we get a winter storm cold enough and wet enough to drop snow in the Santa Cruz Mountains. Most winters, even when it might snow in the East Bay on Mt. Hamilton, the closest we get to snow is freezing rain. We're just too close to the coast. Actual snow on the ground is therefore exciting and wonderful, not just to me, but, seemingly, to every resident of the Santa Clara Valley. The usual paltry three to six inches doesn't last long once the clouds clear and the sun rises, so thousands of people apparently call in sick or skip class to go play in the snow while it lasts. By the time I get to work, get in the truck and get up the mountain on "snow patrol," the early birds have usually beaten me to it. The loveliness of the smooth, unblemished surface has already been destroyed. The precious few occasions of being first on scene of the fresh snow therefore stick in my memory.

"Snow patrol" can be kind of fun. Everyone is excited and happy. They are throwing snowballs and trying to build snowmen. Little kids jump and roll and stamp and curiously put snow in their mouths. Families show up with sleds and toboggans, but no hats or mittens. Visitors whom we would otherwise never see make their first visit to the mountains. A complete gridlock of parked vehicles, stuck vehicles and vehicles trying to turn around quickly develops at gate SA08 on Umunhum Road. Rangers spend their time doing traffic control, and opening and closing the gate to allow space for vehicles to turn around. Fortunately the snow often starts at right about the elevation of the gate, so the snow isn't terribly thick, just the traffic. I prefer Umunhum snow patrol to Loma Prieta snow patrol. We have no gate where our property starts on Loma Prieta Way, just big signs on either side of the road saying, "Area Closed. Resident and Authorized Vehicles Only." On snow days we station a ranger at this point, which is also the junction with Mt. Madonna Road and a broad flat with plenty of parking. But no snow. The snowline is usually about a quarter mile away up the road.

2/21/11:Loma Prieta at Mt. Madonna: Pretty warm compared to the past week or so when we had a winter storm come through. Most of the snow fell last week while I was on vacation, but it has continued cold and two days ago we got more snow on Umunhum and Loma Prieta, so have had rangers on "snow patrol" the last three days. At least we have gotten smarter and we are allowing people to park here and then walk up into the "closed area" to play in the snow. The problem is that people don't want to walk.

They see all the "resident" vehicles driving through and they want to do the same. At least the snow starts just above here. Engine 4 was stuck up at the five-way junction, at Loma Chiquita, when I got there. They too must have been out doing a lookie-loo at the snow. They had given up trying to extricate themselves and were waiting for another engine to come and pull them out, which I was amazed actually worked. I was sure they would have to bring in a bulldozer to get the engine out. Their right rear tires were completely off the road and sunk into the axles in the mud. The chief didn't look happy. I didn't stop to chat.

One snowy day some years ago, I got up to gate SA08 early enough that I wasn't really needed. There were only a half dozen cars so far, and I knew a second ranger was en route because we expected a big turnout. I grabbed my chance to drive up and check the base. The snow, just a couple inches thick at the gate, got thicker as I drove up the road, and shortly passed the visitors whose footsteps I'd been following. Continuing up, I started to realize that I should turn around because the snow was getting too deep for me to feel comfortable driving. Of course, there was no place to safely turn around and I would, instead, simply have to back up. Fortunately Larry appeared. I was so relieved to see him. He had his little snow plow mounted to the front of his pickup and was doing his civic service, as well as allowing his family to drive to and from their house. He was cheerful and talkative, seeming nearly as excited about the snow as any city dweller. Today he was wearing a big plaid jacket over his characteristic overalls. He said he had already plowed up to the yellow gate and now was working his way down. He backed up to a wide spot and we scooted past each other.

Parking where Larry had stopped plowing, I geared up to walk to the Airforce Base on the summit of Mt. Umunhum, hurrying so I wouldn't miss it. I didn't want anyone spoiling my special pleasure in walking up the road slowly and alone through the beautiful, unsullied snow. It was a bright blue morning, still well below freezing, but with very little wind and not a cloud in the sky. It must have been quite windy during the night, however, because, sticking out horizontally from every bare branch and every strand of wire was a matching icicle. The gray pines with their ten-inch long needles were surreally beautiful. The chain-link fence was an artwork of prisms and mirrors. Railings had icicles; the edges of buildings had icicles; twisted, mangled piles of debris had icicles. All the ugliness of the old base was hidden by snow and transformed by the ice. I shuffled forward very slowly, silently and peacefully, stunned by this ephemeral icy wonderland, my eyes agog, my mind Nirvana. An old ranger, her time mostly spent, wandering out into the deep cold snow, but not into the storm and not seeking death, but rather into beauty, and seeking life, beautiful life.

I pulled myself away and returned reluctantly to the truck. Someone had been there in my absence. Huge round footprints, the "M" shaped impressions of toe pads neatly incised in the soft snow, came out of the bushes below the road, circled my truck, and descended back into the bushes. A mountain lion. Cool. I will remember this day the rest of my life.

27. Search and Rescue

My first winter with the District, in 2002, was a wet one. It rained and rained and there were flooded roads and downed trees and mudslides, and we were kept busy clearing plugged culverts and fixing water bars. I was still quite new to the job and was not patrolling on my own yet, and so was riding around with Cory one evening when dispatch called with a report of a bicyclist who had been swept off his feet and carried downstream while trying to cross the creek in Stevens Canyon. It sounded like he had managed to save himself and get across the creek but was now stuck on the far side. His friends, who were calling in the report, were going to make their way back up the Canyon Trail and not try to follow him across, but they were worried about their friend soaking wet and possibly injured, stuck on the far side of the creek in a driving rainstorm with night falling. Cory and I headed for the end of the canyon along with every CDF, County Fire, County Parks, and SO unit in the vicinity. What a mess! All those vehicles and personnel stampeding up to the washed-out bridge at the end of the road. The bridge had washed out a few weeks earlier, meaning that all the would-be rescuers were stranded, with their rescue vehicles and rescue gear, on the east bank of the creek, while our victim was reportedly on the west bank, on the other side of 50 feet of angry churning water. Now what?

As a complete neophyte, I was in the fortunate position of not having to make that decision. I could just stand around in my rubber boots and banana slug raingear and wait to be told what to do. I remember Tony was on scene and he sent one of the rangers back to the office to get the ATV to patrol up the Charcoal Road, which ascended Skyline Ridge on the far side of Steven's Creek. Charcoal Road's bridge, somewhat farther down the canyon had not yet washed out. Maybe the stranded guy would think to make his way over to Charcoal Road. Then Tony detailed Cory and me to patrol up along the east bank of the creek, without trying to cross, looking to see if we could find the guy or find some other way across the water. We loaded up and headed out into the night and driving rain. We crossed through the yard of the final house on our side of the torrent, then plunged into the undergrowth and fallen branches of the thick redwood and douglas fir forest. The embankment was muddy and slick as were all the branches and brambles, and the slope under our feet was getting steeper as we progressed. We couldn't see a thing beyond the tiny beams of our flashlights and almost certainly could not have yelled loud enough to be heard over the thunder of the rain and the booming of the river. This was great, I thought, this is what this job is all about—rescuing people trapped by adverse circumstances. I bet I'll be doing this all the time. It was fun being part of a rescue, getting to participate, even though my part was so tiny and rather silly and entirely futile.

Cory and I were soon soaked through, and well before our imposed time limit was up, we came to the point where the cliff of the long-ago landslide dived straight into the roiling water of the creek, and we turned around. On our way back to the Incident Command Post, we came upon the homeowner of the last private in-holding of the canyon, who asked us what was up.

We quickly explained the predicament. "Would you like to use my bridge?" he asked. What?! "Yeah, it's just a little foot bridge, but it is still up. If that would be of help..." How could we have missed seeing this? How could we have not known about this? When we got back to the IC with the neighbor, it turned out that other rescuers had independently discovered the bridge just minutes before. So now, perhaps several hours after the original call, with the access problem solved, a rescue party, not including me, was assembled to go hike up the far bank and bring back our presumably badly injured, hypothermic and helpless victim.

They found him just a few minutes up the other side, striding along, heading out. He would have been out sooner, he explained, except that he had spent some time searching for his expensive bicycle, which had been torn from his grip in the current and washed downstream. He was fine, wasn't hurt, didn't need any help, but could use a ride back out to his car, if that would be all right. So the finale to our big rescue was pretty anti-climactic. County Roads replaced the washed out bridge the following year with a monstrous structure that looked fit to withstand the 100-year flood, just to save all us professional rescuers from future embarrassment at our inability to cross swollen rivers, I suppose, since there are no further homes higher up the canyon. The victim's bicycle was never found; it's still out there somewhere cemented into the creek bed or at the bottom of Stevens Canyon Reservoir.

We had more recent and also weather-related search and rescue job in February of 2011. George, my West Valley College Intern, and I had been on "snow patrol" all day up at the residence gate on Umunhum Road, basically doing traffic control and helping people turn around in the six inches of snow. I was already tired from hours of cheerfully helping under-prepared visitors negotiate the strange white stuff, and assisting my intern, whose combination of unbridled enthusiasm and know-it-all bravado were starting to get on my nerves. Then about seven p.m., with the afternoon coming to a close, and darkness impending, came in this call to aid three young men lost and off trail in Sierra Azul. One of them had a working cell phone and had managed to get out a call to 911 before losing contact. They were reportedly parked at Kennedy Road, so George and I headed over to the Kennedy trailhead, found their truck, ran the plates and checked out the interior. (Why run the plates? Why check the interior? No particular reason. Just being thorough, since we had so little else to go on.) The dirt patrol road heading up the ridge was slippery on the frozen mud under the fresh layer of snow, but it was wide and pretty well graded and we continued on up as night descended.

Meanwhile, Rangers Henry and Gabe loaded up the motorcycles and headed for the Incident Command now being established at Alma Bridge Road at the bottom of the Priest Rock Trail. Rangers Tina and Patty came all the way down from Skyline and went to check the Woods Trail starting at Jacques Ridge. Thick snow halfway up El Sombroso, despite the truck's "snow and mud" tires, stopped them. George and I made it up just past the Priest Rock Trail junction in about a foot of snow before I chickened out and turned back. George looked more nervous and apprehensive than I, but, of course, wasn't going to say so and was urging me on, "but only if you think it is safe."

Back at the Priest Rock junction we met up with Henry and Gabe on the motorcycles. They were struggling through the snowdrifts on the small motorcycles and had almost quit, but they wanted to reach us. They too tried to continue across the ridge to El Sombroso, but were stymied. So we had now checked all the drivable roads of Sierra Azul, and had seen neither hide nor hair of our lost guys. It really did look pretty hopeless. What

would be the point in checking them over and over again? Poor
Zack was doing a stint as Acting Supervisor that month and was
down at the incident command post on Alma Bridge along with
the full complement of Sheriffs and County Fire and so forth.
Who knows what they were doing. There was nothing left to do.
How were we supposed to find these guys after dark, off trail, in
steep brushy terrain in the snow? It was stupid. Some would-be
rescuer was going to get themselves lost or hurt.

Then we heard that we had a CDF helicopter en route.
Okay, that might work. Then we heard it had broken down.
Then there was an hour or so of sitting on our hands, the four
of us (me, George, Henry and Gabe) stuffed into the cab of my
truck trying to stay warm, while we were "standing by." Then
we heard we had a CHP helicopter en route from Napa. Once
the helicopter arrived on scene, the search part was over in 15
minutes. They had found them. Unbelievable, but true. One of
the lost guys, upon hearing the helicopter overhead, had thought
to hold up to the sky the only source of light they had, the lighted
screen of his cell phone, which the spotter on the copter saw.
Their spotlight revealed three young men a half-mile off trail,
down in a steep gully off the side of the ridge on which runs the
Priest Rock Trail.

Communicating with me and the other rangers in the patrol
truck by radio on the mutual aid channel, the spotter directed
us down the Priest Rock Trail to a spot directly above the three
men. Using the copter's loudspeaker, the spotter was able to
direct them up the side of the ridge toward the truck before the
chopper ran short on fuel and had to leave. There had been
a lot of relief and excitement when the guys had been found
and while we were getting positioned. All of a sudden there
was a plan and we felt like we knew what we were doing and
things seemed to be under control. There was some inevitable

confusion about using the mutual aid channel, of course. Was everyone now supposed to get on the mutual aid channel, or was it supposed to be exclusively for communication with the helicopter? For example, if I had a question for the IC, was I supposed to switch back to the District primary channel, or stay on the Mutual Ad channel? Incidents of this sort, when we are working with several different agencies—the very sort of multiple-agency response incidents that mutual aid radio frequencies are designed to handle-- don't come up that often and every situation is novel, so patience and professionalism are important. This was only time I have ever worked with a CHP helicopter and I was very impressed with their crew.

Once the helicopter left we suffered a would-be dark and silent hour of waiting while our lost guys presumably made their way toward us crawling through the brush up the steep snowy hillside. It was frustrating because we couldn't communicate and didn't know if they were still making progress, but the IC kept calling demanding updates. We, of course, had the truck's spotlight and the truck's loudspeaker, but we didn't know if these were audible or visible to the hikers. There was some strong muttering in the cab, especially from George, about mounting a rescue party to go out on foot looking for them. Why were we just sitting here? We should go out and look for them, etc. We flashed our lights, ran bursts on the siren, and called encouragement on the loudspeaker, but heard no response from out of the dark. George kept hopping on and off the truck bed calling out into the night and waving the handheld spotlight. Finally, just as the re-fueled helicopter reappeared, three soaking wet young men crawled out of the chaparral and, it was over.

They weren't injured; they weren't even hypothermic, not after a half-mile climb straight uphill through the brush. All the same, the medics were waiting down at the Kennedy Road trailhead to check them out. Just a lot of scratched limbs, and the next day, undoubtedly, three horrible cases of poison oak. Why had they gone off trail in the first place? Their story was that the snow down in the gully had looked so much deeper and thicker than the thin stuff up on the windblown ridge top. And then, once they had slid and jumped all the way down in there, climbing out had looked so awfully difficult, that, compounding their first bad decision with another, they had tried to make their way down canyon. Their little caper cost a lot of local agencies a lot of money in fuel and overtime, but at least it had a happy ending. I can now tell the entertaining story of the three stupid young men who got themselves lost in the snow, rather than the sad tale of finding their frozen bodies three days later.

Technically, search and rescue events fall under the prevue of the Sheriff's Office. When we have a missing person reported, especially a missing child or a mentally or medically compromised adult, after doing a cursory search of their vehicle (if any), their last reported location, and the area in-between, we will usually call for the SO to respond and take over. Ninety percent of the time the "lost" people are "found," or they turn up back at their car on their own, long before we even get around to calling the Sheriff. Some "lost" people don't even realize they are supposed to be "lost" and that their loved ones are panicking, and four or five rangers are en route to look for them. Their route might have taken them much longer than they anticipated, and they were unable to get out on their cell phone to call their anxious friend or relative. Like medical calls, lost person calls are another potentially applicable time for the weekend OST adage, "Respond slowly. Maybe it will be over by the time you get there."

Mini-searches for separated members of hiking parties are a nearly weekly occurrence at Rancho. Invariably, just when

I'm about to set out on a nice quiet foot patrol somewhere in the boonies, some kid will go missing at Rancho between the Farm and the parking lot and I will have to return to my truck and return to Rancho to go search. Quite often the person is located before I even make it back off the freeway. Finding a truly lost and scared child should be very gratifying, but often the kid is oblivious of their "lost" status, simply waiting quietly where they thought they had been told to wait. They are sometimes more scared of being in trouble with their parents than they are worried about any danger they may have been in.

Cell phones have just about eliminated the job of the county sheriff's volunteer search and rescue teams and their affiliated ham radio operators. Cell phone coverage and certainly satellite phone coverage is now so universal that a lost or injured hiker can simply call for rescue themselves, directly from their location. No need any more to make a difficult decision about whether to try to have the injured trip member hobble out on a badly sprained ankle or, alternatively, have everyone sit tight while sending out for rescue, (which, on an extensive backpacking trip could be a multi-day process.) Just dig out the phone, punch in the magic number and in an hour or so the helicopter, or truck, or wheel litter will appear and solve the problem for you.

Who needs those Ten Essentials anymore—map, compass (what's that?) extra clothes, raingear, extra water, whistle, water purification, fire starter, flashlight, extra batteries, matches, etc. All you really need is a phone. Oh, and a GPS device, and a SPOT device, and a pedometer. Why not? All this technology will surely spare the modern-day hiker from the need to actually know how to read a map, or to know the name of the park they are in, or the name of the trail, or the land management agency or the county... Does knowledge of such information really matter any more? After all, it's right here in my iPhone. I can just look it up…oops no reception. I just click on this icon and … oops, low battery. Damn!

A working phone is a godsend in the event of a serious or life-threatening injury in the backcountry, but it's a plague in the front country. Hikers in no danger of expiring from heat, cold, thirst, or exhaustion have phoned in for us to come get them. I certainly don't mind giving first aid or a ride out to some sufferer I happen upon while patrolling, but I do think that many visitors are all too quick to reach for their phones at the first hint of danger or suffering. How about planning ahead and preparing?

Search and rescue team members are the polar opposite of the un-prepared cell-phone dependants. These are the guys loading up in the parking lot for a ten-mile day hike with enough equipment for a mountaineering expedition. Yes, they have all the tech devices, but also a full complement of survival gear, and well-stuffed first aid kits, "just in case…" They have an emergency action plan and a leader and a sweep. They know the mileage and the elevation gain and the water sources. They've all certified in wilderness first aid as well as hundreds of hours of training in low-angle rescue and man tracking and grid search techniques. They are falling over themselves in their readiness to help that lost and injured someone. I feel bad for them. Like us rangers, by the time they assemble and organize and report to an incident, the action can be almost over. While I have occasionally ended up at "staging," standing around together with S&R volunteers waiting for deployment, I can recall only one event when we actually ended up working together.

I think it started in the morning when rangers found a vehicle still parked in the Purisima Creek parking lot from the night before. They did an ATC (attempt to contact) based on the information from the license plate and eventually ended up making contact with the parents of the registered owner of the vehicle. The missing person, a young woman, was potentially suicidal; she had attempted suicide before. By the time I made it up to the IC in the Purisima Creek parking lot, it was late afternoon and other searchers had already checked the preserve trails and roads at least once. San Mateo County Sheriff was on scene with their incident command operations bus, as well as the Sheriff's volunteer search and rescue team, including several dogs trained to sniff out and find missing people. Around dinnertime the Red Cross showed up with free food and hot coffee for all the participants. With all these rescuers and all these different agencies, the scene could easily have become chaotic, but because the incident had evolved slowly at first, with new rescuers reporting over the course of the day, and because the weather was fine, a cold and clear January day, communication and organization were easier. Naturally there was still a lot of standing around and waiting.

Eventually I got assigned to a team of "man-trackers" and we got sent to re-check the entire length of the Purisima Creek Trail. This being mid-winter, it was already cold and dark by the time we started, and it got colder and darker as we descended into the canyon. We went slowly, closely checking for correct-sized footprints and looking for places where someone appeared to have left the trail. We called the missing girl's name and shined our flashlights up into the trees. Given this girl's history, I was really hoping not to find anything, and I didn't think we would. After all, this trail had already been checked once in the daylight. The best hope at this point, I figured, would have been the dogs, and our team didn't have one. The night was cold, well below freezing, and I got uncomfortable every time we stopped to investigate a side creek or deer trail. Our lost girl, if alive, must surely be unconscious with hypothermia, no matter how warmly dressed. Hours later, around midnight, we reached the bottom of the trail and were picked up by a van. After driving all the way back up through Half Moon Bay to the parking lot on Skyline Boulevard, we were released. I still had to return my patrol truck to the Foothills Field Office and then drive home, so it was almost the next morning by the time I got to bed. Other rangers worked almost two days straight on this incident, catching a few hours of sleep in their patrol trucks. The search continued, in a reduced fashion, all the next day, wrapping up only at dark. We didn't find the girl, or any sign of her.

The next morning, two full days and three nights after her car had first been seen in the parking lot, the girl came walking up the trail. Ranger Bart happened to be walking down the trail and met her. She was lightly dressed and not wearing shoes and it took a minute for him to realize who she was. I think speculation about where she could have been all that time centered on a small shrubby hollow, not far from the parking lot, that the dogs had been interested in, and which later seemed likely from the vague directions the victim was able to provide. Fire medics, of course, came and checked her out and she was fine—cold, hungry and thirsty, but not hypothermic. How is that possible? How could she have missed all the commotion of the search if she was that close? Had she been in a drug-induced coma? How could we have missed finding her less than a half mile from the IC? Here's the real lesson of this incident, I would say: finding lost, unresponsive people in thick woods is well neigh impossible, and human searchers would do well to really trust, and believe in, the testimony of the dogs.

28. Volunteer Projects

7-16-11: Ravenswood: Preserve Partner volunteer project here today, repainting the observation platforms, or at least the far one. I also did this the last time, a couple years ago, and we only got to the near one, plus the far one has some graffiti on the deck I'd like to hit. I drove out there last week and blasted it with the fire pumper to knock off some of the loose paint and old spider webs. (Later) Project only lasted a half day and was all crew leaders, so they were all clued in and hard working. We ran out of paint. It didn't seem like most surfaces had ever seen more than one coat of paint, which is odd, because I think we have a platform-painting project out here every other year. As with any painting job, most of the time is spent prepping. Since we finished early, I walked some of the braver souls out across the pickle weed to the tidal channel. It was low tide and hardly muddy at all. They had no idea it was walk-able, and had imagined it would be a lot squishier.

One fun way to work in the Open Space without having to quit your day job is to be a volunteer. I will almost certainly return to being a District volunteer after I retire, maybe as a Preserve Partner or a Trail Patrol Volunteer, although probably not as a volunteer working in the Administrative Office, bless those guys' hearts. When I was hired as a ranger, District policy required that I quit my docent position with the Spaces and Species program up at Alpine Pond at the Daniels Nature Center. No double dipping, I guess. I therefore promptly signed up to be a guide with Hidden Villa's Farm and Wilderness program. Both programs offer nature knowledge field trips to elementary school aged children, and they depend on volunteers with kid-friendly interpretive skills. I volunteer at Hidden Villa (a wonderful place in Los Altos Hills with a summer camp and a Community Supported Agriculture program, and a social justice agenda, which you can read more about online) every other Thursday during the school year. Maybe when I retire I will make it every week, like the other amazing, talented, inspired and fun-loving people I work with there.

Those adjectives would pretty well describe the character of your average District volunteer as well, which is why I think all rangers love volunteer projects. What would you rather do: drive around in a truck by yourself all day looking for off-leash dogs and writing tickets, or spend the day with a bunch of friends getting the invasive broom out of a meadow while sharing stories and swapping wisecracks? Eat a solitary sandwich in the cab of your truck, or share a social meal, including snacks provided by Mac, the District's amazing, super-human volunteer coordinator?

The Preserve Partners program is the District's volunteer trail crew. They have a couple of projects scheduled every month, building split-rail fences and retaining walls, clearing slough and building "burritos" to improve the trail bed, planting and watering native plants, constructing and installing tree cages to protect baby oaks, and lots and lots of pulling broom. Outside groups such as churches and schools and scouts also call up Mac wanting to volunteer, and he finds projects for them. Although new people sign up or show up at almost every project, many of these guys have been at it for years and are mutual friends. Many long-standing Preserve Partners have gone on to be trained as Crew Leaders, meaning that they get additional training in maintenance skills and safety concerns and Workers'

Compensation procedures. Other long-timers go on to be ARMS volunteers (Advanced Resource Management Squad). This status gives them the right to operate independently. They can adopt a broom patch in a preserve of their choice and have at it any time they want. We issue them a weed wrench and a parking pass and they can schedule their own volunteer projects, including, however, only other ARMS volunteers.

5-8-05: Yesterday was fun. I had a volunteer project pulling broom at St. Joseph's Hill. I restricted myself to pulling the really little stuff, avoiding the weed wrenches altogether, trying to spare my back. No problem as there was plenty of broom of all sizes. The three teenage girls here to fulfill their service hours required by their high school were all but useless. Weren't they embarrassed to just sit listlessly chatting while others worked? Of course, the dad chaperoning them did the same thing. One of the docents came out at lunch and gave a talk on the history of the Los Gatos area, particularly the towns of Lexington and Alma that got drowned by Lexington Reservoir. I thought he did a good job, and some of the other volunteers also seemed interested, but the three girls looked completely bored. Other than my frustration with them, I had a good day.

Aside from the Preserve Partners, most of the volunteers we see or hear from are with the Volunteer Trail Patrol (VTP). These come in four varieties—foot, horse, bike, and dog. They complete a lengthy training to learn some basics about the District's lands and its mission, its funding and its organizational structure. They also learn how to confront visitors who are breaking the rules. The volunteers who will be patrolling with their animal or machine get special training to make sure they are able to handle their horse or dog or bike while dealing with a violator. Back in my bike patrol days I got to help once or twice with the horse VTP training. It takes a very calm, mild-mannered, and well trained horse to be able to safely ride the crowded trails at Rancho or Fremont Older. In particular, these animals have to be able to tolerate speeding bicycles whizzing past them from behind. Most horses (and people) don't like this. My part in the training was to hide behind the water tank with my bicycle and then come from behind and pass the horses. Other rangers, Lars, I think, have helped out with the general VTP training, and Matt has helped with the dog-walking volunteers.

VTP training grads are issued a nice nameplate, a T-shirt, a District ballcap, and a really dorky looking vest. The vests look like the pinnies we used to have to wear for team sports in high school. Aside from seeing the volunteers out in the preserve, and stopping to chat for a while, we mostly hear from them via messages left on the field office answering machine, where they report maintenance concerns—downed trees, plugged culverts, broken fence rails. With more pressing concerns, such as medicals or suspicious circumstances, they are supposed to call directly to Mountain View Dispatch.

Another group of volunteers, the docents and Outdoor Education Leaders, lead all the District's interpretive programs: the school field trips, the scheduled nature hikes open to the general public, and the informal drop-in times at the Daniels Nature Center on summer weekends. I rarely run into any of these guys, partially because of the concentration around Russian Ridge and Skyline Ridge and the Nature Center, and partially because many of the hikes are on weekends, days when docents know better than to schedule hikes in "the core" --Rancho, Fremont Older, and Pichetti, the preserves where I spend most of my time—because the parking will be a problem.

One of my favorite volunteer projects is the Earthday wildflower survey in Sierra Azul. We tramp around the same four routes, year after year, identifying and recording the plants in bloom. Thank goodness some of the interpretive docents turn out for this volunteer project, because the level of botanical knowledge required often exceeds my own and that of many of the usual trail crew volunteers.

Sam, the weekend OST, is undoubtedly the field staff member who knows the volunteers the best. He works all weekends and is assigned to all volunteer project out of the Foothills office. During the week, many of his days are given over to preparing for the upcoming weekend volunteer project: surveying the site, buying the materials, and loading the truck. While I may be assigned to just one or two volunteer projects a year, and greatly look forward to each of them, for Sam they are just another day at the office. He's probably pulled more broom than any other District employee.

One of the most disastrous and thus most memorable volunteer projects I can recall was a fence installation project on the north side of the Wildcat Loop Trail in Rancho. The north side of the Wildcat Loop is a series of long, well-graded switchbacks. There is something about long, well-graded switchbacks that ignites impatience and frustration in the human heart. When running downhill, seemingly zigzagging endlessly back and forth, a runner, looking downhill, can see below him the trail coming back the other way. Rather than finishing the switchback, going all the way to the pointy end and making the sharp turn, the runner might instead leave the trail and cut straight downhill, "cutting" the switchback. This is such a pervasive practice that, in well-used parks, the ends of nearly all the switchbacks are cut off with little cheater trails. That is why you often see a short stretch of fence on the outside of the trail for the last 20 or 30 feet leading up to a switchback. We're trying to keep the people on the trail. Otherwise the whole stretch of hillside becomes a wide, denuded, and eroded running track.

So, on the day of our project we headed out to put in four or five pressure-treated four-by-four posts and bolt split rails between them to prevent further switchback cutting on one of these eroded corners. It looked like a fun project to my crew of volunteers; at least it didn't involve broom. I started hiking up the trail from Rogue Valley with most of the volunteers carrying shovels, digging bars, clamshells and Seymours (clever hinged devices for scooping loose dirt out of the bottom of deep, narrow postholes.) We were to measure and mark where the posts would stand, and start digging the holes. Meanwhile Sam, after waiting for a few stragglers still walking in from the permit parking lot, would drive the toter slowly up the trail. The toter has two rubber treads, like a bulldozer. You steer it by gripping hard with either your right or left hand to apply the breaks to the corresponding tread. It's not that hard once you get used to it, but it takes concentration. You really have to pay attention because the velocity is pre-set and all you are doing is steering, trying to keep the toter in the middle of the trail.

The toter today was loaded with all the split rail fence building stuff: the electric drill and portable generator, the case of drill bits, the eight-inch bolts and their nuts and washers, the Sawsall and extra blades, tape measures, post levels, a chainsaw for cutting the rails to fit, chaps, helmet, extra chain, and more. Piled around of all this, and held down with straps, were the posts and rails.

My crew arrived at the work site and began measuring three eight-foot segments and digging with two people on a hole, trading off rock barring and scooping. The ground was really rocky, and progress was slow. I went back to see what was keeping Sam. as the other volunteers had now arrived. He was struggling to keep the toter balanced on the uneven trail with the large, ungainly load, but we were almost there, so we continued. I can't remember what caused it, whether one of the long rails hit a tree, or Sam just got distracted, but just one switchback short of the worksite, the toter got too far over to the side of the trail, balanced on the lip for a second, and then rolled over. Everything came unstrapped, and all the contents spilled out and slid down the hillside and sifted down into the duff. No one was hurt, but everyone abandoned digging holes and came to help clean up the mess. The worst clean-up chore was finding and collecting all the spilled nuts and washers. Four or five of the men, working together, managed to upright the toter and get it back on the trail. Nothing was broken; everything was all right, so we went back to work, but we had lost at least an hour. We were now short of time to finish the project and there was a sense of urgency.

After levelling and tamping in the first three posts, and marking and starting to dig the next three, we discovered that not one of the rails we'd brought was actually eight feet long. They were all seven feet nine inches or seven feet ten inches. Oh no. Now what? Should we go back to the pile of rails in the yard and see if we could find some slightly longer ones? No, there wasn't time. Should we somehow try to fudge the error by drilling the bolt holes at an extreme angle? No, that would not be acceptable; it would look shoddy. With resignation we started to dig out the posts we had just planted, just as it started to drizzle. We got a couple of new holes dug before we gave up; I seem to recall that some other foreseeable and un-accounted-for measuring error showed up, sapping the last of our resolve. We felt very foolish. What a waste of time. We decided to carry out the rails and posts so as not to overload the toter again; at least we had learned that much. After finally deciding to start, the toter made it halfway down the hill before running out of gas. Maybe it had leaked some fuel while it was upside down. It was just the final blow to the most miserable and frustrating volunteer project ever. Everyone knows the story.

29. South Area Outpost

11-21-07: Alma Bridge Road, Gate SA19

I was surprised to hear at the staff meeting today that the District is purchasing some property here on Alma Bridge Road, the Beatty property, which has a nice big flat, where we might build the long-awaited "South Area Office." I thought they were looking to put it in Bear Creek Redwoods, maybe at the site of the old seminary buildings, where Governor Jerry Brown was a student in the 1950's. I do agree that Alma Bridge would be the better spot as far as getting on Highway 17 and over to Hicks, but not so great if I wanted to get up to Summit, since you can't go south on 17 without first driving all the way around the reservoir. Bernie said he wants to see this office operating at least out of portables within two years. I don't. I know I live in denial, but I really don't see the huge need for a South Area Office. The main argument in favor is that it would cut response times. I don't care about that. To me an hour's wait is reasonable. Why do we have to have instant response? My real concern, of course, is greedy: I don't want to lose my own patrol access to the southern part of the District.

As it turned out, Bernie got his wish. Officially called the South Area Outpost, it operates entirely under Bernie's auspices out of the Foothills Field Office. It didn't end up on the Beatty property or at Bear Creek Redwoods, but just off Hicks Road in Sierra Azul, in the former landlord's house next door to Cory's ranger residence. Bernie's time frame was only off by two years, twice as long as promised, but not bad by District standards.

3-15-11: The SAO is now up and running, at least sort of. Tony couldn't get my evaluation to print yesterday, to his immense frustration, so he had to email it to me at FFO to print. I guess the phones there keep going out too. The place really is a pit—a tiny two-room shack over 80 years old with additional rooms progressively tacked on with low ceilings that sag in the middle, floors that bow and wave, bubbly linoleum, ancient cupboards, and a cracked and calcified shower stall. I know crew has supposedly been down there this last month, but all work looks to be outside, brush clearing and a new sidewalk up to an old shed that is the new "wet room." A new coat of paint would really help, especially inside.

Cory and his wife and kids moved out within the month. It was just too great a loss of privacy having their front door now just yards away from the new field office, with patrol trucks and personal vehicles coming and going at all hours seven days a week. They bought a house down in Morgan Hill. Cory, Sandy, Chantal, Terry and Tony moved to the new southern digs. Zack, Henry, Lars, Matt, Bart and I remained at FFO. Although still officially in the Foothills patrol district, standard operating procedure now specified that the FFO would patrol just Rancho, Fremont Older, Pichetti, Pulgas, and Ravenswood, while the SAO would patrol all of Sierra Azul, St. Joseph's Hill, Bear Creek Redwoods and El Sereno. I was not a happy camper. I was largely cut off from the wild and wooly south and restricted to tame and boring Rancho and environs. Even worse, I had chosen my torture. We had been given the choice—in order of seniority-- of staying at the FFO or moving to the SAO. I just couldn't justify the time and gasoline to drive all the way to Hicks Road every day, almost an hour each way, when I could continue to report to Rancho. Bernie got his wish and I was screwed.

3-19-11: Given the new SAO, the preserve assignments also had to be redone so that rangers assigned to the north, like me, wouldn't be assigned to a southern preserve, like El Sereno. I put down Pichetti as my first choice, although I felt guilty taking it away from Henry again, but then it went to Lars! Lars got both Pichetti and Pulgas, "because he asked for them." I got Windmill Pastures and Stevens Creek Nature Study Area, two areas without any action at all. This just gives more ammunition to my thoughts of moving to Skyline. I talked to Lane about it. He's been down here playing supervisor for the last three weeks since Bart is still out on sick leave. He pointed out a couple of other factors to consider in my decision. I would probably have to switch days off since the only one willing to trade to FFO was Tina, who has Monday and Tuesday off instead of my Thursdays and Fridays. The Skyline rangers have some crazy handshake agreements about the schedule, resulting in a rigid structure of lates and earlies that could interfere with my swimming, and, finally: it is a lot longer drive up to Skyline.

A little wheeling and dealing and I got Pichetti back from Lars. I had been working on eliminating the Italian thistle on the Zinfandel Trail for a few years and felt committed to my project. I could always have pulled thistle in Lars' preserve, of course. It's amazing how petty one gets during a time of perceived loss and shortage. Meanwhile I asked Bernie about how to get moved to the Skyline Field Office (SFO).

3-28-11: I talked to Bernie this morning about moving to SFO. He advised against it. His main argument was that I would be bored and lonely because there are so few visitors up there. He had worked up there and couldn't wait to leave. Maybe he thinks I'm more of an extrovert than I think I am. After a whole day working at Rancho, I'm tired. Being "on" all the time—friendly, receptive and engaged, is an effort. It doesn't feel false or fake, just tiring. I'm just as happy pulling broom.

It was flattering to have both Bernie and Tony begging me to stay at FFO, but the lure of SFO was strong. I had been a ranger for almost nine years and had barely scratched the surface of Skyline. Theoretically, rangers are interchangeable. Superintendents can borrow and swap rangers to fill for one another when one or the other area is short. We are also expected to have a reasonable knowledge of the SFO lands in case we get called up there for a medical or a search or a fire, but in fact, I get lost or get the truck stuck almost every time I visit, because I don't know which roads are actually drivable, and I don't know my way around. Skyline Rangers have the same problems when called down into the FFO lands. Then an opportunity arose to go to SFO for three weeks while one of their rangers was down at FFO playing supervisor. It was perfect timing. Here are a series of log entries from that period:

4-24-11: Easter Sunday and I am finishing my first week on Skyline. I am testing the waters, considering changing offices. I've actually been having a real good time, doing a lot of foot patrol and seeing a lot of new country. Everything is very green. I know a lot of that is because it is spring, and it is also green in the Foothills area, but the lushness of the mountains and particularly the coastside are extraordinary. Yesterday I was down in the western part of Purisima Creek and then came back up Lobitas Ridge onto Irish Ridge and then on out "King's Grove," which it turns out is an "emergency use only" access. Ignorance is bliss; it made a nice loop. There is a little community in the Irish Ridge area with an organic farm and little fields of green with furry, lichen-encrusted fences. So very idyllic, I thought I was in Ireland. Then today Tina and I did a foot patrol in La Honda Creek. It was totally foggy and misty and the road was obliterated by long lush grass. We got lost in the fog. I felt like Sherlock Holmes out on the moors.

4-25-11: Another awful weather day here on Skyline. It is misting heavily and visibility is about 100 yards. It is sunny and warm down in Foothills. I went to Coal Creek and hiked the Crazy Pete's Loop, plus the Alpine Road Bypass. This whole thing seems like a horrible mess to me. Alpine Road washed out in the early 1990s and San Mateo County never fixed it. Meanwhile, the bicyclists started making a use trail around the slide, so when we bought the land, we had this horrible un-planned use trail already in place and, rather than shut it down and build a real trail, we made it a designated trail. Meanwhile, the bits of old Alpine Road above and below the "bypass" are still considered San Mateo County road and we are told not to cite on them. "Dirt Alpine" is actually still in pretty good shape, but the bypass is a disaster—a miserably steep, slimy, muddy gully. Ranger Gabe recently led a volunteer project to close off some of the use trails the bikers have cut in addition to the official bypass. He seemed pretty discouraged about the whole thing.

5-18-11: Rancho, top of the PG&E Trail: From here I look down over the mega-city of the greater Bay Area, with the shrunken puddle of San Francisco Bay in the middle. There are a lot of trees, it is true, down there in the suburbs, but they are all unnatural. That flatland used to be marshes and savannahs. At night the extent of the city is more evident; the whole flatland is a blaze of lights. Turn 180 degrees and look west and from the vista points along Skyline Boulevard you see no urban area, no lights at all except for a few giant turd-houses calling attention to themselves on the ridges. Your eye is pulled to the ocean, which looks so huge and grand and close.

In the end, after a lot of vacillation and endless discussion, I ended up staying put in the Foothills office. I still have many regrets, and part of me still wants to go. I feel like a coward and an old stick-in-the-mud and keep thinking about what I have given up. I want to walk again through those meadows of long green grass hung with mist. I long to go exploring up more of those creeks through silent cathedrals of pillar-like redwoods and massive Douglas firs. Maybe because of the thick forests of tall trees, coupled with the frequently foul and foggy weather, my general impression of Skyline is of intimacy, of close-up views of droplet covered moss and tiny colorful mushrooms. This parade of delicate close-ups is then suddenly broken by a clear, sunny day on Russian Ridge with the vast expanse of ocean to the west and all the golden Johnny Jump-ups aglow in a sea of grass. The lands of Skyline are undeniably beautiful.

I also miss the southland, now mostly off-limits to me. I love the coastal-influenced chaparral down around Loma Prieta at the far southern limit of the District, where we border with lands of the Open Space Authority. Deep in a steep canyon, my "secret" redwood grove is hidden, probably scorched now by one of the recent fires in that area. Up above the canyons, the chaparral is luxuriant, impenetrable, and hung with crispy dry Old Man's Beard. Limestone rock outcroppings and small stands of scrub oak break up the monotony of gracefully folded hillsides. The Monterey Peninsula forms the southern horizon, and Monterey Bay sparkles in the foreground. My impression is of a mini-American Southwest, with a bowl of arid, pale blue sky filled with intense sunlight. It may not be as lush as the preserves along Skyline Boulevard, but it is beautiful, rugged and remote. I could have chosen Skyline or I could have chosen the southland, but I chose neither. I had my reasons, but were they good ones? Mostly, I'm afraid, I didn't want to risk losing what I have, the mostly-happy, mostly-contented rut I've fallen into.

I also have decided not to seek a supervisor position. I went through the application and interview process for the last open supervisor slot, which went to Bart, and found, by the end, that I really didn't want it. I love being a ranger. I think I might hate being a supervisor. As a supervisor, I would sacrifice a good part of what I like best about the job (patrol time, to be spent out on the land) in favor of more time spent doing what I like least about the job (forms, and paperwork and computer time). As a supervisor I would have to actually know and pay attention to obscure and boring details about uniforms, meal breaks, time off requests, fitness time, purchase order forms, work order forms, cite amendment forms and so on. I would have to have truly memorized the Rangers Operations Manual and the Safety Manual and the Illness and Injury Prevention Plan. Supervisors are also supposed to be the "big picture" people at accident scenes, the leader who avoids patient care and other immediate and obvious jobs, and stands back to coordinate the overall scene. I no longer aspire to that role. As an "older adult," I ascribe more and more to the adage "play to your strengths," and my strengths are basic and hands-on. The supervisor job is one level removed from the immediate action, up there in the paperwork and rulebook jungle hovering just slightly over my head, and I don't want it. I can say that with no regrets. I will remain a simple ranger, tried and true, to the end of my days.